COMMUNIST LOCAL GOVERNMENT

COMMUNIST
LOCAL
GOVERNMENT

A Study of Poland

Jaroslaw Piekalkiewicz

Ohio University Press: Athens

To my parents and Jan, in memory

CONTENTS

LIST OF TABLES

LIST OF TABLES

x

PREFACE

Communism, among other things, is the theory of forceful and rapid industrialization and urbanization. As such it presents one of the options in the general movement of humanity to what is loosely described as "modernization." But industrialization and urbanization under communist auspices, while bringing undeniable benefits to the population, is also bound to produce "modern" ills, from which all the industrialized societies seem to suffer. To be meaningful and scientifically productive, the effects of industrialization and urbanization must be studied not only at the macro- but also, what is even more important, at the micro- level. This means micro-society and micro-politics and hence local social and political organizations. The literature on the communist local organizations is singularly scarce, with the exception of a few pioneering works, such as Fainsod's and Cattell's. This study is designed to continue in this pioneering tradition and above all to thoroughly describe structures and functions of the communist local government—something which was never well-described before. It is meant to be encyclopedic and detailed in order to provide a starting point for those who want to pursue more specific inquiries into communist politics, social organizations, industrialization and urbanization.

It is no easy matter to study communist local politics. One has to cope with more secrecy of decision-making and communication than is characteristic of most other systems. On the other hand, if one cares to dig there is an abundance of meaningful statistical data even if the series are often broken and incomplete. This study took ten long years with stays in Poland totaling twenty months. It covers the period from 1958, when the Polish local government was "reformed" as a result of the anti-Stalinist limited revolution of 1956, to the end of 1972, when again the local structures underwent basic changes in the wake of the "workers revolution" of 1971 and the displacement of the "ideological" leadership of Gomułka with the "pragmatic" one of Gierek.

The reforms of 1958 were, in many ways, the expression of the true spirit of communist local government—direct participation by the people—although the Party continued its hegemony. After 1960 there was a gradual reversal of political liberalism, but the trend towards deconcentration of the administrative decisions continued.

The reforms of 1972, which end our period of analysis, primarily aim at increased efficiency of local government and professionalization of its staff. As of January 1, 1973, the 4413 communes (gromada—the lowest level of the local government) were replaced by 2400 towns (gmina). The new town is composed of an urban center and the surrounding rural area including several villages. It should be a socio-economic micro-region capable of performing on its territory broad social, production and service functions based on increased budgetary and economic self-reliance. Of specific significance is the creation of the office of the town's manager. The office of manager is the organ of the state administration and the manager is nominated by the chairman of the presidium of the province. The legislative function of the town is vested in the town's council which is directed by the council's presidium and its chairman. The wide prerogatives of the manager, his professionalism and his status as the representative of the central government makes him largely independent of the town's council. The reform seems to increase centralization and it is assumed by the Polish authorities to lead to an increase in efficiency of the local administration. One, of course, cannot yet evaluate the results. However, the reform appears to be a departure from the more "social" character of the communist local government, in which the communist party provided the dominant centralizing force.

The Polish system as it existed prior to 1973 was closer to the typical model of communist local administration as practised in all other communist states, with the exception of Yugoslavia, China and Cuba, which emphasize their own peculiar systemic characteristics. Hence the Polish system was a "typical" communist local government and could be viewed as a "model" with findings applicable to *all* other communist states. It is hoped that this study will be viewed in this fashion by the reader with Poland providing a convenient backdrop to our analysis.

To state that this study took ten years is to negate the period of its germination. In fact, my interest in this subject dates back to my undergraduate days at Trinity College, University of Dublin, Ireland. In many ways it is a result of the criticism of a paper presented to the seminar of Professor Basil Chubb, whose intellectual stimulation in this and other matters is here gratefully acknowledged. No small debt is owed to the late Professor Vaclav Benes of Indiana University whose kind counsel will always be warmly remembered. Certain theoretical eclecticism of this study is due to the influence of Professor Charles Hyneman, also of Indiana, who fertilized many minds of American scholars and who cannot be blamed for the imperfections of this study anymore than for other books produced by his students. I am grateful to him for the wealth of ideas.

During its long process of research and writing many people lost hope that this study ever would be published. Such was not the case with Professor Ethan Allen, for many years the chairman of the Political Science Department of the University of Kansas. His understanding of the problems, his constant encouragement and help in obtaining financial assistance will not be forgotten and it is sad that his untimely death prevented him from seeing the study come to its conclusion.

The help which I received in Poland was so extensive that it would be impossible to enumerate all the individuals who offered data, counsel and allowed themselves to be interviewed. From among the many I will only single out two who epitomize the most helpful and hospitable attitude of the rest. My special thanks go to Professor Grzegorz L. Seidler, then Rector of the Marii Curie-Skłodowska University, for inviting me to spend the academic year of 1961–62 in Lublin and to Docent Jan Szreniawski also of Marii Curie-Skłodowska for being a perfect host and for supplying me over the years with literature on Polish local government.

Those who will read this study should join me in my thanks to Martha Masinton of Lawrence, Kansas, who with her characteristic gentleness and firmness first unravelled the knots of my "scientific" writing. Also my thanks to the staff of the Ohio University Press: Ian Mackenzie, its director, for first recognizing the publishing potential of the work, Holly Mitchell, its managing director, for guiding the manuscript through its many production stages and for being so understanding to my special problems and finally to Susan Schulman, the copy editor, for her sympathetic treatment of my work and her many useful suggestions on style, composition and title.

The study was financially aided by the Ford Foundation in its initial grant in 1961 and by grants from the University of Kansas. The contribution of both institutions was most helpful.

My thanks to my wife Maura, who had the perfect right to get absolutely fed up with what came to be known in my family in the early years of the manuscript as the "Rady Narodowe Tango," but who did not and to my children Ellen and Andrzej, who only knew that daddy was writing the "Book."

Finally, the contribution of P. M. S. must be mentioned, without whose help most of the interviews conducted in this study would have been impossible.

No individual or institution enumerated above can be blamed for the results of this work, but equally well I am the only one to be praised, if any praise is due.

Jarosław A. Piekałkiewicz

Lawrence, Kansas. June 15, 1973

COMMUNIST LOCAL GOVERNMENT

INTRODUCTION

Western Studies of communist political systems avoided for many reasons serious treatment of communist local government. This subject presents many difficulties; lack of systematic data and the inability of Western scholars to get into "the field" are the most obvious of many obstacles. Local government in general lacks the "glamour" of government at the national level. And yet an understanding of communist politics will never be complete without an investigation of the political process at the local level, because without it we can not conceive how the communist government operates in relation to the ordinary person who depends on local administration for nearly all of his services, which are provided in our own systems not only by government but also by private enterprise. The role of local administration in the communist countries is that much more important, disregarding even the specific character of communist local government as political mobilizer.

Polish local government functions in a state[1] controlled by an authoritarian movement which denies a moral or ideological, but not always a practical, necessity or obligation to tolerate other parties or groups offering different solutions to political, social, and economic issues; it is a movement which proclaims as its ultimate goal the creation of a society with total and exclusive acceptance of the movement's philosophical and moral tenets. The movement can be easily identified as the Communist party. The government dominated by it in view of the party's monistic goals tends toward centralization. With this tendency in mind and because of the very word "authoritarian," which suggests a uniform, monolithic structure of political institutions, the reader may be in doubt as to the value of a study of local bodies in such a rigid, icebound framework. Are not the central directives executed down the line without a murmur or possibility of change? Are not the local bodies just simple cogs in the grinding machinery of the total state? There may be some justification in such an attitude, and it is only right, at the outset, to ponder these questions.

3

The comparison of an authoritarian government to a well-run machine is suggestive and illustrative, but it is at best only a dream of the top leaders and a literary metaphor of doubtful practical value. In reality, no man is a perfect cog and no local body is identical to another. The variations are perhaps smaller, less striking, and of a different character than under the truly democratic system of government,[2] but no less significant and deserving of thorough investigation.

It is an erroneous oversimplification to treat and reject the communist pattern of government as a pathological variation of democracy; it is an oversimplification which results from value judgment and places democracy on the pedestal of the universally accepted perfection in the best tradition of belief in the natural law. One has to bear in mind that one-third of the population of our globe lives in communist states, and that in large parts of the world, as in Africa and Asia, the Soviet system is regarded not as the evil perversion of democracy but as the alternative political system in the age of mass industrial society.[3] The communist political and economic solution presents for many, perhaps even to their own regret, a much more reasonable path to achieve quickly the benefits of industrialization made mandatory by the twentieth-century psychosis and to cope with the social and moral problems which industrialization brings in its wake. The issue is not always "freedom" but more often "economic justice," or even simply "well-being." And indeed, it is not surprising that the communist solution is viewed as an alternative to liberal democracy, considering the fact that both have their common roots in the same premises of eighteenth-century Western philosophy.[4] As an alternative the system must be studied in depth because it presents a choice, not only of the philosophic approach to government and the role of the individual in society, but also of different administrative procedures and technical means for settling local affairs.

Accepting the separate identity of the communist political system with the full understanding of the implications of this classification we must not be blind to the many similarities to other modern governmental systems. As much as it is a mistaken simplicity to deny the communist system its completely independent life, it is also no less confining an approach to disregard in our indignation the existence of many of the same problems on both sides of the ideological barricade which would permit us to construct a bridge of understanding necessary for any mature comparison. The similarities between the two types of technologically advanced societies are more numerous than the Communist party militants or, for that matter, the ultraconservatives in the West care to admit. It is not at all unusual for these similarities to exist, considering that both systems to a large extent originated because of and developed side by side with industrialization and urbanization. Although both sides are equally eager to blame the ideology of the other for its own social and economic shortcomings, the problems created by rapid industrialization and urbanization are as prominent in the West as in the East, and it is exactly in this sphere that the two meet. Shortage of adequate housing expressed either in terms of high rents, slums, or overcrowdedness, alcoholism and drug addiction, the growing rate of traffic accidents, the difficulties in policing large urban centers, or even just plain hooliganism and vandalism, to mention only a few, are constant headaches of the "city fathers" not only of New York or London but also of Moscow and Warsaw. Most of these problems have nothing to do with the ideological inclination of the national government but result from the pressures of urban life on the individual in such a way that he often finds himself alienated from society and society's values, communist or democratic. It could be argued that the mass movement of the rural population to urban centers is responsible, at least in part, for this feeling of alienation. This movement has taken place in all modern or modernizing societies, and its effects underline the great similarities of the human race across national or ideological borders. The Polish peasant of the 1950s in a big industrial complex as Katowice, Poland, was no less bewildered and lonely than the nineteenth-century Irish immigrant in Gary, Indiana, or for that matter the twentieth-century Black from the deep South in Chicago. Nor do these problems end with one generation. The alienation felt by their parents is often transferred to the offspring and tends to express itself in a more violent form because the children, already born in the cities, consider themselves rightful members of the urban community and are ready to battle the old, established and privileged strata of society.

There are also similarities of what we may call a technical

nature, such as theory and practice of public administration, problems of a large bureaucracy, relationship between central and local government and budgeting, financing, and taxation. We must not try to deny of course that the dominant approach to government colors these technical matters, but beneath the mantle of ideology we still have to deal with similar problems of local bodies. The local government in a communist or democratic state still has to find the means to finance new road and bridge construction, slum clearance, park and recreation centers, and more than once it has to extort the funds from local industry and from the province, as well as the national government. The awareness of this fact is not entirely limited to people in the West. There are also voices heard to the same effect in Poland, coming as they are through the maze of ideological jargon:

Among the organizational-technical elements, there are also those which appear independently from the political aims, and even independently from the basic socio-political system of a state, because they are, so to speak, an expression of physical necessity.[5]

These independent elements are most likely to appear in low-level institutions, the operation of which is considerably free from involvement in the ideological struggle.

However, even the strictly political issues tend to show astonishing similarities through the thick foam of ideological phraseology. The means used may be different, but local politics under communism is no less free from struggle for power than its democratic counterpart. There is a clash of personalities between individuals, party interference in strictly administrative affairs, collision between lower and higher levels of government, and competition between different organizations, branches, and organizational men. Communism as well as democracy has its share of dedication, self-sacrifice, and a fine civic spirit as well as of corruption, bribery and theft of public property. Neither is free at the local level from political behavior at its most debased display, but both also enjoy its highest sublimation.

An investigation of Polish local government presents a good case study of the impact of rapid industrialization on local government, provided of course, that we take into account all the specific aspects of the communist framework. The industrialization process is illustrated by the movement of population out of agricultural employment: the 60% of population depending on agriculture for its livelihood in 1931 decreased to 38.7% in 1960 and further to 29.5% in 1970.[6] In 1950 newcomers from the countryside composed about 1/3 of the total population of Łódź and about 1/4 of Warsaw.[7] The total natural increase in the Polish countryside between 1950 and 1957 was completely absorbed by the cities.[8]

The process of industrialization had already started in Poland at the end of the nineteenth century, and it was accelerated in the period between the two world wars. However, despite this constant industrial development Poland was still predominantly agricultural in 1939, as was most of East-Central Europe with the exception of Czechoslovakia in her Czech part. The economic dependence on agriculture was augmented by the staggering war destruction of industrial capacity which the region suffered between 1939 and 1945. Therefore, at the end of the war Poland could have been considered as an underdeveloped part of the world in so far as the industrial facilities existed, although the country had the great advantage of cultural and educational development and, concomitantly, a greater social awareness for modernization.

Poland also suggests some striking similarities to underdeveloped regions in her political and social characteristics. Like many new emerging nations the country was subject to nearly 150 years of foreign domination which kept her in semicolonial subjugation and produced lasting social and political effects.[9] The disruption of the national life in the crucial nineteenth century when the Western European masses were brought into political participation left Polish society in a state of individualistic fragmentation in which the only political consensus was the desirability of national independence. After this goal was achieved in 1918, the country sadly lacked political leaders with experience to cope with her tremendous administrative, political, and economic problems. To most Poles independence meant the license to be free to disagree, and they had very little understanding and preparation for orderly self-government, in which freedoms could only be maintained with corresponding duties of responsible citizenship. They regarded political controversies as a matter of moral principles, distrusted and could not comprehend the necessity of compromises and adjustments between many wills and interests. The society also developed a hearty dislike for *all* governments, civil servants, and police in particular, during its long and bloody fight for independence. Poles became masters in civil disobedience, law evasion, as well as antigovernment conspiracies and plots. Nobody paid much attention to laws and regulations. These were viewed as instruments of oppression crushing the noble expression of individual freedom.[10] The law, government, and officials were regarded as existing above and apart from the society and not as an expression of popular participation. Even some of the leaders of the state and the higher civil servants behaved in a haughty manner, as if they were foreign rulers and not servants of their own society.

The political instability was augmented by the lack of a middle class which for many long-standing historical reasons was slow to develop in Poland. There was nobody to fill the void and to provide the social and political communication between the upper classes of rural nobility and urban intelligentsia and the masses of peasants. The working class, although well organized and conscious of its role, was too small to provide the necessary leadership.

Administratively, the country in 1918 was in the impossible situation of having to cope with three different systems of law and three different structures of local government. There was also a great shortage of trained administrative personnel, since only a few Poles were permitted to serve under Russian or Prussian rule. Only the Austrian part which had some local autonomy within the Austro-Hungarian monarchy developed a native Polish officialdom. In addition, the recruitment of the civil servants between 1918 and 1939 was proceeding very slowly, especially at the lower ranks, due to inadequate salaries and because of a practically nonexistent middle class, which in other countries traditionally staffed the civil service. All these social, political, and legal difficulties were slowly resolved in the twenty-year period of independence (1918–1939), and the new generation of Poles born in a free country could hopefully look to a national life cured from the scars of foreign domination. However, the shock of the Second World War and the five long years of German and partial Soviet occupation disrupted the growing fabric of Polish society. Once more conspiracy, plots, and antigovernment activity were the order of the day. The law was there to be circumvented, officials and police distrusted and hated. Once more the antigovernment and, to some extent, antisocial characteristics developed during previous foreign domination were to be reaffirmed. The losses in population resulting from the unprecedented terror, genocide, transfer of territories, and forced emigration affected most the educated classes and bled Poland white of her technical and scientific personnel.[11] The war left Poland a human and economic desert and her rebuilding was no less a task than that by some of the new nations, and perhaps with no more resources.

The immediate postwar development did not produce stability. On the one side the communists, with little support within the country but aided by the powerful Soviet army and the security forces with the whole mighty Soviet Union behind them, were determined to establish their dictatorship and reshape Poland along communist lines. On the other side the equally determined nationalist forces, well-trained in their long struggle against the Germans and supported at least at the beginning by a large segment of the population, fought back bitterly. The civil war lasted for three long years[12] and produced wounds of bitterness and a cleavage in the Polish nation much more serious than the experience of the German occupation. Pole fought Pole and the normal brutality of the civil war imprinted itself firmly on many minds. The local administration established by the communist government was disrupted time and again, and many government officials were executed by the nationalists,[13] adding to the difficulty of finding trained personnel since many others would not serve the communists.

Finally when the armed struggle ended, the country was more divided than ever before. The communist government was regarded by many Poles as a tool of Russia, hatred of which went back to the Tsarist occupation of Poland after the partitions, notwithstanding the communist doctrine and social, economic, and political revolution. This was again a foreign domination and once more it was patriotic to sabotage the government, to disrupt its functions, to oppose its regulations, to bribe the officials and to steal public property. The communist rulers were faced with the enormous task of rebuilding the shattered economy and administration and to achieve the necessary social and political unification under the most adverse conditions. They used a skillful mixture of brutal force and persuasion, indoctrination and propaganda. Their successes can only be measured alongside their failures and with the understanding of the odds working against them. Local government was in the very frontline of this long battle and the study of it should disclose interesting insights into the communist political tactics as well as illumination as to the efficiency of communism in the process of national unification and economic construction.

The study of Polish local government, then, is necessary to the understanding of the communist system in that country, and by implication it is vital as a case study for a full comprehension of the working of the communist political system and an insight into communist political tactics. The communist system in turn must be investigated in depth, not as a passing curiosity but as an alternative system in the age of industrialism.

NOTES TO INTRODUCTION

[1] The author uses the term "state" to mean a body of people occupying a definite territory, and politically organized under one government not legally subject to external control, and not a part of the federal union as in the United States.

[2] The author does not feel that this title could be unconditionally applied to all the state (part of the federal union) and local governments in the United States, and perhaps a comparison, for example, of the Mississippi government prior to the 70s with the communist political system of Poland would reveal many striking similarities.

[3] For an excellent discussion of this subject see: Marshall D. Shulman, "Changing Appreciation of the Soviet Problems," *World Politics* 10, no. 4 (July 1958): 499–511.

[4] This point is made very forcefully and convincingly by J. L. Talmon in *The Origin of Totalitarian Democracy* (New York, 1961).

[5] Maurycy Jaroszyński, *Zagadnienia Rad Narodowych* (Warszawa, 1961), p. 69. The growing influence of rationalism and empiricism in the study of administrative law in the communist countries of East-Central Europe and the USSR dates back to the 1956–1960 period. Leaders in this movement were scientists in the USSR, Hungary, and Poland. Bulgarians, Rumanians and East Germans did not carry on independent research but utilized the findings of their other East-European colleagues. The Czechs were, until 1966, somewhere between these two groups. After 1966, they moved rapidly to the leading position. Of course the Yugoslavs, and on the other end of the spectrum, the Albanians, are

classes in themselves. See also: Jerzy Starościak, *Wprowadzenie Do Prawa Administracyjnego Europejskich Państw Socjalistycznych* (Warszawa, 1968), pp. 25–62.

6 *Rocznik Statystyczny* (Statistical Yearbook), (Warszawa, 1963), p. 31, table 18, and for 1970 figures *Rocznik Statystyczny* (1971), p. 87, table 14. See also Włodzimierz Wesołowski, "Stara i Nowa Klasa," *Kultura* 6, no. 45 (November 10, 1968): 4. Wesołowski's figures are: 60.6% for 1931 and 38.4% for 1960 (the year of the last population census). He must be using slightly different criteria to mine.

7 Ryszard Turski, *Dynamika Przemian Społecznych w Polsce* (Warszawa, 1961), p. 27. See also an excellent study of one small town by Dr. W. Narojek. In Zawodzie (an assumed name) in World War II nearly the whole Jewish population, composing 4/5 of the population of twenty thousand persons, was exterminated by the Germans. By 1961, Zawodzie had a population of eleven thousand, mostly newcomers from the villages (Winicjusz Narojek, *System Władzy w Mieście* [Wrocław, Warszawa, Kraków, 1967], p. 20).

8 Turski, *Dynamika Przemian*, p. 27.

9 The Polish Commonwealth, as it was then called, was divided among Prussia, Russia, and Austria, by the three partitions of 1772, 1793, and 1795.

10 This spirit of anarchy was always a characteristic of Poles and could even be blamed to a large extent for the loss of their national independence. That this is still true today, at least among the intelligentsia, is the opinion of Jarosław Iwaszkiewicz, well-known Polish writer, in his answer to the question posed by *Polityka*: "What changes took place in the character of Poles during half a century of their independence?" ("Przemiany Polaków," *Polityka* 12, no. 45 [November 9, 1968]: 1). Also in the same number of *Polityka* see a most interesting article along the same lines by Andrzej Szczypiorski, "Polska 1918," p. 9.

11 In 1939 the total population of Poland was 35.1 million (*Mały Rocznik Statystyczny* [Warszawa, 1939], p. 10, table 2). The 1946 census revealed only 23.9 million left (*Rocznik Statystyczny* [Warszawa, 1955], p. 23, table 1). Out of the total loss of 11.2 million as many as 5–8 million were killed, the rest being the population of the territories lost to the Soviet Union, mostly of Byelorussian and Ukranian nationality, and political emigration to the West.

12 From 1945 to 1949. It may be disputed here if the term "civil war" really applies. However, the bitterness of the fighting and the losses on both sides, which ran perhaps as high as 300,000 to 400,000 killed makes the term, in the opinion of this writer, quite appropriate. It is often referred to as such in Poland, for example see Andrzej Burda, *Rozwój Ustroju Politycznego Polski Ludowej* (Warszawa, 1967), p. 12, and Zbigniew Załuski, *Czterdziesty Czwarty* (Warszawa, 1968).

13 The government admitted that it lost altogether 100,000 army, police, and civil personnel in the civil war. During the twentieth anniversary celebration in 1965 the KWB (Internal Security Corps) was credited with 755 military operations in 1945 alone, during the course of which 81 armed underground groups were liquidated (*East Europe* 16, no. 8 [August 1965]: 50. Even in 1968, the then First Secretary of the Polish United Workers' Party, Władysław Gomułka, returned to this subject with considerable bitterness (see Władysław Gomułka, *Stanowisko Partii Zgodne Z Wolą Narodu* [Warszawa, 1968], pp. 15–17).

LOCAL GOVERNMENT IN THE COMMUNIST THEORY OF STATE

THE SOCIALIST STATE

The understanding of the role and function played by local government in the communist state is necessary, indeed vital, for the full comprehension of the communist political system. But we must start our discussion by defining the state in Marxist terms. According to the teaching of Marx, followed by Engels, Lenin, and other communist theoreticians up to the present day, the traditional state is nothing more than an expression of the power of the dominant economic class; a machinery by means of which that class imposes its rule on other exploited classes. It is not an organization of the whole society in equal partnership but only a weapon designed to preserve and defend the existing economic structure. The state is a direct outcome of private ownership of the sources of production and class conflict resulting from it. The class which controls the means of production, or in other words the wealthy, controls also the political structure, the state. With the change in ownership, the political power also changes hands and is transferred to the new economically dominant class:

> The antique state was, therefore, the state of the slave owners for the purpose of holding the slaves in check. The feudal state was the organ of the nobility for the oppression of the serfs and dependent farmers. The modern representative state is the tool of the capitalist exploiters of wage labor.[1]

Therefore the state cannot be the neutral arbiter of the social and economic conflict of individuals and groups, but by definition it is only and exclusively the device by which one class protects its own selfish interest and keeps other classes in economic and political bondage.

Liberal democracy is only *formal* democracy, the Marxists claim, because it provides only *formal* equality: that equality which is written into the constitution but which cannot achieve its practical realization so long as economic inequality exists, so long as the rich by virtue of owning and operating all the means of production can control the government and the livelihood of the poor. The poor will never be equal to the rich, neither economically, socially, nor politically. He who controls the means of production, he who controls the wealth of the society controls the state. True democracy is only then possible when the people themselves take over all the sources of production and social wealth and own them in common. True democracy is only achieved after the final proletariat revolution.[2]

The first act of the proletariat after the victorious revolution must be the abolishment of private ownership of the sources of production and transfer of that ownership to the whole society. With the destruction of the economic base which nourished the dominant economic and political position of the bourgeoisie, the class division should also automatically disappear. Following Marxist reasoning, the state itself as the tool of oppression of one class by another should simply evaporate. This is exactly what is advocated by anarchists who wish no state and no political authority whatsoever, but free and willing cooperation of individuals organized in autonomous groups of producers.[3]

Marx takes sharp issue with the anarchists and argues that the workers need to retain the state even after the revolution and employ it in much the same way as it was used against them. The state remains the state with all its functions of repression, but now its sharp edge is directed toward the bourgeoisie. The capitalists will not freely resign their will to dominate and the proletarian state must keep them in check by its power as well as defend itself against the predictable attacks of international reaction. After the revolution the workers constitute the dictatorship of the proletariat, which in its basic political function is no different from any other type of dictatorship. This time, however, it is the dictatorship of the great majority of working people suppressing the tiny minority of excapitalists and, therefore, the new order can claim to be the closest approximation of true democracy.[4]

Marx in his theoretical consideration, having retained the state even after the victorious proletarian revolution, is faced with an excruciating dilemma. On the one hand, he admits the practical necessity of maintaining the state machinery; on the other hand, his own analysis proclaims the state to be an instrument of oppression which the proletariat fights to nullify. He is fully aware that if the workers employ the political vehicle of liberal democracy, even restricting it to their own class under the dictatorship of the proletariat with the exclusion of the excapitalists, there is no guarantee that some unscrupulous leaders and bureaucrats would not use their position and power to exploit and enslave the workers once more. After all, the elections could be manipulated after the revolution in much the same way as they were under the old bourgeois state, the officials could be corrupted, the press controlled by one group and even the sources of production could be used for the benefit of the few instead of the welfare of all. Marx's anguish is evident in his *Civil War in France*. The working class simply cannot employ the mode and structure of a liberal democratic state; "the working class cannot simply lay hold of the ready-made state machinery, and wield it for its own purpose."[5] *The new state has to be born*—a political system which would insure the true representativeness of government, one which would permit a direct control of public officials, a new state which would provide the means for true democracy and not only the sham faculties of the liberal fraud.

The problem is how to construct this new proletarian state: What structure should it adopt? Marx finds his answer in the historical example of the Paris Commune,[6] which he greets as the dawn of a new political era. "Vive la Commune," he shouts enthusiastically, "that sphinx so tantalizing to the bourgeois mind."[7] Lenin follows closely on the heels of his Master:

> The Commune is the form 'at last discovered' by the proletarian revolution, under which the economic emancipation of labour can take place. The Commune is the first attempt by a proletariat revolution to *smash* the bourgeois state machine; and it is the political form 'at last discovered' by which the smashed state machine can and must be replaced.[8]

The Paris Commune was an assembly of municipal councilors elected in the wards of Paris by universal suffrage, with the dual function of legislating and executing its own laws. It was a combination of parliament and government in one and the same body. The administrative officials, including the police, were agents of the Commune and, in principle, were revocable at all times. The councilors of the Commune themselves were also recallable by their electors at short notice. All public officials, legislative, executive, judiciary or administrative, were paid compensation equal to the average worker's wage.

The Commune was overpowered before it developed its plan for national organization, but it established the theoretical foundations for all future communist states.[9] In Russia the experience of the Commune was reproduced, not necessarily as a conscious theoretical development, but rather as a spontaneous act of the 1905 and 1917 revolutions. It took the form of the workers' organizations called the "Soviets,"[10] which in 1905 were mostly strike committees, with the exception of a few which assumed some characteristics of local parliaments and executives. In the chaos of the 1917 revolution, the Soviets spread all over the territory of the Russian Empire and were constituted in factories, army units, cities and villages, performing in many places the functions of local government on a completely or semiautonomous basis, existing side by side with whatever authority was maintained by the disintegrating Russian state, formally headed by the Provisional Government.[11] Lenin immediately recognized the spiritual and theoretical bond of the Soviets with the Paris Commune and intended to found his new Bolshevik state on their framework.

True democracy, democracy prophesied by Marx, is a state founded on the structure of Soviets and it is not a repetition of the bourgeois political institutions, but a new original creation of the working people, "exactly a case of 'quantity being transformed into quality': democracy, introduced as fully and consistently as is at all conceivable, is transformed from bourgeois into proletarian democracy; from the state (a special force for the suppression of a particular class) into something which is no longer the state proper."[12] The Bolsheviks constructed this "new democracy" when they took power by the "coup" in October, 1917, but the whole Soviet state system did not develop fully until the victorious conclusion of the Civil War in 1920.

THE UNIFIED STATE ADMINISTRATION

The structure of the new proletarian or socialist state as it evolved from Marxist writings, the experiences of the Paris Commune, and the Russian Revolution, is a pyramid of councils, beginning at its base with the commune, which covers the territory of a few villages or one small town or urban settlement; then the county, an area which is composed of several communes; the province, which includes several counties; the republic in the states with the federal structure (the USSR, Yugoslavia, and Czechoslovakia); and finally, the national parliament, which in theory is the top council of the whole country. The membership of each council is elected by the population of the territory under the council's authority. Each council, in turn, elects its own executive committee which directs the work of the administrative departments of the council.

Theoretically, the councils are not just another type of bourgeois self-government with limited prerogatives; they belong totally to the *unified state administration*. There is no formal division between the central government and noncentral governments, which are supposedly self-governing; hence, it is argued, the working class rules and runs the machinery of government *directly* on all levels of administration and policy-making. Each council represents the local population and, at the same time, is the *only* organ of the central government in the given locality. The local officials elected by and representing the locality are also the officials of the central government. The administrative departments of the councils in addition to performing the functions of their own local governments are also the territorial branches of the central ministries. The unified state administration based on the popularly elected councils supposedly insures a mass, grass roots participation in the administration of the whole of the socialist state and direct public control of the state officials.

THE SOCIALIST DEMOCRACY

The socialist state resting on the pyramid of councils insures, the communist doctrine claims, freedom from the abuses of liberal democratic parliamentarism. Workers, peasants and working intelligentsia elect their own representatives to legislate on their own local matters, as well as in the affairs concerning the larger territory, and by degrees eventually the whole nation. They vote not for a relatively unknown member of the bourgeoisie, a name on the ballot, a lawyer, a doctor, an industrialist, or a professional politician who does not have the feeling for the needs of the working class and who goes to the distant capital to engage in endless petty talk, but they elect their own kind, their neighbor, their co-worker, whom the whole village or city ward knows, respects and trusts:

> We cannot imagine democracy, even proletariat democracy, without representative institutions, but we can and *must* imagine democracy without parliamentarism, if criticism of bourgeois society is not mere words for us, if the desire to overthrow the rule of the bourgeoisie is our earnest and sincere desire, and not a mere 'election' cry for catching workers' votes, ...[13]

The same representative of the little community, village, or city ward, may become through election by his council the executive officer of the commune, county, province, or even the nation. He keeps constant close contact with the people and, being revocable by them at all times, he cannot develop any bureaucratic habits. In theory, the officials should be subject to frequent rotation and nearly all proletarians should at one time or another try their hand in the executive at various levels.

Thus, the whole population is brought into the administration of their own affairs:

> The Commune substitutes for the venal and rotten parliamentarism of bourgeois society institutions in which freedom of opinion and discussion does not degenerate into deception, for the parliamentarians themselves have to work, have to execute their own laws, have themselves to test the results achieved in reality, and to account directly to their constituents. Representative institutions remain, but there is *no* parliamentarism here as a special system, as the division of labour between the legislative and the executive, as a privileged position for the deputies.[14]

The unified state administration based on the pyramidical structure of councils, the local parliaments, and the local cabinets, provides for direct participation in government by all the working class people. The law is not only made and executed in the distant national capital but brought down to the level of the ordinary citizen at all grades of local government, which is at the same time one and unified with the national government. Democracy is the fact of everyday existence:

> You do not understand what it means to rule. You think that to rule means to sit in the government. The people's rule has a wide aspect. The pyramid of political power starts from the top and ends in a commune . . . . Not only here, in Warsaw, at the top, are the state's problems decided, but also down there below.[15]

The decisions are made at all levels and the whole state structure is an aggregate of semiindependent communes bound in theory together by wider and wider circles of local councils with progressively higher and higher authority and larger and larger territorial jurisdiction.

DEMOCRATIC CENTRALISM

The term "democratic centralism" is often confusedly understood as applicable only to the internal affairs of the Communist party. It is, however, the fundamental principle binding together the structure of the Communist state. The principle may be defined as it is by two Polish writers in the following manner:

> The principle of democratic centralism means binding together in complete unity the necessary amount of centralism with the true democracy . . . which is indispensable for the fulfillment of the aims of the socialist state.[16]

The philosophical spring of democratic centralism lies undoubtedly in Rousseau's "General Will,"[17] with the strong undercurrent of its doctrine in the concept of the Jacobins, who influenced Marx and Engels so much. It achieved its first practical expression in the dictatorship of the Convent of the French Revolution,[18] was explicit in the planned state structure of the Paris Commune, only to be finally crystallized by Lenin, who injected it into the organization of the Bolshevik party. Lenin, following closely the logic of Marx's *The Civil War in France*, also plainly intended to employ democratic centralism as the binding force of the socialist state:

Now as the proletariat and the poor peasants take state power into their own hands, organize themselves quite freely in communes, and unite the action of all the communes in striking at capital, in crushing the resistance of the capitalists, and in transferring the privately-owned railways, factories, land and so on to the entire nation, to the whole of society, won't that be centralism? Won't that be the most consistent democratic centralism and, moreover, proletarian centralism?[19]

This "proletarian centralism" was employed by Lenin in the Bolshevik state and, following the example of the Soviet Union, it was copied by all the communist countries. It is implicit in their constitutions, although only two of them, the fundamental law of the Chinese People's Republic and of the German Democratic Republic, declare it "expressis verbis."[20]

In theory, democratic centralism permits free discussion of all the issues progressing from the lowest council, the commune, by stages up to the national assembly and descent of binding decisions down again gradually step by step from the central authorities back to the commune. In other words, free discussion takes place at all the levels of the government up to the time when the final decision based on these deliberations is made by the national government or any other higher authority in the hierarchy and passed down to the subordinate bodies.

In practice, in the structure of the councils, the principle of democratic centralism is employed as a tool by which obedience to the central government is insured, permitting, at the same time, the use of local initiative and taking account of regional peculiarities. The councils have freedom of action within the framework of their legal prerogatives and subject to the general directives and supervision by the Communist party, with the provision that all the higher units of government within the councils' structure can annul, suspend, or reverse all regulations, bylaws, and other decisions of the lower bodies, including the elections of officers, if they are not in accordance with the law and what is generally defined as "the principle line of the policy of the state." The principle line is only specified in ambiguous terms as a policy designed for the building of socialism. Under these circumstances, it is obvious that any higher body can completely control the actions of the lower units in all matters and this, of course, frustrates the very essence of the concept of local self-government and democracy as understood by Western political theorists. There is no sphere of local government activity which could be completely free by irrevocable right from the directives of the central authority, should it desire to exercise fully its prerogative impregnated by the logic of democratic centralism. The degree of autonomy of local initiative is always prescribed by the central government and in the final analysis by the leadership of the Communist party, which alone decides which mixture of *democracy* and *centralism* promotes best the dynamics of the socialist state without endangering the stability of the Communist rule.

THE REVOLUTIONARY DYNAMICS OF THE SOCIALIST STATE

The socialist state is not a stable institution bound in its internal relations by the limits determined by the constitution, but it is considered to be in constant revolutionary ferment in its dynamic development on the continuum from capitalism to communism. Each period of its existence is only a transitory stage leading to the final clearly prescribed goal. Its character changes with its development; and "the interference of the state power in social relations becomes superfluous in one sphere after another, and then ceases of itself."[21]

Immediately after the revolution the proletariat abolishes the bourgeois state and establishes the dictatorship of the proletariat, which is a highly centralized organization used to suppress the capitalists and to defend the revolution against all internal and external attacks. The socialist state in this early period must be strong and cannot permit decentralization of its power, but is forced to set the balance between democracy and centralism in favor of centralism. The socialist democracy, as understood by the communist theoreticians, does not include participation by elements considered hostile to the revolution since "it is contrary . . . to the essence of democracy to leave freedom of political action to anti-socialist forces; freedom for free play of political tendencies foreign to us."[22] For a long time after the revolution "the anti-socialist forces" persist. There are not only individuals of bourgeois origin, but also some members of the working class who show evidence of attachment to "bourgeois mentality." This is due to the fact that the socialist society "has its origin in capitalism, that it develops historically from capitalism, that it is the result of the action of a social force to which capitalism gave birth."[23] Communism cannot be achieved in one day—it cannot even be achieved in one generation.

Eventually, socialism takes roots; more and more people are converted to the belief in the scientific truth and historical inevitability of communism. The communists and their followers grow into a powerful majority internally and internationally; and "since the majority of the people itself suppresses its oppressors, a 'special force' for suppression is no longer necessary!"

> In this sense, the state *begins to wither away*. Instead of the special institutions of a privileged minority (privileged officialdom, the chiefs of the standing army), the majority itself can directly fulfill all these functions, and the more the functions of state power are performed by the people as a whole, the less need there is for existence of this power.[24]

The institutions through which the people take over the power of the state are their local councils; and, hence, with the progress of a socialist state from capitalism to communism, more and more governmental functions are transferred from the central to the local authorities.

With time, the class conflict becomes less and less drastic[25] and the character of the socialist state changes from the dictatorship of the proletariat to the state of the whole nation:

> One of the basic assumptions of the new program of the CPSU (Communist Party of the Soviet Union) is the assertion that the dictatorship of the proletariat institutes only one of the phases in the development of the socialist state, characteristic exclusively for the superstructure of the transitory period from capitalism to socialism. The next phase of the development of the socialist state, which follows the elimination of the exploiting class and the formation of the socialist base and is connected with the gradual passage from socialism to communism, is characterized by the existence of the state of the whole nation. It is a new and higher link on the road of transformation of the socialist state into communist self-government.[26]

In addition, the program of the Communist party of the USSR adopted at the XXII Party Congress made it plain that the increasing role of the Soviets leads directly to the establishment of the future communist society. It declares that "during the construction of Communism the role of the Soviets will increase, as the Soviets are the all-embracing organization of the people; the expression of its unity."[27] The councils will also serve as a training ground in public administration for millions of working people, training them at the same time in self-discipline and responsible citizenship in preparation for the self-rule in the final communist stage.

However the final achievement of this red paradise, in which the "government of men" shall be supplanted by the "administration of things" is still far away. In pure communism the state will cease to exist, since there will be no need to suppress individuals who refuse to submit voluntarily to the spirit of communist cooperation. With the disappearance of capitalism internationally and with all nations becoming communist, (an eventuality scientifically inevitable according to Marxist dialectics), the socialist state will not be required to maintain its centralized power, necessary at present for its defense against the international forces of reaction. The state will "wither away" and become a free association of communes and social organizations. In the meantime however, in the present understanding, the theory of "withering away" of the state means the transference of certain functions, hitherto performed by the central government, to the councils and different social organizations. Although this process is thought to be "withering," in fact, it is only deconcentration,[28] which increases the role played by the councils in the whole structure of the communist government. The Communist party alone determines how much of "withering" or deconcentration can be permitted at any given time; the party alone is the final arbiter of the dynamics of the socialist state. It is conscious of the correct proportions between a dictatorship and a democracy, because "there exist limits (to this relationship) prescribed by the objective disposition of class forces, which cannot be traversed in one or other direction." And "the proportions between dictatorship and democracy shape themselves differently in separate countries in relationship to the disposition of class forces on the internal as well as international scale."[29] In each communist country the native Communist party is the only force capable of determining accurately the stage of the country's development toward communism,[30] since only the party is:

capable of assuming power and *leading the whole people* to socialism, of directing and organizing the new system, of being the teacher, the guide, the leader of all the working and exploited people in organizing their social life without the bourgeoisie and against the bourgeoisie.[31]

DEMOCRACY AND THE NEW SOCIALIST MAN

There is no other social or political force but the Communist party capable of guiding people scientifically to the historically predetermined goal of communism; and, hence, there is no reason for the communists to share their power or to permit competition for it with any other political or social group, although they may tolerate for tactical reasons the existence of other, minor political movements, providing they acknowledge without any reservation the communist leadership. The socialist democracy does not include open political competition. It is only fair to mention that communists view democracy differently from us in the West. They assume that economic abundance is the primary desire of mankind and that only communist organization of production is capable of creating the necessary magnitude of goods and services. Then, they claim, by a curious switch of logic, that the communist system itself is widely desired and that what is widely desired is automatically *democratic*. Their democracy means limited discussion within the framework of Marxism-Leninism; a limited choice of execution but not of major direction, which is always strictly defined in a "scientific way," as interpreted by the party and in turn for the party by its top leaders. Democracy and freedom mean acceptance of the communist way of life.

Obviously, if democracy means free acceptance, but of only one political, economic, and social doctrine, the hope of ever achieving communism, the highest stage of democratic development, must rely on the ability to "educate" the masses in subscribing without any reservations to the communist faith. Communists do not expect this complete acceptance to be achieved easily or over a short period of time, but "in striving for socialism," they are convinced that eventually:

it will develop into communism and, therefore, that the need for violence against people in general, for the subordination of one man to another, and of one section of the population to another, will vanish altogether since people will *become accustomed* to observing the elementary conditions of social life *without violence* and *without subordination*.

In order to emphasize this element of habit, Engels speaks of a new *generation*, 'reared in new, free social conditions,' which will 'be able to discard the entire lumber of the state'—of any state, including the democratic-republican state.[32]

The state cannot wither away completely until the education of the people progresses to the point "when society adopts the rule: 'From each according to his ability, to each according to his needs,' i.e., when people have"

> become so accustomed to observing the fundamental rules of social intercourse and when their labour has become so productive that they will voluntarily work *according to their ability*. 'The narrow horizon of bourgeois right,' which compels one to calculate with the heartlessness of a Shylock whether one has not worked half an hour more than somebody else, whether one is not getting less pay than somebody else—this narrow horizon will then be crossed. There will then be no need for society, in distributing products, to regulate the quantity to be received by each; each will take freely 'according to his needs.'[33]

The socialist state, therefore, must engross itself constantly and unrelentingly in the process of indoctrination, or as it is euphemistically called—education of the masses, in their preparation for communist democracy; it must create *the new socialist man*. The councils as the mass organizations of the people, play an ever increasing role in this remolding of society. They also perform, apart from their important position in the theoretical structure of the state, many other vital practical functions.

The state according to Marxist theory is the outcome of economic conditions and is an expression of class conflict. It is a structure maintained by the owners of the sources of production to suppress the lower classes and to permit their economic exploitation. Even the liberal democracy, which the Marxists admit is the most sophisticated of traditional states, is nothing more in its function than another political organization of repression. It is still used by capitalists to exploit the workers, who are cheated out of their rights by fraudulent elections, corruption of the state bureaucracy, and deceitful propaganda. True democracy can only be attained by a proletarian revolution, which transfers the sources of production from private to public ownership and, therefore, abolishes the exploitation of man by man; and by the structure of independent freely elected councils, the mass organization of workers, peasants and working intelligentsia, which are part of the unified state administration guaranteeing true public participation, electiveness of officials, and their vigilant control by the people.

The structure of the councils gives the socialist state its unique character, different basically from any other state—a semistate, which eventually will wither away under the pure conditions of communism. In the dynamic process of development from capitalism to communism the councils play an important role, taking over the increasing amount of the functions of the central government. They also train the people in administration and the civic spirit and in the free acceptance of communist scientific interpretation of historical, economic, and social progress. They prepare individuals by changing their very nature for entrance into communism. They help to create the "new socialist man." The structure of the councils, acting each independently in its own sphere, should not be confused with the notion of federalism. The councils are strictly unified in one indivisible state machinery with the relationship of different levels determined by the principle of democratic centralism. The correct blend of democracy with centralism is decided upon by the communist party alone, fully aware through the wisdom of its leaders, in which particular stage of development the society finds itself at any given time.

In practical terms, the councils with their semifree discussions and elections permit the flow of information between the population and the leaders, as well as disseminate orders of the central authority and facilitate their easier acceptance. The great number of people participating in the activities of the councils provides the communist government with a multitude of supporters, even if in many cases unconscious of their true role. It renders the exclusive reliance on force for political reason unnecessary. The councils are the theoretical basis on which the communist claim to "true democracy" rests; they are vital in the process of development from capitalism to communism and in practice help to keep the communist leadership in power, allowing at the same time for a degree of administrative, economic, and political efficiency, which could hardly be maintained without such a device.

NOTES TO CHAPTER I

[1] Frederick Engels, *The Origin of the Family, Private Property and the State,* (Chicago, 1902), pp. 208–209.

[2] V. I. Lenin, *The State and Revolution,* in *Collected Works,* vol. 25 (Moscow, 1964), p. 472.

[3] The main propagator of this idea was Pierre Proudhon (1809–1865), French socialist and political writer, often regarded as the father of anarchism.

[4] See Karl Marx and Friedrich Engels, *The Communist Manifesto* (New York, 1955), especially pages 31 and 32; also Lenin, *State and Revolution,* pp. 435–436. For the excellent discussion of the functions of the socialist state and the difference between socialism and anarchism see Mieczysław Maneli, *O Funkcjach Państwa* (Warszawa, 1963), chapter 4; and also Jerzy Wiatr, *Społeczeństwo, Wstęp do Socjologii Systematycznej* (Warszawa, 1968), chapter 6.

[5] Karl Marx, *The Civil War in France* (London, 1933), p. 37.

[6] The Insurrection in Paris, March–May, 1871.

[7] Marx, *Civil War in France,* p. 37.

[8] Lenin, *State and Revolution,* p. 432.

[9] In this sense, the author uses the term "communist" to mean the state ruled by the Communist party, although in the strict Marxist terminology the communist stage of development does not yet exist, but according to the proclaimed ideology, is to be attained sometime in the future. Strictly speaking, the present "communist" states are either "people's democracies" or "socialist" in the transitional stage evolving toward communism. The main difference between socialism and communism lies in the mode of distribution of the National Product, which in socialism is divided in agreement with the following principle: "From each according to his ability, to each according to his work," and in communism is distributed accordingly: "From each according to his ability to each according to his needs." Also, in communism there is no state.

[10] Russian word for "council."

[11] Among the best known and most active were the St. Petersburg Soviet, presided for some time by Leon Trotsky after the arrest of its first president Khrustalyov, and the Moscow Soviet. For a description of the activity of the St. Petersburg Soviet see Lev Trotskii, *My Life; An Attempt at Autobiography* (New York, 1931), chapter 14.

[12] Lenin, *State and Revolution,* p. 419.

[13] Ibid., p. 424.

[14] Ibid., p. 424.

[15] Władysław Gomułka, *Przemówienia, 1959* (Warszawa, 1960), p. 494 (author's translation). On the same subject see also Zdzisław Jarosz, *System Wyborczy PRL* (Warszawa, 1969), p. 8.

[16] Kazimierz Sand and Marian Błażejczyk, "Z Teorii i Praktyki Samorządu Robotniczego w Polskiej Rzeczypospolitej Ludowej," *Annales Universitatis Mariae Curie-Skłodowska* 7, no. 3 (1960): 102.

[17] See Talmon, *Origins of Totalitarian Democracy,* chapter 3.

LOCAL GOVERNMENT IN THE COMMUNIST THEORY OF STATE

18 Henryk Groszyk, "Geneza i Istota Centralizmu Demokratycznego," *Annales Universitatis Mariae Curie-Skłodowska* 4, no. 5 (1957): 332.

19 Lenin, *State and Revolution*, pp. 429–430.

20 Article 2 of the Chinese Constitution states: "The National People's Congress, the local people's congresses and other organs of state without exceptions practice democratic centralism" ("The Constitution of the People's Republic of China," in S. B. Thomas, *Government and Administration in Communist China* [New York, 1955], p. 183, appendix 4. For G.D.R. see K. Sorgenicht et al., eds., *Verfassung Der Duetschen Demokratischen Republik. Dokumente. Komentar.* 2 vols [East Berlin, 1969] 2: 239).

21 Frederick Engels, *Herr Eugen Dühring's Revolution in Science (Anti-Dühring)* (New York, 1935), p. 315.

22 VI Zjazd Polskiej Zjednoczonej Partii Robotniczej, *Uchwała O Dalszy Socjalistyczny Rozwój Polskiej Rzeczypospolitej Ludowej* (Warszawa, 1971), p. 27.

23 Lenin, *State and Revolution*, p. 458.

24 Ibid., pp. 419, 420.

25 Stalin, presumably in order to justify his purges, claimed that with the development of the socialist state the sharpness of the class conflict increases. Today this theory is completely repudiated.

26 Sylwester Zawadzki, "Spór o Istotę Dyktatury Proletariatu," *Państwo i Prawo* 18 (October 1963): 664 (author's translation). On the same subject see also Wiatr, *Społeczeństwo*, p. 344 and Jarosz, *System Wyborczy*, pp. 60–61.

27 *XXII Zjazd Komunistycznej Partii Związku Radzieckiego* (Warszawa, 1961), p. 603.

28 The author feels that the term "decentralization" includes as much administrative as political dispersion of the decision-making process, e.g., the decentralized political system in the United States. In view of the highly centralized political structure in the communist countries the author prefers to use the term "deconcentration" and feels that it is a more appropriate term to describe the communist experience in the dispersion of decision-making. This same term is used by Professor W. Sokolewicz in his *Przedstawicielstwo i Administracja* (Warszawa, 1968), p. 15.

29 Zawadzki, "Spór o Istotę Dyktatury," p. 664.

30 This independence from the dominance by the Soviet Union dates back to the Polish and Hungarian revolts in 1956. Today Marxist politicians and theoreticians use the term "the Socialist Commonwealth" to denote the large degree of independence from Moscow's dictation, although they often are willing to admit the applicability to their own circumstances of the Soviet example as the first socialist country. On the other hand, the events in Czechoslovakia in August, 1968, proved that the Soviet Union and the other four East European communist countries did not shun from even a military intervention when developments in a neighboring country threatened their own system maintenance. The argument for the invasion was of course the Czechoslovak counterrevolution.

31 Lenin, *State and Revolution*, p. 404.

32 Ibid., p. 456.

33 Ibid., p. 469.

2

THE POLISH LOCAL GOVERNMENT

THE LEGAL AND HISTORICAL FOUNDATION

The body of law on the basis of which Polish local government acts is extremely large. The communist regime was established after a thousand years of historic existence of the Polish state. It introduced many sweeping changes but at the same time was forced to build on the already existing tradition and precedent. Some of the laws affecting local government originated as far back as the thirteenth century, such as those laws relating to village planning.[1] Laws and regulations adopted in the nineteenth century are still very much in effect; for example, those dealing with such matters as village communal property. A large bulk of pre-war Polish law is in use today. It would not serve our purpose to discuss that vast collection, and we shall limit ourselves to only a few of the more important statutes which established and defined the present system.

The councils, called in Poland National Councils (*Rady Narodowe*),[2] were organized in 1944 by an act of the underground communist-sponsored Home National Council (*Krajowa Rada Narodowa*), dated January 1, 1944, and a further act of the Home National Council, dated September 11, 1944,[3] which replaced the old system of local self-government, retaining from it, however, the method by which the heads of provinces and counties were appointed by the central authority. Organized by the communist underground and operating directly after the liberation from German occupation, the national councils played an important role in the communist take over of the country. Their functions far exceeded the legal limits of a new administrative organization. Even before the adoption of the new Constitution, the act of March 20, 1950[4] established the elective principle of the chairmen of the presidia of the national councils, making the Polish system identical in principle with the Soviet model.

The Constitution of the Polish People's Republic, enacted in

1952, declares the system of the national councils to be the foundation of the Polish state.[5] It affirms the three-stage division of noncentral government and three types of national councils, which are classified according to the scope of their territorial jurisdiction: communes, counties, and provinces; and which correspond roughly (in geographical terms only) to municipal or township, county, and the state governments in the United States. Each of the governments on all three levels is headed by an elected council.[6] The elections to the national councils are regulated by the act of October 31, 1957,[7] describing the manner and establishing the guiding principles concerning the number of councilmen to be elected at each level of local government. The most important reorganization of the national councils was achieved by the act of January 25, 1958,[8] which incorporated and superseded all the previous acts concerning the national councils, with the exception of the 1957 electoral legislation. The act is more embracing and comprehensive than the previous legislation, and it enlarges on the general provisions of the constitution. In keeping with the tendencies of decentralization after the Polish "revolution" of 1956,[9] it transferred many activities directed up to then by the ministries of the central government to the prerogatives of the national councils, increased considerably their economic independence, and delineated the competence of the national councils at all levels. Of fundamental significance was the designation of the county as the pivotal unit of the whole structure. The serious legal weakness of the act is its general and often vague wording, reading in part like a propaganda pamphlet. The act does not specify many matters in concrete terms but leaves them to subsequent legislation by the Council of State[10] or the Council of Ministers. One has the impression that the composition of the act, in keeping with the theory of permanent revolution, consciously permitted important changes in the spirit of the law, if not in the letter, by delegated legislation without the true parliamentary control or the necessity to promulgate new parliamentary acts.[11]

Recognizing some of its deficiencies and following the directives of the VIII Plenum of the Central Committee of the Polish United Workers' Party,[12] the parliament in 1963 amended the act of 1958.[13] The most important changes include the establishment of long-term economic planning in the lower councils, the widening and legal determination of the coordinating functions of the councils in relationship to other state organs, the strengthening of the role of sessions and standing committees as well as of the councilmen themselves, and the regulation of the position of the industrial and trade associations (firms) within the councils' structure. Today, then, the legal foundation of the structure and general functions of the national councils rest on the act of 1958 as amended in 1963. In addition, there are a number of specialized acts regulating different activities of the councils, as for example the budget law of 1970, which will be discussed below in relationship to these functions.

THE GENERAL STRUCTURE

The national councils are organized on a territorial basis and correspond to the historical administrative division of the country according to provinces (*województwo*); counties (*powiat*); cities (*miasto*); settlements (*osiedle*); and communes (*gromada*).[14] They form the pyramid of importance and authority, with the commune councils at the bottom, then up through the counties and cities to the provinces, and finally to the National Parliament (*Sejm*), which can be regarded theoretically as the national council of the entire country. In our consideration we will disregard the parliament, which, although logically at the top of the national council pyramid, is not a unit of local government. By the term local government we mean exclusively the government of any particular subdivision of the country and not the state organs forming the central government of Poland.

The smallest unit of Polish local government is a commune. There are 4,671 rural communes (*gromada*) and 55 urban settlements (*osiedle*) in Poland.[15] A rural commune may consist of varied numbers of villages. The size of the population varies from below 1,000 to above 5,000 with the largest number of communes in the population range of 2,000 to 3,000.[16] The average size of a commune is about 35 square miles. Settlements and many small towns have the administrative status of a commune. The settlements are small urban communities which do not have a city charter, and this is really only an historical difference between them and the small towns.

Theoretically, the county national councils form the pivot of the whole structure of local government. The functions and powers of local government not specifically delegated to the provinces or communes are reserved for the county national councils. There are 317 counties in Poland.[17] Some have less than 10 communes (73 counties) others more than 31 communes (5 counties). The largest proportion of counties have from 11 to 20 communes (201) and the average county has 15 communes.[18] Seventy-four larger cities are excluded from the jurisdiction of the counties and form counties of their own.[19] They have the functions and rights of the counties, excluding the activities connected with agriculture, and in addition they operate urban services and public utilities.

Poland has 17 provinces. The number of counties within the provinces varies from 34 in Poznań to 14 in Szczecin.[20] The population of a province is on the average between 1 and 2 million, with the biggest population (3.7 million) in the province of Katowice. The smallest in population is Koszalin with about 800,-000.[21] The average area of a province is from 9,000 square miles to 15,000 square miles. The biggest, the province of Warsaw, has over 16,000 square miles, and the smallest, the province of Opole, has about 6,000 square miles.[22]

The five largest cities, Warsaw (pop. 1,309,000), Poznań (pop. 470,000), Łódź (pop. 762,000), Wrocław (pop. 524,000), and Kraków (pop. 585,000)[23] are excluded from their respective provinces and form their own special administrative units, with the status of provinces. They are divided into city wards (Warsaw 7, Poznań 5, Łódź 5, Wrocław 5, Kraków 6)[24] which have the administrative status of counties. City wards exist also in other large cities which have the status of a county. These wards are on the administrative level of urban communes.

THE GENERAL FUNCTIONS

The constitution and the act of 1958 declare the state power to reside in the working people of cities and villages. The national councils at all levels are the organs of that power and express the people's will.[25] They direct the economic, social and cultural activities of their territory and are competent in all matters of state power and administration not specifically reserved for other state organs.[26] In principle, each council is the most universal organization of the local population and at the same time the only general organ of government representing the state power on its territory. It has therefore the dual function of caring for the needs of the local population and development of the locality as well as of implementing a realization of the national goals and enforcement of the directives of the central government. Theoretically, these two tasks are not separate since the concept of unified state administration excludes the possibility of conflict of interest between the locality and the state. The socialist state—being the state of the people—always acts in their interest.

The role of the councils is not considered to be that of administrators only, but also of *masters of the house*, responsible for all the economic, social, and cultural activities in their localities and, therefore, for all the functions of the socialist state, organizational as well as educational. They act first of all directly: they issue generally binding norms, establish policies for their own organs and institutions, determine production in their local industries, and coordinate activities of other bodies. They also perform their role by indirect influence, stimulating initiative of individuals and the whole population, and organizing meetings, conferences, and social and cultural affairs. They engage in propaganda and actively seek support for their own activities as much as for the goals of the state and programs of the Communist party. The national councils are the administrators combined in one unit with the social and political organizations.

The functions of the national councils include extension of the protection of law and order. They assist in the enforcement of criminal law, administrative regulations, and peace in public places and issue their own ordinances in these matters, and regulate traffic, fire protection and questions of public health. The councils are assisted here by the citizens' militia (*Milicja Obywatelska*), the centralized police force under the control of the ministry of internal affairs, but with the general supervision of and coordination by the councils. Also included in the duties of the national councils is the protection of the "people's democratic system as established by the constitution of the Polish People's Republic, and the in-interest of the state against enemy espionage and terrorism,"[27] although the organs of state security[28] are specifically excluded from the supervision of the councils. The law requires the councils to support the communist rule of Poland.[29]

In economics, the councils direct the activities of the territorial state industries, farms, service and trade organizations; regulate and stimulate production of individual private and cooperative agriculture, trade and crafts; supervise local building trade and administer dwelling houses and institutions of communal econ-omy; construct and conserve roads and streets and operate road and city transport; engage in irrigation and direct water economy. The councils also have important functions in education and cul-ture, providing physical plants for schools and universities, ad-ministering libraries, museums, and "palaces" of culture. In health and social welfare, they operate hospitals, clinics, senatoria, kin-dergartens, orphanages, and old people's homes. They are also active in the promotion of tourism and physical culture and op-erate rest homes, camps, swimming pools, stadiums, recreation centers, and other facilities for sports. The councils not only have responsibilities in regard to their own organs, but are also required to control and coordinate the activities of all the state, cooperative, social, and private institutions in their territory.

THE COUNCILS' MEMBERSHIP AND FUNCTIONS

The national councils are elected by the population of the terri-tory under their jurisdiction for a four-year term, the same as the parliament. Although the law of 1958 (as amended in 1963) does not require the election to the councils to take place together with the election to the parliament, this practice was followed in the 1965 and 1969 elections. In 1972, the new Gierek administration called for election, but only to the parliament, breaking the old established pattern.

The council deliberates at sessions called by the presidium (the executive committee), which decides, after consultation with the chairmen of the standing committees, on the agenda. Any other gatherings of councilmen do not constitute the council and have no legal validity. The first session of the new term is organized by the outgoing presidium and is opened by its chairman. It elects its own presidium for the duration of the council's term. The normal meetings of the council are chaired by the meetings' chairman and the records are kept by the meetings' secretary, both elected for one or more sessions. Half of all the members of the council constitute a quorum, but for the election or recall of the presidium or any of its individual members the presence of 2/3 of the membership is required. Resolutions are decided upon by a simple majority of those present and voting in an open vote. The council may employ a secret ballot in some matters and is required to do so for the election of the members of the presidium. Generally all the seatings are open to the public, which must be informed of their time, place, and subject matter. The chairman of the meeting can order a secret debate if in his opinion the interest of the state requires it, or a secret debate can be called on the proposal of the presidium. Persons from outside the council can address the meeting at the discretion of the chairman, and the chairman may also order directors of the state or cooperative institutions not administered by the council to furnish any information required for the debate. Meetings usually take place in the permanent seat of the council, but the presidium is empowered to organize a session in any other location (e.g. a factory) or a joint meeting with another council. Each session usually lasts only one day, although, legally, longer sessions are permitted.[30]

The council adopts its own rules and within the general framework of the 1958 statute is free to regulate a large number of matters regarding its own operation. Of these the most significant are the rules pertaining to the election of the chairman and the secretary and to the specifications of their functions. Also of vital importance are the council's own rules on the introduction of proposals, manner of debates including questions and closure, as well as voting and counting procedure. In addition, the council is empowered to set up its own committees and to define their role during the sessions. The minutes of each session, signed by the chairman and the secretary of the meeting, must include a description of the session with the summaries of *all* the speeches and debates and the *full* text of all proposals. In seven days their copy must be delivered to the presidium of the higher council, and the minutes of the province national council to the Office of the Council of Ministers.[31]

The formal expression of the activities and the will of the council takes place through the council's resolutions and acts. The resolutions are general directives addressed to the presidium, lower councils, and the population in general. The acts are legal norms binding on the territory under the jurisdiction of the council.[32] The acts can be divided into the council's own acts, which originate from the initiative within the council itself (the councilmen or presidium), and those acts which stem from the resolutions or acts of the higher council (*Sejm*), the Council of State, or the Council of Ministers. In this case the higher body initiating the normative action of the council usually sets up the general framework determining the scope and nature of such an act.

COUNCILMEN

The whole concept of the national council as the link between the population and the state power, or as it is called in communist terminology, the people's power, rests to a large degree on the role and functions of the councilman. He is, on the one hand, required to represent his constituency, within the well-specified limits of the communist party monopoly of power, and on the other hand, he is expected to perform the role of catalyst mobilizing the population for the achievement of the goals of national and local programs. He is legally obliged to fulfill this role by the oath taken on the first session of his council.[33] Any activity in violation of this oath does not carry the protection of law normally accorded to the councilman and, in certain cases, he may even be deprived of his mandate.[34] In other words, if he engages in actions openly contrary to the communist party ideology and goals as expressed in the program of the Front of National Unity,[35] he courts arrest with the waiver of his immunity. The oath specifies in no uncertain terms the councilman's duty "to contribute toward strengthening the bonds between the state authority and the working people." In order to fulfill this task he must explain to the population the goals and directives of the state and the party and agitate for their acceptance as well as for their smooth execution in accordance with the orders of the national council, its presidium, and other superior state organs. He is expected to mobilize the local population for political, social, and economic change and development stemming from the logic of the communist doctrine. By virtue of his oath, he is compelled to deepen the unity of the Polish nation. The communist sociopolitical theory implies that unity here is meant in its organic implication. The individual is supposed to merge himself with the social body organized along the lines laid down by communist teaching and perform willingly and unquestionably the assigned tasks for the good of the whole. The councilman is then required to participate in the education and creation of the new socialist man who accepts his specified role in the organically unified society. He cannot be a follower of popular demands, but must be an active leader and formulator of public opinion, stimulating, agitating, propagandizing, and organizing in the march toward a future communist society. His action is of special value in the field of economic development in which he is supposed to urge greater production, efficiency, and harder work.[36] In his role as organizer and mobilizer, the councilman should actively cooperate with the local social organizations[37] and with the political parties—especially, of course, the leading party, the Communist party.

The second important function of the councilman is to supply the authorities, in the first place his own council and the presidium, with information as to local attitudes regarding general policies of the state as well as specific local programs and drives.[38] With the centralized control of nearly all the means of communication, such information is of vital importance for the formulation of new and the adjustment of old policies. Here, even if not truly actively representing his constituency, the councilman facilitates some impact of popular demands on the official policies.

The councilman's representative nature permits him and indeed obliges him by law to resolve some of the justifiable local grievances resulting from the obvious misinterpretation of regulations or from the negligence of the local officials. He can lodge an interpellation on these and other matters to the presidium and must receive an answer within a two-week period.[39] Participation in the sessions is obligatory. In addition, the councilman must actively take part in the work of the committees to which he is appointed as well as perform other duties stemming from the work of his council. Willful neglect of his work, at least over the period of six months, entitles the council to abrogate his mandate.[40]

A councilman has "the full protection of the law" during the performance of his duties. The specific regulations of the criminal code prescribe punishment for physical violence against the councilmen or any other physical interference with the activities of the national councils.[41] These provisions protect the councilman from violence or interference by private citizens, but they do not accord him immunity from the action of the state itself. As noted above, his activity in violation of his oath subjects him to the possibility of administrative repression. In practice, any political behavior on his part challenging the established communist monopoly of power will not be granted immunity despite his status as a councilman.

A councilman is entitled to leave with pay from his employment during the session of the national council and during the performance of his other duties. The employer can refuse to grant the leave only with the approval of the shop council (a trade union body) and only if the employee's absence would result in a considerable financial loss to the enterprise. The management must notify the presidium of the national council as to the cause of refusal, and the presidium has the right to intervene at the next superior level of the enterprise's structure. During his leave of absence, the councilman receives his full pay, and the absence does not affect his seniority rights or his annual holiday.[42] There is no provision for reimbursement for the loss of time, and therefore income, for the self-employed councilman (individual peasants, craftsmen, small traders, professional people, etc.). Their duties as councilmen require financial sacrifice, and hence they are less likely to engage in the activities of the national councils. This, it seems, is exactly what the government desires, since they form the most independent group, politically and economically. Most of the other councilmen are, in fact, state employees and are therefore in economic and political subjection to the government, making possible a stricter control of their activities. The councilmen are reimbursed by the national council for their travel and hotel expenses. They also receive from the council a daily allowance of twenty-one *zlotys* in cities which have the status of a province or are the seats of a province, and eighteen *zlotys* in all other places.[43]

There can be only one interpretation of the duties of a councilman. He is supposed to be the agitator and the organizer of public support for the government's policies and to bring to the attention of the council information on public opinion. He settles the minor grievances of his electors. Ideally he should remove the natural conflict of interest (denied, by the way, by communist political theory) between individual citizens and the administration implementing the party program and should educate the citizens into merging themselves with the communist organic society. The law does not grant him immunity to challenge the political monopoly of the communists. The financial reward for the councilman's duties virtually bars the self-employed from participation and insures that most of the councilmen will be easily controlled state officials. The councilman, together with other "activists," provides the useful grease for the party-state machinery in its movement to effect revolutionary change.

THE COMMUNE COUNCIL

The membership of the commune national council is determined by law to be between 15 and 27 councilmen, depending on the size of the commune in terms of its territory and its population. The actual number is established by the resolution of the county national council.[44] In the elections of 1969, 112,267 councilmen were elected to the rural commune councils and 1,294 to the settlement councils.[45] The relatively large territory of the communes, many of them encompassing several villages, combined with the primitive means of transportation and communication existing in rural Poland and the desire, stemming from the character of the national councils, for direct influence and mobilization of the population necessitate an additional link between the village community and the commune council. Such a connection is provided by the office of a village elder (*Sołtys*) elected at a village meeting for the duration of the mandate of the national council (4 years). His election requires approval by the commune council if he is not at the same time a councilman. The council can also recall any village elder whose performance does not meet with its approval. Generally, the elder serves as the mediator and contact between his village and the council. In addition, he performs the important, even if unpleasant, duties of the tax collector, which to a large degree imperils his ability to have the complete trust and support of his co-villagers and may prevent him from mobilizing them voluntarily for the assigned tasks of development. His difficulties in this respect are increased and his prestige diminished by the fact that he does not play any role in tax assessment, but is merely a collector for a distant authority.[46]

The commune council is the Cinderella of the family of Polish local government, and the arrival of the handsome prince is yet at best far away in the future. In practice its activities are limited to the enactment of the annual economic plan and budget, both within the strictly defined framework of the directives of the higher councils (discussed fully in Chapter 5); the election of its own presidium and the collection of taxes. The commune council is also compelled by the nature of the whole structure of local government to generate popular support and enthusiasm for the policies of the central authorities and especially to induce individual farmers to produce the quantity and quality of crops demanded by the central economic plan. Only after performing these duties for the state is the commune council free to provide, out of its own often meager resources, for the needs of the population of the commune. Of course the commune, or rather its bureaucratic arm, also performs a number of strictly administrative functions. It registers permanent and transient inhabitants, certifies copies of official documents, and expresses its opinion regarding citizens' applications to the higher councils and other state offices. The registration of civil acts is in the hands of the registrar offices covering the territory of more than one commune.[47]

In many ways the crucial matter of the relationship between the commune council and the population is the obligation of the commune to collect taxes. The largest of all the taxes imposed on the rural community is the land tax levied on ownership.[48] In addition, the commune gathers entertainment turnover tax, electrification special assessment, and market and other administrative and licensing fees.[49] Up to 1966, the authority of the commune was seriously undermined by the fact that it was only the collector of taxes and of mandatory deliveries of agricultural products to the state. The assessment of these obligations was in the hands of the county council. The quotas for the deliveries were established by the central government. All negotiations concerning tax and deliveries had to be done by the commune citizens at the county seat, often many miles away from the individual villages. In the age of "horse and buggy" which still exists in the Polish countryside, the effort might have required a trip of a whole day's duration. Mistakes in assessment were quite common, and at least thousands of peasants all over Poland spent days every year traveling to and from the county seat.[50] One of the Polish local government specialists thus described the existing situation:

> In the county of Żnińsk alone, there were mistakes in the tax assessments for 1960 to the grand total of over two million *zlotys*. The mistakes were on an average of about one thousand *zlotys* per person, and consequently about two thousand peasants had to appeal in person to the organs of the county national council.[51]

The lack of authority to assess taxes and deliveries was a standard complaint of the members of the commune councils visited by the author. The problem was also well-recognized by the Polish local government specialists, who, as soon as the Statute of 1958 was promulgated, started to advocate more responsibility for the communes in taxation and delivery matters.[52] Starting in 1961 the central authorities also decided to strengthen the position of the communes and permitted them to grant a deferment of payment of taxes of up to three months.[53] In cases of natural disaster the commune was empowered to cut taxes up to 50% of the total assessment.[54] What was most important, however, in 1964 communes in 60 counties were permanently allocated the duty of tax assessment, and an additional 20 communes in the Wrocław province were given the same rights on an experimental basis. In these communes the effectiveness of tax collection increased while the number of complaints by individual citizens decreased. The farmers stopped losing valuable time in making trips to the county seats.[55] Encouraged by the results, the central government transferred, in 1966, all tax assessment duties to the communes.[56] The compulsory deliveries of agricultural products were abolished as of January 1, 1972.

Without any doubt the most important economic function of the commune is the stimulation of agricultural production. Polish agriculture is still conducted predominantly on a private basis.[57] The independence of farmers makes central planning difficult and uncertain. The government has to rely on the commune councils in its drive to fulfill the planned agricultural production. The party, weak as it is in the rural areas, must also depend on the communes for its agricultural program. The United Peasant Party is not a completely effective instrument of communication and agitation because the peasants distrust even this political group, which is supposed to represent them, and do not join the UPP in any great numbers.[58] In its effort to stimulate production the commune organizes propaganda drives, competitions for prizes and medals, and tries to improve the yields and agricultural efficiency by stressing technical education. It provides for the members of the commune the services of the commune agriculturist and, in some communes, those of a zoologist, mechanical instructor, and even veterinary doctor. The state channels through the commune financial stimuli for larger production in the form of bonuses and credits.[59]

Highly important in the drive for greater agricultural production is the organization of the agricultural circles (*Kółka Rolnicze*). The Statute of 1958 and the joint resolution of the Central Committee of the Polish United Workers' Party and the Supreme Committee of the United Peasant Party of June 1960 placed on the communes the responsibility of forming and supporting the circles.[60] The circles are not producers' cooperatives (*Kolkhozes*) and do not involve any pooling together of private land. These are associations of farmers for mutual cooperation and agricultural training. They have a strong tradition in Poland, extending back as far as the nineteenth century, especially in the western part of the country.[61] The specific purpose of the circles is the mechanization of agriculture for which the individual farmers have neither adequate funds nor large enough holdings for effective utilization.[62] The commune council exercises general supervision of the activities of the circles and must also approve all their economic plans and expenditures. It aids the circles by providing free services of agricultural specialists.

The communists' ideological dream and, it seems, their own

practical nightmare is the producers' cooperatives. The cooperatives are based on the principle of commonly owned and cultivated land. The communes, as the state agents in the countryside, should in theory actively promote their organization. The incentives to join are considerable, and the state creates extremely advantageous conditions for the cooperatives. It transfers state-owned land and other property to them for perpetual use without rent. They pay lower land tax and have priority in the purchase of building materials, agricultural machinery, and all spare parts. They are given prime consideration in the allocation of long-term credits. They can request the transfer to their jurisdiction of small industrial and service units, such as flour mills, sawmills, food processing units, and repair shops. They are allowed to organize handicraft production and to sell all their products in their own shops. They are entitled to 20% discount on all purchases of building materials, petroleum products, coal and gas for heating, and on the services rendered by the state machine stations. Many cooperatives have a retirement plan for men over sixty-five and women over sixty.[63] Despite all these obvious advantages, in 1970 there were only 1,071 producers' cooperatives in existence.[64]

The Polish peasants are strongly opposed to collective agriculture and are suspicious of any government drive in this direction. They even distrust the agricultural circles, fearing, perhaps with some reason, that circles are the first step toward fullfledged collectivization. This sentiment was realistically appraised by Mr. Gomułka, the previous first secretary of the PUWP, in the following manner:

> When we tried to hold a meeting in one village, the inhabitants did not turn out because they thought that 'they would come here to tell us to join a comparative,' because the people are afraid of collectivization. Such is the situation in many villages.[65]

Members of the commune councils, themselves peasants, give only lukewarm support to the official policy. The commune is more likely to advocate the formation of other types of cooperatives which do not require collectivization of land, such as dairy, gardening, and mutual loan and saving associations.[66]

The commune council finances all the communal services and utilities from its own budget. For the construction of new utilities, such as water,[67] electricity,[68] and gas supply systems, and for projects such as sports stadiums, state grants are available, if they are undertaken as "social deeds." It is also responsible for the maintenance of local roads, which places a heavy burden on the council. The category of local roads includes roads connecting the seats of the communes with one another and with the seats of the counties, roads between all villages, urban settlements, and towns which are not seats of counties, and roads leading to railroad stations, the sea, rivers, and airports.[69] Most of the construction of dwellings and farm buildings in the Polish countryside is done by private investors. The commune council provides guidance in terms of village building plans and building norms. The county councils can, with the consent of the province council, transfer to the authority of the commune enforcement of the construction regulations, inspection of the existing buildings, and ordering of necessary repairs.[70]

The commune council provides medical care and social assistance to its community, and also directs the fight against alcoholism. Individual farmers were not covered in the Polish People's Republic by state medical and hospitalization insurance until January 1, 1972, when such coverage was extended to all private farmers. As a result about 35% of the total population lived outside the protection of socialized medicine in a political and social system in which medical services were under centralized control. There was no system which would facilitate completely private practice of medical services. According to at least one Polish author, the rural population existed in "a state of health which leaves much to be desired. Over 20% of the children of preschool age are deficient in height and weight. About 3.4% of the inhabitants of villages have tuberculosis, 6.7% have bone diseases and a large percentage of children have rickets and caries."[71] The commune constructs health centers which usually combine all the medical, surgical, and dental services under one roof, and engages doctors, nurses, and midwives. The council's resources are usually too limited to cope with the results of a long history of medical and dental neglect. Also it has difficulty in attracting doctors and other personnel, not only because of the lack of funds for substantial and necessary financial incentives, but also because of the unattractiveness of life in rural Poland (lack of cultural, housing, and educational facilities) and the traditional disrespect for "peasant existence" among the Polish professional class.[72] And, we must remember the state of transportation in the rural areas, where the horse-drawn vehicle over poor roads would take many hours to deliver a patient to the nearest doctor or medical center. Even ambulance service based in the cities cannot greatly speed matters. Progress in this field was being made, but the commune government was not quite capable of attacking the problem in a fully effective manner. This required indeed a massive central government investment and program which was provided by 1968.[73]

Alcoholism is a serious problem in Poland.[74] The commune council is empowered to prohibit the sale of alcoholic beverages containing more than 18 percent of pure alcohol on Saturdays, public holidays, paydays, and market days. It can request the county council to order the total prohibition of the sale of alcoholic beverages containing more than 18 percent of pure alcohol, or even those of as low as 4.5 percent.[75] Anybody traveling in Poland will notice that the use by the communes of this authority is not excessive and that, at best, it may prevent the consumption on some days of pure vodka, but not of other less potent alcoholic beverages. The only effective weapon against large consumption would be a prohibitive increase in price. This would of course diminish the large profits of the state monopoly.[76]

In the field of education the commune council supplies the primary schools, schools of agricultural training, and kindergartens with physical plants and maintenance. It does not control the curriculum, which is determined for the whole country by the ministry of education, or the appointment of personnel. Teachers are salaried employees of the state and not of the local government. Primary education in Poland is by law universal, free of charge and compulsory.[77] This places a heavy economic burden on the communes, which many of them, especially in the rural areas, are not capable of meeting. The 1961 school reform law created additional problems by increasing the time of compulsory school attendance from seven to eight years.[78] At the same time there were many complaints that the school facilities were grossly inadequate, with 10,000 rural schools requiring badly needed repairs.[79] The large natural increase of population added to the pressure on school facilities and it was calculated that by 1965 an additional 30,000 new school rooms must be constructed.[80] Finally, it was recognized by the political leadership that the solution of the problem was outside the financial possibilities of the communes.[81] The Social Fund for the construction of the Millennium Schools was constituted in commemoration of the thousand years of the existence of the Polish state. The Fund organized a vigorous campaign for private contributions. A large part of the donations, although ostensibly voluntary, were obtained through what was in fact a special school tax.[82]

In addition all communes are required to organize and finance public libraries. The libraries' functions are to stimulate an interest in the arts and sciences and to increase the sociopolitical awareness of the population.[83] The commune council also operates small local industries, such as small factories producing building supplies, and works excavating peat, and manages marketplaces, slaughterhouses, and public baths.[84]

All retail trade and the supply of agricultural inputs (e.g. fertilizers) and fuels is in the hands of the consumers' cooperatives, called *Samopomoc Chłopska* whose activities also date back to the nineteenth century. The commune council supervises the activities of these cooperatives regarding the quantity and quality of merchandise sold, prices, and proper accounting. It establishes hours of business for shops and warehouses. The representatives of the cooperatives attend the meetings of the council in which matters relating to their interests are discussed.[85]

A large amount of construction and renovation is achieved in a commune with the help of so-called "social deeds." The population "pledges" finances, materials, and labor for a particular project. The pledge is usually suggested to the public by the council, political party, or some social organization. Then enthusiasm for the project is generated by a strong propaganda effort, and finally the action is legalized by an act of the council. From then on the pledge of institutions and individuals is strictly enforced by the presidium of the council. The state offers financial help for the following actions undertaken as social deeds:

1. Construction of roads—15% of the total cost, and in the case of local roads of special importance, even up to 40%.
2. Construction of local bridges—35%, and in special cases,

with the approval of the province national council, up to 60%.

3. Construction and renovation of the state roads—60%.
4. Construction of new schools, kindergartens, health centers, houses of culture, libraries, public utilities, and sport stadiums—up to 60%.
5. Repairs to commune buildings and other objects classified above—20%.
6. Construction of streets and sidewalks, the planting of trees on streets, the setting up of parks, village greens, and children's playgrounds—20%.
7. For drainage—10% of the renovation work and 30% of a new undertaking.

The state grants must be repaid, with the exception of money appropriated for work on state roads and local roads of special importance. All the materials for the construction should be provided from local sources. Only in case of a lack of some of the raw materials can they be supplied by the province or a ministry.[86]

In reality the money "pledged" for social deeds constitutes an additional tax, easier to collect because part of it is in the form of labor and because it is used for tangible local needs. It is imposed on the peasants in addition to the normal taxes. Above all, the social deeds squeeze out the local resources of materials and labor which are unaccounted for in the already taut national economic plan. This type of tax collection is typical for the agrarian state, in which "frequently the government tries to obtain its income in the form of labor contribution rather than, or in addition to, the tax on production. Thus the labor corvée or compulsory service forms a major source of governmental input."[87]

The functions of the national councils of small towns and urban settlements which have commune status are the same as those of the rural communes, excluding, of course, the control and direction of agriculture and related activities. In addition, they are in charge of the supply of city utilities (gas, electricity, and water), the provision of city services (transportation, street cleaning, garbage collection), and the administration of housing, hotels, shops, theaters and cinemas.

One may conclude that the activities of the rural commune national councils are not very broad and in practice are limited to stimulation of agricultural production, collection of taxes, and maintenance of schools and libraries. The scope of urban communes is larger because of the involvement in the administration of urban services. In all communes the mobilization of the population for "social deeds" plays an extremely important role in the construction of new projects by means of self-help. By their own admission the Polish writers view the commune as the weakest link in the structure of the national councils.[88] One of them, Zygmunt Rybicki, states the following: "Still too many matters, which are in the competence of communes, end with the decisions taken by the organs at the higher level."[89]

The commune to a large degree is left outside the scope of social benefits, and modernization proceeds more slowly in the countryside than in the urban centers. It is as if there were two Polands: one modern, industrial, and socialist; the other agricultural, independent, and in many localities, especially in the Eastern provinces, backward. Industry and the cities take the major part of the investment, leaving the villages to fare for themselves. This is not to say that the peasants live in poverty. By comparison with the prewar rural conditions, they fare much better today.[90] They benefited by the land reform, which increased their holdings (1944–1949). Heavy war losses and postwar industrialization— even if paid for by the exploitation of the population during the Stalinist period—relieved the chronic prewar underemployment in agriculture by diminishing the rural population and providing urban jobs for the remaining surplus. The material position of the peasants is today much better than that of the majority of the workers. This is due to their hard work on their own land, the ownership of which they are not about to relinquish,[91] and to the reasonably just prices set by the government for agricultural products. The communist leadership recognizes that in order to increase food production, so vital to the general growth of Poland, it has to insure a peaceful relationship with the peasants and to offer them reasonably high material incentives.[92] Even a slight change in the precarious balance may lead the farmers to employ their powerful weapons, economic boycott and decreased production.[93]

The position of the commune national council may be usefully compared to that of native administrators in a colony—representing the central authority, but not quite trusted by it; enforcing the central government's policies, but not with complete enthusiasm; directing the local activities, but not having the confidence or the esteem of the local population. The council is subject to pressure from both sides and tries to perform a balancing act between the two, often pleasing no one. In this situation it is not at all surprising that the councilmen of the commune do not show too much willingness to participate in the activities of the councils. Theirs is indeed a thankless role.

THE COUNTY COUNCIL

The actual size of the membership of the county national councils is determined by the province national council, varying from 50 to 60 councilmen in the ordinary counties and from 50 to 80 in the cities with county status.[94] In the elections of June, 1969, 17,639 councilmen were chosen to serve in the county councils.[95]

Legally (and in general terms) the county council is the basic unit in the structure of Polish local government. All functions, duties, and activities of the national councils system which are not specifically assigned by law to other levels of local bodies belong to the prerogatives of the county council. The state organs at the county level, as a rule, decide most administrative matters in the first instance, with the province and other higher administrative bodies serving as the level of appeal. The direct management of most economic, social, and cultural affairs should be concentrated at the county level, although the transfer of functions from the province government to the county councils "should be undertaken gradually with consideration for the local specifics."[96] The county council coordinates, within the broader coordination of the province, all activities of its subordinate councils—commune, settlement, and town. It specifically supervises the total agricultural production of the county through the commune councils and the county technical and specialist services.

The state farms and the state machinery stations[97] are under the direction of the province national council. Control by the county council of them is limited to approval of their plan of work and the general supervision of their activities. The county council operates and conserves the county drainage system, but all new construction is in the hands of the province national council. Most of the county councils have a veterinary station, and many counties operate, in addition to this, veterinary centers in some of the communes. Agricultural research and advice stations and the fight against pests and crop blight are directed by the province council with the cooperation of the county council, whose activity is limited to enforcement of the regulations. The duty of the county council to extend special help to the Agricultural Producers' Cooperatives is realized by allocating to the cooperatives free of charge the services of the county agricultural specialists and by insuring that the cooperatives are given priority in the supply of machinery, fuel, fertilizers, and long-term loans. All cooperatives are required to undergo formal registration with the county council.

The county council supervises industries which produce exclusively for the county needs. The same enterprises, however, are united in the province associations, which coordinate their performance. Hence the county industries have two bosses, independent of one another. This arrangement leads to constant friction between the county council and the province associations. The associations plan production, decide on production technology, and check on accounting and financing. The economic plan of an individual enterprise forms a part of the total plan of the county council. The profit or loss of each enterprise enters the county budget. The county council has a right to influence planning and to enforce the fulfillment of the production quotas. It is not at all clear what exactly is meant by "influence the planning." In practice the relationship between the county council and local industry is different in various counties[98] because of the unclear regulations on this matter,[99] and it often depends on the personalities and political standing of the people involved— the members of the presidium as well as the directors of the enterprises and of the associations. (This problem will be discussed below in connection with planning.)

The building and financing of Workers' Housing Settlements is in the hands of the county council or the city council, although the design and actual construction is performed by the province enterprises. The Workers' Housing Settlements are not exclusively designated for occupation by physical laborers, as the name would suggest. On the contrary, they house all who can secure an allocation from the county or city council, regardless of occupation. Most of the individual building in the countryside is performed by county or private construction firms. Production of building materials for exclusive use in the county is organized and directed by the county council.[100] The building of new hard-surface local roads is also in the hands of the county council, since it possesses the necessary concentration of machinery and technicians. Often the actual construction is performed with the labor and part of the capital provided by the commune as a "social deed." The maintenance of local roads is undertaken jointly by the commune and county councils, the county donating machinery and some of the funds and the commune the rest of money, labor, and materials.

The retail trade and craft services in Poland are conducted by state, cooperative, and private enterprises. The county and city councils run state shops directly and regulate the activities of cooperative and private shops, especially with regard to licensing, hours of business, assortment of goods and services, and allocation of shop space. Restaurants, coffee shops, bars, and bakeries are administered by the county or city councils.

All employees are covered by the state compulsory insurance system, which provides in addition to health and hospitalization services, unemployment and maternity benefits, and disability and old-age pensions. It is administered independently of the local government by the Social Insurance Administration, which has branch offices in all counties. The county social service is concerned only with the destitute who are not covered by insurance. Since the communes and towns take care of their own charges, the county deals only with marginal cases and helps communes if they encounter financial problems in the administration of their benefits. All property owners, including individual farmers, have to cede their property to the state in order to qualify for social aid. The county hospitals are of a general type, and special cases are referred to the province hospitals. The county operates clinics for tuberculosis, skin diseases, and venereal diseases. These provide treatment, but not hospitalization. The county councils and cities with the status of a county operate ambulance and first-aid stations. Apart from providing transportation and medical services, these stations also study the causes of accidents and suggest ways for their prevention.

In the field of education the county council supplies buildings, equipment, services, and utilities to high schools and trade schools. Like the commune council, it does not influence school policies, curricula or hiring of personnel. Theaters and cinemas are mostly administered by cities and towns, and only mobile units are under the direction of the county. Most of the counties operate their local museums.

The county national council, although theoretically having a pivotal role in the Polish local government structure, in practice is secondary to the province council. It is not so independent and free from control by the province as the letter and spirit of the law suggests.[101] There is hardly any reason to allocate direction of agricultural services and state farms to the relatively remote province authorities. County supervision of local industry has little impact since the actual management is in the hands of the province associations. Province "coordination" means in fact detailed instructions and close supervision of the county work. The county is an executor of the higher will rather than an independent agent. Most of the purely administrative functions as well as the enforcement of state and province regulations are concentrated at this level. On the other hand, the county performs many administrative functions which, according to the general principle of the structure of the Polish local government, should belong to the commune. The commune, however, is considered unreliable from the political as well as the functional point of view. All in all, the county council is the most important unit of local government in administration and in the enforcement of state policies, but not in the decision-making process.

THE PROVINCE COUNCIL

The Election Statute of 1957 sets the membership of the province national council at between 80 to 120 councilmen, with the actual number for each province decided upon by the Council of State.[102] In the election of 1969, 2,500 councilmen were chosen to serve at the province level in the 17 province national councils and the 5 councils in cities with province status.[103]

The most important functions of the province national council are the formulation of the general policies and the coordination of the activities of all national councils in the province. In the field of economics it directs regional industry and building enterprises, state farms, state farm machinery and drainage enterprises, state road transport enterprises (trucking and buses, excluding city transport), and state consumer and industrial wholesale trade (excluding wholesale enterprises covering more than one province). Furthermore the province council directs building and conservation of state roads and bridges and controls all regional industry in its territory. Regional industries include most of the consumer-goods industry, as distinguished from "key industries," which are all producer-goods industries, and very large consumers' goods enterprises, which, it is held, must be centrally directed.

The enterprises of the province are grouped in associations. An association is composed of all factories producing the same commodity, and there are, for example, the Association of Shoe Factories, the Association of Dress Factories, and the Association of Meat-packing Factories. Each association is directed by a board formed by all directors of the factories in the association, the chairman of the board, and the vice-chairman. The association coordinates production, supply of raw materials, and the distribution of produced commodities. The province council directs the industry through the associations. The key industry is required to coordinate its activity with the province council. In practice, this cooperation is limited to reports on activities and the contribution of funds for specific projects.

It is part of the province council's work to direct the state farms and the farm machinery stations as to the planning of their production, employment, supply of raw materials and machinery, finances, and accounting. It collects their profits and covers losses. Most of the province councils operate state drainage enterprises which supply services to public and private investors. All road transportation in Poland is in the hands of the enterprise called State Automobile Transportation (*Państwowa Komunikacja Samochodowa*). The province branch of PKS is under the administration of the province council. It operates trucking firms and bus services covering the territory of the province. Long distance buses and trucks are run directly by the central board of PKS in Warsaw. The city bus service is supplied by the city council.

In education, the role of the province council is limited to enforcement of regulations and to furnishing buildings and services to places of higher learning. But, the province council operates directly the province theatre, central library, museum, and palace of culture. The province hospitals are usually specialized, caring for example for tubercular cases, and mental patients. In addition, the province operates its own health resorts and institutions for people in need of special social care, such as orphanages and old peoples' homes. The distribution of drugs is under the strict control of the province council.

According to the Statute of 1958 the province national council is entrusted with only a limited number of functions involving direct operation. Its main duty is coordination of the activities of the subordinate units of local government and the formulation of general policies for the province. In actual practice, however, the terms "coordination" and "formulation of general policies" are broadly interpreted, and the province council issues detailed instructions, regulations, and bylaws binding on its territory and controls closely all activities of the county and commune national councils. Although the statute specifies to the contrary, the province, and not the county, is the principal unit of local government. In our personal observation, we noticed that the officials connected with the province national councils were doubtful as to the ability of the lower bodies to run their own affairs efficiently. This attitude was based on the assumption that the educational and cultural levels of local councilmen and the qualifications of local councilmen, officers, and members of the staff are too low to warrant the transmission of responsibility from the province to the county level. In turn, a similar approach is taken by the county in regard to its communes. This argument may be valid from the point of view of administrative efficiency, but it contradicts the basic principle of genuine local self-government.

THE CITY COUNCIL

The city national council of each of the five cities with the status of a province has the same prerogatives and functions as the ordinary province councils, excluding the activities connected with agriculture. Similarly, the cities with the status of county enjoy the same privileges and carry out the same duties as counties. In all cities divided into city wards, the city national council is empowered to transfer many of its functions to the ward council, which performs them in addition to its normal activities. The city council must, however, retain the prerogative to issue legal acts, and decisions regarding taxation and fees, and to administer enterprises, property, and facilities serving the whole city.[104] The city wards have less independence than counties and communes due to the compactness of a city and the fact that most of the city services are conducted as one individual unit.

THE PRESIDIUM

The national councils elect their own presidia, which are their executive organs. The presidium is subject to control by its own council and to control by the presidium of the next higher level in the local government structure.[105] It is composed of the chairman, vice-chairmen, secretary, and the members. The chairman, vice-chairmen, and secretary are full-time employees of the council and as such are state officials. The members serve on a part-time basis only. The election of the chairman requires the approval of: the council of ministers in the case of the chairman of the province council or the chairman of the city council with province status; the chairman of the council of ministers in the case of the chairman of the county council or the city with the county status; the presidium of the province council in the case of the chairman of the city council or the city ward which does not have the status of a county; the presidium of the county council in case of the chairman of the commune council.[106]

A national council has the power to recall, at any time, its presidium or individual members of the presidium and to elect a new body, or new members. The elected persons assume their duties directly upon election. This also applies to the chairman, even though his assumption of office requires the approval of a superior state organ. The Statute of 1958 does not specify any time limit in which the approval must be decided upon. The chairman loses his powers automatically on notification of the refusal of approval, and the council must conduct a new election. The

Statute does not have a provision for determining the course of action if the council elects the same person again. There were instances of such cases, and they resulted, as one Polish jurist pointed out, from a lack of understanding of the law by the councilmen. The law excludes the possibility of appointment to the position of chairman of the presidium of an individual who is not acceptable to the superior organ of government. Members of the presidium do not have to be elected from among the councilmen and the persons elected from outside the council do not have to be initiated into its membership.

The presidium represents the council when the council is not in session. It executes the resolutions of its own council and enforces the regulations of all superior state organs. In particular, the presidium does the following: prepares and calls together the sessions of the council, acting in coordination with the chairmen of the standing committees; formulates the proposals for the economic plan and budget and, after their passage by the council, supervises their fulfillment; directs and coordinates the activities of the departments of the presidium and the council's own enterprises; and issues regulations for the execution of existing acts. Apart from its functions as an organ of the national council, the presidium performs many duties as an organ of the unified state administration. To mention only a few, it plans the recruitment to the army, determines fees for many communal services, allocates state land for individual housing, cemeteries, and state parks, negotiates common investments with the presidia of other national councils, and provides state grants to social organizations. The presidium forms a collective body.[107]

Only in cases of emergency is the chairman of the presidium empowered to issue regulations. They must be validated by the whole presidium at its next meeting. In practice, the presidium divides among its members the functions of directing the departments of the council and of supervising the lower councils in such a manner that each member is in charge of certain departments and certain counties and communes. Half of the total number of members of the presidium constitutes a quorum, and the decisions are made by a simple majority in an open vote.[108] The work of the presidium is determined by the internal statute of the council and by the general directives of the presidium of a superior council. The presidium establishes a timetable in which it determines, in advance, the subjects of the meetings for a given period. The meetings are called together by the chairman. They are usually held once a week or one in ten days. The discussions are not open to outsiders, but the chairman can invite persons other than members if he feels their advice would be useful for the topic under consideration. In special cases the presidium may hold open meetings outside of its normal seat such as, in a factory, or at village meetings, or may call together a conference with other state organs, for example the State Control Board. A copy of the minutes of each meeting must be delivered in seven days to the presidium of the superior council.[109]

The presidium acts formally by passing resolutions. The most important resolutions require consultation with appropriate standing committees of the council. All resolutions can be declared void by the Council of Ministers or the presidium of the superior council if they are in conflict with the law or the general policies of the state.[110]

The chairman of a presidium occupies a special position in the local government structure. He is the official representative of his council as well as the representative of the state. Thus he is the head of the state administration in his locality. He prepares, calls together, and chairs the meetings of the presidium, opens the sessions of the council, and signs all the resolutions of the presidium. As head of the administration, the chairman is the superior of the employees of the local government, and it is his duty to control personally the economic planning and financial matters, and to supervise the activities of the bureau of internal affairs, including the political police. The chief of the Citizens' Militia (M.O. – the police) is required to inform the chairman of all activities of his force. Many acts of the central government allocate to the chairman the responsibility for their fulfillment. For example, in 1958 the Chairman of the Council of Ministers required the chairmen of the national councils to organize the commissions of employment,[111] and, in 1959, to cooperate with the State Control Board.[112] The chairman is not only dominant inside the council, but is also often directly charged with enforcing the regulations of the central government, and in reality, he is responsible for the realization of the general policies of the state.[113] The Statute of 1958 does not specify the duties of the secretary, apart from the requirement that he should sign, together with the chairman, all resolutions of the council and of the presidium.[114]

All the members of the presidium are required to "toil" for the welfare of the Polish People's Republic and the working people, to obey the law, and to behave in a "proper" manner during the performance of their duties, as well as in their private lives.[115] All the full-time members of the presidium are treated as state civil servants and are accorded special protection of the law, which prescribes punishment for interference with their duties. They receive salaries, expense accounts, leave with pay, pensions, and free medical care. The work of the part-time members of the presidium is considered to be a social obligation. They do, however, enjoy the same benefits as the ordinary councilmen.

PRESIDIUM OF THE COMMUNE COUNCIL

The rural commune elects to its presidium the chairman and not more than three part-time members.[116] The presidium of the urban commune (settlements and towns) has, in addition, one vice-chairman. The secretarial and organizational work of the presidium is performed by the secretary of the bureau of the commune national council, who is not an elected official or a member of the presidium, but a government employee appointed by the chairman of the presidium of the county national council.[117] The functions of the presidium are not very extensive, and a large part of its work is specially connected with the assessment and collection of taxes[118] and the consequent supervision of the village elders in their tax and fees collection.[119] The direct control of this collection is in the hands of the finance department of the county council. The commune presidium is expected to provide moral support for the elders and to pressure them if they are reluctant to carry out their duties.

The presidium of the commune council administers the commune property. The council may transfer the actual management to the village in which the property is located. The presidium supervises the activities of the consumers' cooperatives, especially concerning the supply of commodities, storage and transportation of compulsory deliveries, and the establishment of new shops, stores, and other cooperative enterprises. It conducts inspections of all these facilities and informs the board of directors of each cooperative of the results. The board must take action in fourteen days on the recommendations of the presidium. The presidium enforces the fire prevention regulations, organizes and helps the voluntary fire brigades, and provides them with equipment, stations, and alarm and communication systems. It is the duty of the presidium to render help to the "organs of public security," which are the Citizens' Militia (ordinary police), the Corps of Internal Security (special army units for fighting internal unrest), and the Office of Security (*Urząd Bezpieczeństwa*—political police). This duty also covers cases in which actual physical assistance is required. The presidium is also charged with keeping the peace.[120]

All the strains and stresses of responsibility of the commune council are concentrated in the person of the chairman. His official position is that of a faithful servant of the state. His peasant origin influences his allegiance to his own community and mitigates the harshness of the government's policies. Most of the chairmen interviewed expressed a feeling of frustration, resulting from their awkward position, especially with regard to the collection of state dues. The material rewards for the job are modest. The pay scale normally ranges from 1,500 to 2,300 *zlotys* monthly.[121] The chairman's position as head of administration is undermined by the fact that the secretary, the head of the commune bureau, is nominated by the higher level of local government. It is argued that the low educational level and lack of administrative experience of the chairmen of the communes requires the services of a professional secretary. (In my opinion, the political unreliability of the chairmen and the council in general should be considered as a partial explanation of this arrangement.) His salary matches that of the chairman (about 1,500 *zlotys*).

Corruption is not at all unheard of in Polish local government, and the commune council probably has more than its share. It ranges from the mild form of settling matters over a drink to the more serious arrangements of a power group within the commune which allocates to itself the most attractive consumers' goods, often for resale at higher prices, and which can be bribed to modulate the citizens' obligations to the state and to the law.[122] The low pay of the commune officials partly explains the corruption.

PRESIDIUM OF THE COUNTY NATIONAL COUNCIL

The county presidium has a maximum of six members: the chairman, one vice-chairman, a secretary and not more than three part-time members.[123] Because the county council is the basic unit of state administration, the activities of the presidium are mostly connected with actual administration. It maintains close contact and supervision over the presidia of the commune councils, approving in particular the elections of their chairmen. It oversees, through its financial department, the collection of taxes and has the right to recall a village elder whose performance as a collector is not satisfactory. In the field of economics, the actual supervision of the industries located in the county is often performed directly by the departments of the province.[124] The county presidium is charged with the utilization of local resources and with the organization and stimulation of "social deeds," for which it allocates prescribed state funds. It issues licenses for vehicles and drivers, for the organization of dances and fairs, and for the exercise of private trades and crafts. In addition it registers all enterprises in the county.

The chairman of the presidium of the county council may be regarded as the most important administrator in the structure of local government and as a mediator between the province and the communes. He is in constant close contact with the province presidium and is not too far removed from the commune officials. He serves as a necessary link between the two, explaining to the province the local difficulties and pressing on the communes for a better performance. Generally speaking, he is overworked and often unappreciated by both sides. However, the government does recognize his usefulness, and by Polish standards he is well paid. His monthly salary is from 3,500 to 4,200 *zlotys*. In addition, he receives free housing with all utilities furnished and other fringe benefits accorded state officials. The vice-chairman and the secretary have salaries ranging from 3,200 to 4,000 *zlotys*.[125] The vice-chairman and the part-time members of the presidium spend most of their time touring the countryside and serving as controllers, agitators, and organizers. The secretary directs the county departments and performs the unpleasant and frustrating task of listening to complaints and receiving petitions. The working day of the county presidium is spent dealing with the petty matters which compose the greatest bulk of administrative business of any county. The central government's "crash" programs (which are often chaotic) of economic and industrial development stretch the working capacity of the presidium to a near-breaking point. They force the presidium to act under great duress and place it in a state of constant emergency, in which the normal administrative process is interrupted. This, of course, leads to disorder and extreme inefficiency.

PRESIDIUM OF THE PROVINCE NATIONAL COUNCIL

The law sets the membership of the presidium of the province council at a chairman, two vice-chairmen, a secretary and four part-time members. Theoretically the presidium is the executive organ of the province council. In practice, it dominates the council (see Chapter 3), and, as the powers of the local government are concentrated in the province council, it dominates the whole province. The presidium is the most important power group in the whole structure of the national councils. It enjoys a large degree of autonomy in economic matters, but its decision-making process in administration and politics is strictly controlled by the central government and the Communist party. The degree of its freedom of action depends largely on the political and personal standing of its members, especially its chairman, and on their initiative and their willingness to take political risks.

The chairman of the province council is a state dignitary of high standing, and he is accorded all the reverence that was given to the prewar *wojewoda* (state-nominated head of a province). He is indeed a powerful man, who belongs, politically and economically, to the elite. His monthly salary of 5,000 to 6,000 *zlotys*,[126] although comfortable, is not unreasonably high by comparison with other well-paid employees in industry, science, or government. But, he receives a monthly supplement of 1,500 *zlotys* and the staggering sum of 100,000 to 120,000 *zlotys* yearly for "representation."[127] The vice-chairman and the secretary are paid monthly salaries of 4,800 to 5,500 *zlotys*.[128] All these functionaries have at their disposal official cars with chauffeurs, state-paid residences, and other fringe benefits. Many of them are engaged in other important state and party functions. The chairman, as a representative of the Polish People's Republic, performs many ceremonial duties. He is invited to open new schools, factories, roads, and bridges and to review military and industrial parades. He welcomes the representatives of the central government and the representatives of foreign powers visiting his province. He opens the sessions of the province national council and represents the state at these sessions. He is responsible for the legality of the actions of local government. He approves the appointment of parish priests. He is regarded as being equal in rank to a vice-minister in the council of ministers.

The vice-chairmen spend much of their time traveling about the province taking part in sessions of the county councils, attending conferences, and supervising the work of subordinate councils and economic units. The secretary directs the vast bureaucracy of the province. The members of the presidium of the province national council are extremely busy and important men belonging to the ruling class and rather remote from the population. This is especially true in the case of the chairmen. They are the men who make Polish local government work, and their position is powerful and secure as long as their councils tick the same beat as the central clock in Warsaw.

PRESIDIA OF THE CITY NATIONAL COUNCILS

The presidium of a City Council is composed of a chairman, a secretary, and a varying number of vice-chairmen: three in the city of Warsaw, two in the cities above 100,000 inhabitants, one in all other towns, city wards, and settlements. There are four part-time members in the five cities with province status and three in all other cities and towns.[129] The functions of the city presidia are similar to the functions of the presidia of other councils at the same level, with the exception of the presidium of

Warsaw, the capital, which requires a large number of ceremonial duties and accords a special status to the chairman. The chairman of the presidium of a town is usually on a higher educational level than the chairman of a commune, and he has more personal authority. He is also of better political standing and is therefore considered to be more reliable.

DEPARTMENTS

The administration of the affairs of local government is performed by the departments of the presidia of the national councils. At the same time, the departments are local branches of the central ministries. The presidia establish departments as prescribed by the regulations of the Council of Ministers.[130] The activity of a department is directed by the presidium of the national council, by the corresponding higher department and, in the case of a province department, by the corresponding ministry.[131] A department is not an exclusively passive agent of a presidium, but is required to act in accordance with the law.[132]

The staff of the departments are members of the state civil service and as such are subject to all civil service regulations. On the average, a province has a staff of about 850; a county, of about 140; an urban county, 250; a small city, 14; a settlement as well as a commune, of only about 7.[133] A department is headed by the chief, who is appointed by the presidium with the approval of the competent minister or the chief of a comparable department of the higher national council.[134] He is responsible for his actions to his presidium as well as to the superior department. This duality of responsibility, often impossible to balance, predisposes many chiefs to surrender whatever decision-making authority they may have to the members of the presidium in charge of the supervision of their departments.[135] This unhealthy situation impedes the performance of the administrative branch, as an extremely busy member of the presidium with his organizational-political work is required to inquire into minute routine matters. From a supervisor he becomes an administrator. He is often called upon to settle issues requiring a certain professional sophistication which the presidium member may not have. The chief, because of his training and long years of practical experience, should be well qualified to rule on the problems at hand, but he prefers to resign his authority to the higher political force—the presidium—and to protect his position in relationship to his superior department. What is more, generally speaking, the chief usually has little time to devote himself to his real task, that of directing the branch of administration. He spends unending hours attending sessions of the council, meetings of the presidium, and various other "gatherings of the faithful" and conferences resulting from the political and "revolutionary" character of Polish local government.

The commune does not have separate departments, but has only one bureau. It is staffed by an accountant, a clerk for economic matters, a clerk for general administration, and a public registrar.[136] The bureau is headed by the commune secretary, a professional civil servant nominated by the presidium of the county council. The qualifications for the office of secretary require that the candidate have either a high school education and two years of practice in the state administration, or a primary school education and at least three years of practice in state administration, and that he pass a special examination. In addition, the post of secretary can be occupied by any person who has been a member of the presidium of a national council at any level for at least three years. The secretary directs the administration of the commune, attends, in an advisory capacity, all sessions of the council and meetings of the presidium, and prepares the proposals for the resolutions of the council and the presidium. He must sign all the resolutions of the presidium as well as of the council. In addition he is the public notary for the commune. His position at his own level is relatively much stronger than that of the department's chief. The institution of the commune secretary was conceived in order to provide the commune with the permanent help of a professional administrator. In view of the often low qualifications of the presidium members and of the other employees of the bureau, such a solution seems to be highly justifiable. The political control nature of the secretary's office, mentioned above, and the fact that he is nominated by and depends for his job on the county presidium no doubt reflects on the political unreliability of the commune.

COMMITTEES

The national councils establish their own standing committees. Their membership consists of councilmen and persons from outside the council, but councilmen must number at least half of the total membership of each committee. The council elects its committees at its first session, and it appoints the chairman from among the councilmen serving on the committee. The members sit on the committee for the whole four-year term of the council. The councilman is obliged to accept his election, and legally all councilmen participate in the work of at least one committee, although this is not always strictly enforced in practice. Some councils request the large local enterprises to nominate candidates to the committees. The council has the right to recall a committee man and to appoint another person in his place.[137] In accordance with the instructions of the Council of State, each committee ought to have at least nine members at the province level, seven members at the county level and five members at the commune level.[138] The actual size of a committee above the specified numbers is decided by the council itself. The maximum membership is, of course, limited by the provision that half of it must be formed by councilmen.

The functions of a committee are determined, in the first place, by the nature of the committee, which is decided upon by the council.[139] In general terms, they are required to maintain constant contact with the population in order to secure popular participation in the activities of local government, and for this purpose they are granted the right of legislative initiative. Furthermore, they investigate problems and practicality of legislative proposals as ordered by the council or requested by the presidium. They also exercise control over the activities of the departments, enterprises, and institutions directed by the council and within the corresponding functional spheres of the committees.[140] The actual day-by-day activity of a committee is prescribed by the rules drawn up by the committee itself and approved by the council, which also supervises the committee's work and demands periodic reports. The presidium is required to assist the committees and to consult with the appropriate committee or committees in the preparation of important normative acts, especially before the session of the council. It should also invite the committee chairman to the meetings at which it proposes to discuss matters within the sphere of the committee's functions. The committee may offer suggestions and proposals to the presidium, and the latter must inform the committee of its decision within a month, explaining the reason in case of a refusal of action.[141]

The control of the corresponding departments by the committees is especially evident regarding administrative efficiency and faithful fulfillment of acts and decisions of the council. The department chief must attend meetings of the committee if invited to do so, and he must take action on the committee's recommendations, informing the committee within the month of his decisions on these matters. He is also required to request the committee's opinion before undertaking any important decision within his department. Some of the proposals, as specified by the Council of State or the presidium on the council's directives, have the characteristics of binding instructions. The chief may, however, appeal them to the presidium, which has the authority of a final ruling.[142] We may note here that for all decisions the formal responsibility lies with the department and the presidium, and not with the committee, even if the latter submitted the original proposal or was consulted in the matter. The advisory character of the committee is plainly visible.

A committee has the right to investigate the activities of all economic and social bodies directed by the council. It also exercises the right of "social control" over the state organs, institutions, and economic units of the central government. The term "social control" is not defined by the 1958 statute, but the Polish writers suggest that it includes all matters affecting local government and also all actions of social character.[143] The "right to investigate" gives the committees authority to probe into all the activities of the institutions subordinated to the council. The council, on the recommendation of a committee, can issue a direct order to the institution in question. "Social control" involves the units of the central government which are not directed by the local government. The committee is empowered to investigate only those activities which directly involve local government. The council may ask for changes and improvements on the basis of "social control" performed by its committee, but it cannot order the units of the central government to follow the council's advice. The committees' legal and political importance within the whole national councils concept is emphasized by the fact that their existence and functions are regulated, if only in broad terms, by the constitution itself, which declares in article 43:

> The national councils establish committees for specific activities. These committees of the national councils maintain constant and close ties with the population. They mobilize the population for participation in the tasks of the council and exercise on the council's behalf social control and they also originate initiative in the council and its organs.

The committees then function as an additional link between the population and the authorities. They are one more mass organization—larger than the councils themselves by the inclusion of noncouncilmen in their membership—through which special policies are channeled. Their members are expected "to go to the people" and to mobilize them for local projects. They transmit from the population to the authorities, in a manner similar to the councilmen, the grievances, signs of support or opposition which can in turn be translated into appropriate action at the council, presidium, or departmental level. They form an important additional line of information, so vital, as pointed out before, to the efficient functioning of the communist state. Through their controls of administration they might help in diminishing bureaucratism, sluggishness, and illegality, although they cannot eradicate their institutional roots. Finally, they add to the council's work a useful degree of functional "expertness," as they engage for their elected four years in a constant study of specific issues, and as their membership includes as a rule many professional and experienced people from within and outside the council. Their advice should at least guarantee action within the realm of technical possibilities. In the last analysis the committees' usefulness depends on the vigor of their members and the characteristics of each locality. Their importance should not be overstressed, but neither should they be relegated to the land of insignificance. They can function well, and if they do not, their members and the political atmosphere are to blame. They will command our attention again in the following chapters.

ADMINISTRATIVE COMMITTEES

The local administration in Poland is permeated with a considerable number of committees, boards, colleges, and councils which perform advisory as well as semijudicial and appeal functions and which introduce a social or professional character into administrative procedure and arbitration.[144] The most important, if only because most of the citizens are bound sooner or later to be affected by their actions, are the criminal-administrative colleges. They are not in the strict sense administrative courts, but rather are comparable to the police courts or the justices of the peace in the American judicial system. They adjudicate petty crimes and misdemeanors which carry a warning, fine, or short prison terms as their penalty and which permit the right of appeal to the normal court or a higher criminal-administrative college.[145] They do not belong to the judicial structure, but are attached to the national councils at county (first instance) and province (appeal) level. The presidia of the councils determine the general policies of the colleges, including the severity of penalties within the legally stated limits, and require reports on their activity. The province presidium can annul a verdict of the college and submit the matter for new trial with different membership on the judging panel.[146] The membership of the colleges is elected for a term of four years by the respective national council from a list of candidates submitted by the presidium. The list should first of all include candidates proposed by the political and social organizations and by the "workers" of socialized economy (factories, state farms, administration, and so on), no doubt to insure the political reliability of the colleges.[147] The importance of the colleges is significant, at least in terms of quantity, as they deal with two-fifths of all the reported crimes in Poland.[148] They are attached to the administrative branch, and their political character would annoy many a pure jurist. Even in Poland they are subject to serious criticism.

Other administrative committees include tax committees for arbitration of tax assessments formed at county and province (appeal) level and composed of councilmen, tax administrators, and members of the public elected by the county council or, for the appeal committees, by the province presidia; and the county and city (in city-counties and city-provinces) housing committees, which hear appeals from the decisions of the departments of housing affairs, with a membership of which one-third must be appointed by the presidia from the trade unions. The rent appeal commissions are appointed by the county and city presidia from among the civil servants, trade unions, and the tenants. The military draft committees are formed by the county presidia and the appeal committees by the province presidia, and they are staffed by the military, the department of internal affairs, and the medical profession. The social-medical committees for decisions on the compulsory treatment of alcoholics are appointed by the county presidium. The committees for fight against speculation and transgressions in trade, with membership constituted by the county presidia (city or city-ward), are chosen from members of the Citizens' Militia (police—M.O.) and social and professional organizations (trade unions, women's league, youth organization). The committees for opinions on private trade and industry permits act by order of the county presidia with membership representing the council's committee on population supplies, the interested departments, craft guilds, and the association of private industry, trade and services. In addition there are a number of committees at all levels of local government dealing with such diverse matters as hunting, stock breeding, agriculture, protection of flora, protection of cultural objects, state decorations, transportation, budget discipline, discipline of work, and, finally, science. Most of these committees provide a certain degree of protection for the individual citizen from abuses by the administration, but they also add to the already large net of state control of local government affairs. Their close identification with the executive or administrative branch impedes their function as independent appeal boards. The character of these committees once again proves the communist party's unwillingness to create genuinely independent sociopolitical bodies. Their membership includes a large number of civil servants (members of the presidia and departments), creating new demands on their already overtaxed time and thus damaging the efficiency of the administration. Each Polish local government official of any stature is involved in a number of committees and social actions in addition to his regular and exacting work as a political "revolutionary" agitator and public mobilizer. The efficiency of his professional work can only suffer.

The inner working structure of the national councils presents in practice quite a different picture from that suggested by the logic of the theory of communist local government. Partially because of the vagueness of the 1958 statute itself and the contradictory controls built in it which violate the basic concepts of the system; partially because of the delegated legislation permitted by the statute; and finally for reasons of political atmosphere, the weight of power in terms of functions and decision-making shifted markedly upward from the commune to the county and from the county to the province. The commune, originally conceived as the basic unit through which the population takes care of its own government, became the outpost of the state, enforcing its policies in an alien environment. The county, originally thought of as the pivot of the whole system, changed to a subservient agent of the province and was relegated from its decision-making status to a purely administrative function. The province, theoretically the level of coordination, purloined the real power and became by far the most important and dominant factor in the Polish local government structure.

The shift in real power and in meaningful functions within the council itself is no less significant. The executive branch, the presidium, far from being the servant of the council proper, became its master. Most of the decisions regarding local administration are made by the presidium and not by the council, the latter meeting only for a few days each year. The province presidium plays, of course, the dominant role in relation to the county and commune presidia. The collective character of the presidium is vitiated by the distinction between full-time and part-time members. There is no doubt that the full-time members, salaried civil servants, dominate this body and that among them the chairman is not equal to his colleagues, but is indeed the undisputed boss of the presidium as well as of the whole council. The chairman represents the council outside. He also represents the state. He is the head of the administration and personally controls the most important local government functions, such as planning and economic matters, and the business of the bureau of internal affairs, which even gives him some supervision over that evasive organization, the political police. He is given responsibility for the realization of the general policies of the state, and many specific duties are placed upon his shoulders by the central government. The commune chairman is an exception to this general rule—he has to share his power with the county-nominated professional secretary. Other members of the presidium serve as lieutenants of the chairman rather than as his copartners.

The departments, and especially the departmental chiefs, placed by the division of responsibility between the anvil of the presidium and the hammer of the central government ministries, tend to subordinate their expertise in administrative decisions to the political command of the presidium. They hope by this avoidance of responsibility to escape the blows which may strike them from one of the two bosses. The "revolutionary" character of communist local government places heavy demands on the presidium and the departmental chiefs assigning second priority to the purely administrative functions and thereby impairing the efficiency of their execution. The dogma as specified by the central authorities and the party takes precedence over the pragmatism and reality of the local situation. The standing and administrative committees instead of providing an independent channel of information and social control, become an extension of the establishment. Polish local government has lost its raison d'être in the shift of decision-making power from the lower levels to the province, from the council to the presidium, and, within the presidium, from the presidium's collective to its chairman. The system of national councils has become a pyramid of authority, with the commune chairmen as its weak base, through the county chairmen and the province chairmen in an ascending order to the Council of Ministers, with the prime minister as its apex. This pyramid of authority which emerges from the structural and functional organization is enforced by the system of popular participation and representation, a topic which we must consider in our next chapter.

NOTES TO CHAPTER II

1 Piotr Typiak, *Praca w Gromadzie* (Warszawa, 1960), p. 108.

2 In Polish "narodowe" means "of the nation," and the word "nation" combines two meanings: that pertaining to the Polish nation and also another signifying people. The name "national councils" indicates the councils' identi-

fication with people as well as the whole nation, not just one class or one sector of the population.

3 *Dziennik Ustaw Polskiej Rzeczypospolitej Ludowej*, no. 5 (1944), entry 22.

4 *Dziennik Ustaw*, no. 14 (1950), entry 130.

5 Poland, *Constitution*, Arts. 1 & 2.

6 The commune councils were not established until November, 1954. The Act of November 25, 1954, *Dziennik Ustaw*, no. 43 (1954), entry 191.

7 The Regulation of Elections for the National Councils, *Dziennik Ustaw*, no. 55 (1957), entry 270.

8 *Dziennik Ustaw*, no. 5 (1958), entry 16. Subsequently, the act will be referred to as the act of 1958.

9 In October, 1956, Poland, under the direction of the newly elected First Secretary of the Communist Party, Władysław Gomułka, obtained a large degree of internal independence from the Soviet Union and accelerated the process of "de-Stalinization" characterized by "pragmatic communism" with limitations on political terror, insistence on persuasion and deconcentration of administration. Since 1962 there was a gradual reversal of this trend in terms of political repression, but with concomitant constant deconcentration of administration. Eventually, the frustration of the 1956 goals and expectations lead to the 1970 upheavals and fall of Gomułka.

10 *Rada Państwa*, the body elected by the parliament, referred to sometimes as the collective president of the Republic, with important legislative functions when the parliament is not in session.

11 The communist state is considered to be in a turmoil of perpetual revolution. The party constantly initiates new policies, which are directly executed by the government. Formal legal normalization follows after a certain, often considerable, lapse of time. There exist side by side two collections of norms, the legal ones on the statute books and another set of rules consisting of party programs and instructions. The frequent and obvious discrepancies between the legal norms and party policies are undesirable from the point of view of administrative expediency and are embarrassing to the official propaganda of "socialist legality." In order to circumvent this dilemma, the communist lawmakers write their acts in an obscure, unclear, and confusing manner, consciously leaving many loopholes through which they can introduce changes. The laws remain the same, although the policies twist in all directions. The law opens itself to many, even contradictory, interpretations. Milovan Djilas, at one time a communist lawgiver himself, bears evidence to this practice: "With the passage of time, they (the Communist leaders) became familiar with this kind of difficulty, so they always left loopholes and exceptions in their laws, in order to make evasion easier. . ." (*The New Class* [New York, 1960], p. 89).

12 *Polska Zjednoczona Partia Robotnicza*, the name of the Communist party in Poland.

13 *Dziennik Ustaw*, no. 28 (1963), entry 164.

14 See appendix 1, diagram 1, Structure of the National Councils of Poland.

15 *Rocznik Statystyczny* (1971), p. 58, table 3.

16 Ibid., p. 83, table 8. An average commune has a population of 3,000 and a yearly budget of 1,066 thousand *zlotys*. (Adam Wendell and Zygmunt Zell, *Rady Narodowe W PRL* [Warszawa, 1968], p. 20).

17 *Rocznik Statystyczny* (1971), p. 58, table 3.

18 Ibid., p. 56, table 18. "An average poviat has 787 square kilometers and

a population of 70,000. . . . The scope of the functional activities of the poviat can be best illustrated by these figures from a five-year plan for an average poviat: 300 million zlotys in investments, construction of 6 industrial enterprises, 3,000 dwelling rooms, 100 school rooms, 80 hospital beds, and 18 kilometers of roads." (Krzysztof Ostrowski and Adam Przeworski, "Local Leadership in Poland," *The Polish Sociological Bulletin*, no. 2 [1967]: 54).

[19] *Rocznik Statystyczny* (1971), p. 58, table 3.

[20] Ibid., p. 55, table 18.

[21] Ibid., p. 69, table 4.

[22] Ibid., pp. 70–78, table 5.

[23] Ibid., p. 69, table 4.

[24] Ibid., p. 55, table 18.

[25] Poland, *Constitution*, Article 1; the act of 1958, article 1.

[26] The act of 1958, Article 3.

[27] Statute of October 13, 1956, "Change in the organization of the central organs of public administration on public security," article 1, *Dziennik Urzędowy*, no. 54, entry 241, in Stanisław Gebert, *Komentarz do Ustawy o Radach Narodowych* (Warszawa, 1964), p. 42.

[28] Political police which is part of the Ministry of Internal Affairs. It is popularly known by the Poles as "Bezpieka."

[29] See for example the *Constitution*, Article 1, paragraph 2.

[30] Stanisław Gebert, *Komentarz do Ustawy z Dnia 25 Stycznia 1958 o Radach Narodowych* (Warszawa, 1961), p. 157.

[31] Act of the Council of State, May 12, 1950, *Monitor Polski*, no. 47, entry 651 and separately for the commune national councils: Act of the Council of State, December 11, 1954, *Monitor Polski*, no. 118, entry 1660.

[32] Resolutions may be called "internal acts," in deference to the normative acts which may be named "external acts." The normative acts can be further subdivided into general acts binding the whole population of the council's territorial jurisdiction and personal acts directed toward specifically named individuals or group of individuals (see chapter 3 and also Henryk Rot, *Akty Normatywne Rad Narodowych i Ich Prezydiów* [Warszawa, 1962]).

[33] The Statute of 1958, Art. 46, par. 1.

[34] Gebert, *Komentarz do Ustawy o Radach Narodowych*, p. 293.

[35] The broad political organization controlled by the Communist party and uniting all political parties and social organizations for the purpose of running single-list elections on the basis of one communist sponsored electoral program (see chapter 3).

[36] The Law of 1958, Art. 48, pars. 1 & 2.

[37] Ibid., Art. 48, par. 3.

[38] Ibid., Art. 48, par. 1, and Art. 49, par. 1.

[39] Ibid., Art. 49, par. 1 & 2.

[40] Ibid., Art. 47, and Gebert, *Komentarz do Ustawy o Radach Narodowych*, p. 298.

[41] The Law of 1958, Art. 50, par. 1. Art. 1 and Art. 19 of the "Little" Criminal Code (*Dz. U* [1946], no. 30, entry 192) deal with the counterrevolutionary activities and Art. 115 and Art. 117 of the Criminal Code deal with all the other cases. See also Gebert, *Komentarz do Ustawy o Radach Narodowych*, p. 300. The provisions of the "Little" Criminal Code were of specific significance during the civil war (1945–1949), when the nationalist guerilla forces executed a number of functionaries of the national councils. In April 1968, the "Little"

criminal code was abolished, but most of its essential provisions were retained in the new Penal Code (*East Europe* 17, no. 5 [May 1968], p. 54).

42 The Regulation of the Chairman of the Council of Ministers, May 7, 1958, *Dziennik Ustaw*, no. 13, entry 53.

43 Decree of the Council of Ministers, March 10, 1958, *Dziennik Ustaw*, no. 131, entry 52. This allowance is extremely small, since, for example, a dinner in a restaurant costs between twenty and thirty *zlotys*. The restaurant prices are centrally controlled and they are stable over a long period of time.

44 The Election Statute of 1957, Art. 12.

45 *Rocznik Statystyczny* (1971), p. 58, table 4.

46 Peasants everywhere—Eastern Europe, Asia, Africa or Latin America—resent paying taxes much more than the urban population. Their share of government services is less tangible and they tend to be more independent and conservative. From the point of view of mobilization of the rural population and regarding local development, it is vital therefore to separate the roles of the tax collectors and the mobilizers.

47 Zygmunt Rybicki, *Działalność i Organizacja Rad Narodowych w PRL* (Warszawa 1965), p. 186.

48 The land tax was in 1960 4,711 million *zlotys* in the total government revenue of 235,209 million *zlotys* and in 1970 5,139 million *zlotys* in the total revenue of 389,602 million *zlotys* (*Rocznik Statystyczny* [1971], pp. 600–601, table 2 and 4).

49 Rybicki, *Działalność i Organizacja*, p. 185.

50 Wiesław Skrzydło, "Zasady Ustawodawstwa o Radach Narodowych w Praktyce," *Z Problematyki Rad Narodowych* (Lublin, 1961), p. 149.

51 Ibid., p. 158.

52 Apart from Skrzydło article see also writings by Rybicki, Gebert, Zawadzki, Rot, and many others.

53 Regulation of the Minister of Finance, February 1961, *Dziennik Ustaw*, no. 13.

54 *Dziennik Urzędowy Ministerstwa Finansów* (The Official Gazette of the Ministry of Finance), no. 30, March 28, 1961, as quoted by Jan Dusza, *Budżety i Gospodarka Rad Narodowych* (Warszawa, 1962), p. 72.

55 *Rocznik Polityczny i Gospodarczy* (Warszawa, 1965), p. 92.

56 The Statute of October 11, 1965, on the increase of the communes responsibilities in the field of taxation (*Rocznik Polityczny I Gospodarczy* [1967], p. 79). The transfer of the assessment authority provides a good example of the role of the national council in its function of transferring information. The party and the central government apparently took account of the signals flashing from the lower levels of the local government structure and of the dissatisfaction of the commune officials with the existing situation. Undoubtedly, the writings of the academic community also had their desired effect. In a way, the government was in a dilemma. There was a need for increasing the authority of the communes, but the question was would the transfer of the taxation assessments lead to the general lowering of taxes? Also, the low technical level of commune administrators, not always capable of efficient bookkeeping, had to be considered.

57 In 1970 the production of individual farmers accounted for 85.7% of the total agricultural production as compared with 1.3% for producers' cooperatives (*spółdzielnie produkcyjne*) and 12.9% for state farms (*Rocznik Statystyczny* [1971], p. 267, table 2).

58 In 1970 the United Peasant Party had only 286 thousand peasant members, which constituted 72.0% of the total membership (*Rocznik Polityczny I Gospodarczy* [1970], p. 183). For additional information on the political parties see chapter 3.

59 Between 1963 and 1965 special attention was paid to the weaker farms, which received cancellation of their debts and special credits to the value of nearly 1 billion *zlotys*. See *III Plenum KC PZPR* (Warszawa, 1965), p. 55.

60 This obligation was again reaffirmed by the Plenum of the Central Committee in April, 1965.

61 See Andrzej Korbonski, *Politics of Socialist Agriculture in Poland, 1945–1960* (New York and London, 1965), pp. 288–89.

62 Typiak, *Praca w Gromadzie*, pp. 118–19 and Korbonski, *Socialist Agriculture*, pp. 294–95.

63 Typiak, *Praca w Gromadzie*, pp. 146–47.

64 *Rocznik Statystyczny* (1971), table 65, p. 299. The number of producers' cooperatives is decreasing. In 1960 the number was 1,668 (*Rocznik Statystyczny* (1961), p. 201, table 51). Most producers' cooperatives dissolved themselves when forced collectivization was abolished during the Polish "revolution" of 1956. "By March, 1957, 83% of all the cooperatives containing 86% of the members and 87% of the area, had disappeared" (Korbonski, *Socialist Agriculture*, p. 258).

65 As quoted by Korbonski, p. 302. Professor Korbonski further states that "his judgment was incidentally supported by various public opinion polls conducted among the peasants in the late 1950s. . . ."

66 These movements also have a long-established tradition to Polish agriculture.

67 The sorry state of water supply on individual farms (shallow, unhygienic wells) was recognized by the party in 1965. The five-year plan (1965–1970) envisaged state credits for the construction of new wells to the sum of 1.5 billion *zlotys*. In addition to credits the individual farmers received building materials and technical help. The plan provided for the construction by 1970 of at least 200,000 new wells (*III Plenum KC PZPR* [1965], p. 56).

68 Considerable progress has been made in electrification of the countryside. By 1970, 90.8% of the total number of farms had been supplied with electricity as compared with only 33.6% in 1955 (*Rocznik Statystyczny* [1968], p. 264, table 106; and for 1970 *Rocznik Statystyczny* [1971], p. 317, table 102).

69 Typiak, *Praca w Gromadzie*, p. 269.

70 Rybicki, *Działalność i Organizacja Rad Narodowych w PRL*, pp. 184–85.

71 Typiak, *Praca w Gromadzie*, p. 257. Of course the conditions of medical services vary greatly from commune to commune. The author visited one commune medical center in 1961 in the province of Opole in western Poland. It was very well appointed and staffed by young and energetic personnel.

72 In 1967 only 2,466 doctors (in this number only 1,918 lived in the villages) out of the total of 43,086 practiced in the agricultural countryside. (The figures for 1960 were 1,929 and 27,569 respectively). There were only 2,011 dentists from the total 12,300 (in 1960 1,355 out of 9,316). (*Rocznik Polityczny i Gospodarczy* [1968], p. 546 and for 1960, *Rocznik Statystyczny* [1961], p. 350). In 1970 there were 2,508 health centers; 1,304 medical clinics, staffed by one doctor, assistant surgeon, or nurse; and 955 midwifery clinics in the rural communes (*Rocznik Statystyczny* [1971], p. 546, table 15). With the total number of communes of 4,671, it seems that every commune had some medical or

midwifery service. At least in technical terms the problem of medical services in the rural areas was solved.

73 Apparently, the government's answer to this dilemma was the provision for the countryside of mobile medical and dental clinics. By 1967, permanent and mobile clinics in rural areas accounted for the impressive figure of 20,258. Finally, the urgent need for improvement of medical services for villagers was sufficiently recognized (*Rocznik Statystyczny* [1968], table 17, p. 499). The indication that by 1968 not everything was yet quite well, was given by the resolution of the Fifth Party Congress, which called for the direction of a larger number of doctors to the village health centers (*Uchwała V Zjazdu Polskiej Zjednoczonej Partii Robotniczej* [Warszawa, 1968], p. 53).

74 In 1964, the annual consumption of alcohol (recalculated into 100% alcohol) per head of population was 2.4 litres (.6 U.S. gal.) as compared to the prewar (average 1933-1937) of .9 (.2 U.S. gal.) see *Rocznik Statystyczny* (1965), p. 483, table 24. By 1970, the consumption increased to 3.2 litres (*Rocznik Statystyczny* [1971], p. 70, table 12). In 1969-1970 the average individual farm household spent 1,140 *zlotys* annually for alcohol and only 1,182 *zlotys* for hygiene and health care (*Rocznik Statystyczny* [1971], p. 582, table 33. One Polish writer reports that in some regions in 1958 the annual expenditure per person for alcohol was 840 *zlotys* while for cultural activities only four *zlotys* (Typiak, *Praca w Gromadzie*, 269).

75 Typiak, *Praca w Gromadzie*, p. 271.

76 The price of vodka is relatively low: a stable price of 96 *zlotys* per litre from 1963 to 1968, while prices of prime beef increased over the same period from 36 *zlotys* to 42 *zlotys* per kilogram (*Rocznik Statystyczny* [1968], table 1, p. 341). By 1970 the price of vodka was increased to 110 *zlotys* per litre while beef to 50 *zlotys*. As of March, 1971, the prices of food were returned to their 1969 levels (*Rocznik Statystyczny* [1971], p. 392, table 1).

77 Poland, *Constitution*, Art. 61.

78 The reform followed closely that of the Soviet Union. The financing of education often has to be done at the expense of other services, such as construction or maintenance of roads, fire fighting facilities, etc. (Zygmunt Żukowski, "Biuro Gromadzkie W Świetle Przepisów i Praktyki," *Problemy Rad Narodowych*, no. 14 [Warszawa, 1969], p. 131).

79 Typiak, *Praca w Gromadzie*, 238.

80 Ibid.

81 The number of primary schools declined from 27,778 in 1937-1938 to the postwar low of 20,119 and then increased slowly to 26,524 by 1964-1965, still about two thousand short of the prewar figure—although the number of primary school students increased from 4,875,300 during the prewar years to 5,207,900 during the 1964-1965 school year (*Rocznik Statystyczny* [1965], p. 393, table 1). By the 1967-1968 school year the number of primary schools increased only to 26,563, while the number of students increased to 5,706,300 (*Rocznik Statystyczny* [1968], table 1, p. 419 and table 13, p. 428). Many schools still had to work on two shifts (Wendel and Zell, *Rady Narodowe W PRL*, p. 128). By 1970-1971 the number of primary schools dropped to 26,126 and the number of students to 5,257,000 (*Rocznik Statystyczny* [1971], p. 469, table 1). The author's own impression of a Polish primary school in Poznań (1971-1972) was that it was working on many shifts and was understaffed.

82 The communes, as well as places of employment, clubs, and social organizations under the pressure by the party and higher national councils,

"pledged" the total sum of a donation which then was divided among their members. After the "voluntary pledge" by their organization the members had to meet their obligation. The fund collected over 7,350 million *zlotys* by which 981 primary, secondary, and vocational schools were constructed (*Rocznik Polityczny* [1965], pp. 499–500).

83 Regulation of the Minister of Culture, January 8, 1956, *Monitor Polski*, no. 69, entry 856.

84 Appendix No. 7 of the Decree of the Council of Ministers No. 611, November 3, 1956, *Monitor Polski*, no. 91, entry 1027.

85 Typiak, *Praca w Gromadzie*, pp. 219–21.

86 Regulation of the Chairman of the State Commission of Economic Planning and the Minister of Finance, June 13, 1956, *Monitor Polski*, no. 52, entry 580.

87 Fred W. Riggs, "Agraria and Industria" in William J. Siffin *Toward the Comparative Study of Public Administration*, ed. (Bloomington, Indiana, 1959), p. 31.

88 In about 75% of the communes the councils do not pass any resolutions concerning education, culture, and health. See Wojciech Sokolewicz and Sylwester Zawadzki, "Wyniki Badania Uchwał Rad Narodowych i Ich Prezydiów," in *Problemy Rad Narodowych*, no. 3 (Warszawa, 1965), p. 155.

89 Rybicki, *Działalność i organizacja*, p. 238.

90 On prewar rural poverty see Korbonski, *Socialist Agriculture*, pp. 17–19.

91 Korbonski cites interesting public opinion polls, conducted in Poland among the peasants in the late 1950s "which indicated that after 15 years of Communist rule the character and beliefs of the peasants had undergone very few changes since the prewar period. Most of them thought that the best way to increase output was to operate their farms on an individual basis; some favored the circles, but very few mentioned the cooperatives" (pp. 302–303).

92 Between 1950 and 1964 the import of wheat increased from 236 thousand metric tons to 2,211 thousand (*Rocznik Statystyczny* [1965], p. 341, table 8). This increase was necessitated by the rapidly growing population which increased between 1949 and 1964 from about 24 million to 31 million (*Rocznik Statystyczny* [1965], p. 13, table 1). The general import of agricultural products for individual consumption increased from the base year of 1960—100 to 145 by 1970. The population in 1970 was 32.5 million (*Rocznik Statystyczny* [1971], table 2, p. 411 and table 1, p. 67). On the other hand, due to the improvement in production the import of grain decreased from 2.9 million metric tons in 1963 to 1.9 million in 1968 ("Między Zjazdami-Rolnictwo," *Trybuna Ludu*, November 9, 1968, p. 3).

93 According to unofficial reports, Warsaw's pressure on farmers in arrears in their taxes and compulsory deliveries resulted in 1962 in peasant unrest in the counties of Koźle, Strzelce Opolskie, Kluczborg, and Namysłów in the province of Opole. "Individual farmers . . . halted harvest deliveries and many collective farmers refused to go into the fields" ("Report of Unrest," *East Europe* 11, no. 5 [May 1962]: 54).

94 The Election Statute of 1957, Art. 11.

95 *Rocznik Statystyczny* (1971), p. 58, table 4.

96 J. Jędrychowski, "Powiat w gospodarce rad narodowych," *Gospodarka i Administracja terenowa*, no. 2 (1962), p. 2 as quoted by: Gebert, *Komentarz do Ustawy o Radach Narodowych*, p. 213. (See also the discussion in chapter 4.)

97 The state machinery stations rent agricultural machinery to the indi-

vidual farmers as well as provide repair services for privately owned equipment.

98 Antoni Hebda, "Wydziały a Zjednoczenia w świetle Przepisów, Praktyki i Propozycji," *Gospodarka i Administracja Terenowa* 2, no. 12 (December 1961), p. 16.

99 Decree No. 533 of the Council of Ministers, *Monitor Polski* (1959), no. 3, entry 13.

100 Ibid.

101 Especially the Statute of 1958, Arts. 19, 20 and 21.

102 The Council of State is a body elected by parliament and performing among other things the functions of the president of the republic.

103 *Rocznik Statystyczny* (1971), p. 58, table 4.

104 The Statute of 1958, Art. 23, par. 2.

105 Poland, *Constitution*, Art. 42, par. 2 and 3. The Statute of 1958, Art. 52, par. 1.

106 The Statute of 1958, Art. 52.

107 Ibid., Art. 56, par. 1.

108 Ibid., par. 2.

109 Gebert, *Komentarz do Ustawy o Radach Narodowych*, p. 320.

110 The Statute of 1958, Art. 70, par. 6.

111 The Regulation No. 45/48 of the Chairman of the Council of Ministers, *Monitor Polski* (1958), no. 17, entry 109.

112 The Regulation No. 220/59 of the Chairman of the Council of Ministers, *Monitor Polski* (1959), no. 104, entry 561.

113 Gebert, *Komentarz do Ustawy o Radach Narodowych*, p. 335.

114 The Statute of 1958, Art. 56, par. 3.

115 Decree of the Council of Ministers, July 31, 1958, *Dziennik Ustaw*, no. 48, entry 236.

116 Decree No. 32 of the Council of Ministers, February 7, 1958 regulating the membership of the presidia of the national councils. *Monitor Polski*, no. 8, entry 41.

117 Decree of the Council of Ministers, December 4, 1959, *Dziennik Urzędowy*, no. 71, entry 448.

118 Up to January, 1972, a large part of the presidium's work was associated with the compulsory deliveries of agricultural products to the state by individual farmers.

119 The village elders collect land tax, local special assessment taxes (for example, the electrification assessment), repayment of bank credits, fees for services of state machine stations, and all other payments collected in villages by the state administration, such as fines, stamp duties, etc.

120 Typiak, *Praca w Gromadzie*, pp. 53–54. I assume that the members of the presidium—or at least its chairman—are armed. I know this to be the case with the chairman of the county presidium.

121 The Regulation of the Council of Ministers, July 30, 1966, *Dziennik Urzędowy*, no. 30, entry 181.

122 Typiak, *Praca w Gromadzie*, pp. 269 and 311. In one commune I visited, all members of the presidium and the secretary, with the exception of the chairman, previously served prison terms for crimes identified by them as mild cases of corruption or bribery. They claimed to be a typical group of commune administrators.

[123] The Decree No. 32 of the Council of Ministers, February 7, 1968, *Monitor Polski*, no. 8, entry 41.

[124] Hebda, "Wydziały a Zjednoczenia, p. 16.

[125] The Regulation of the Council of Ministers, July 30, 1966, *Dziennik Urzędowy*, no. 30 entry 181.

[126] The Regul ion of the Council of Ministers, July 30, 1966, *Dziennik Urzędowy*, no. 30, entry 181.

[127] This fund is semisecret, and the majority of people in Poland are not aware of its existence. I was given this figure by the vice-chairman of the presidium of one of the province national councils. I suspect that the vice-chairman of the province national council and probably the chairman of the county national council have similar, but lower, allowances for representation. In all fairness it has to be said that all these officials do have large expenses which in many cases escape the strictly legal definition of "official expenses" (like wining and dining of American scholars interested in Polish local government).

[128] *Dziennik Urzędowy*, no. 30, entry 181.

[129] *Monitor Polski*, no. 8, entry 41.

[130] The Regulation of the Council of Ministers, October 24, 1961, *Dziennik Urzędowy*, no. 53, entry 300. The regulation determines the following list of departments: (1) province—commission of economic planning, department of building construction, urban planning and architecture, budget-economic, religious matters, finances, communal and housing economy, water resources, trade, communication, culture, legal-organizational, industry, agriculture and forestry, purchasing (of agricultural commodities), employment, health and social welfare, board of education, bureau of internal affairs, commission on prices, committee on physical culture and tourism; in the cities with the province status additionally—department of housing affairs (allocation and management); (2) county—commission of economic planning, department of building construction, urban planning and architecture, budget-economic, finances, communal and housing economy, communication, legal-organizational, education and culture, industry and trade, agriculture and forestry, purchasing, internal affairs, employment, health and social welfare, committee on physical education and tourism; in cities in addition—department of housing affairs; in those which are not divided into city wards—registrar's office; in some counties—department of water resources; (3) in towns and settlements—office of finances, communal and housing economy, general administration, industry and trade, social and cultural affairs, and registrar's office.

[131] See appendix 1, diagram 1.

[132] There is an obvious possibility of conflict between the presidium and the higher department. The conflict is resolved by the higher presidium or by the ministry.

[133] Calculated from the *Rocznik Statystyczny* (1971), table 6, p. 59. This is more or less verified by the author's own observations. What is interesting to note is that the number of employees of the national councils declined steadily between 1956 and 1964, which reflects the government's drive against bureaucratic inefficiency and for reduction of the civil service; for example, the total employment by the councils declined from 165,495 in 1956 to 128,762 in 1964. Relatively hardest hit were the communes, which lost nearly half of their employees and which, in the opinion of this writer, could have least afforded it. This was recognized by the government and by 1967 the staff

of the communes was increased to a total of 31,975, although the decrease in the absolute number of the local government employees continued and it stood by 1967 at 126,685. Evaluating the figures in this context, by 1967, the hardest hit were the counties to which, supposedly, most of the functions of local government were to be transferred (see chapter 4). By 1970 the total number of the local government employees was 125,766, with the decrease at the province level and increase in counties and communes.

134 Regulation of the Council of Ministers, July 19, 1963, *Dziennik Ustaw*, no. 35, entry 20.

135 Skrzydło, "Zasady Ustawodawstwa," p. 148. Evidence of strong involvement of the presidium members in the day-to-day activities of the departments is also found in Eugeniusz Smoktunowicz, "Funkcje Kierowniczo-Koordynacyjne Presidium," *Problemy Rad Narodowych, Studia I Materiały*, no. 9 (Warszawa, 1967), pp. 71–141.

136 In theory the public registrar's office is separated from the local government structure, but in practice at the commune level the registrar is a member of the commune bureau.

137 The Statute of 1958, Arts. 39 and 40.

138 The Act of the Council of State, February 1, 1958, *Monitor Polski*, no. 7, entry 37.

139 The above mentioned Act of the Council of State suggested the formation of the following committees: (1) province and county councils—planning and budget, order and public safety, supplies for the population, agriculture and forestry, building construction and communal economy, education and culture, health, communication, employment and social welfare; (2) by the urban councils—the same as above, with the exclusion of agriculture and forestry; (3) by the commune councils—finance, agriculture and supplies, culture and social welfare, communal property. In addition each council has a mandate committee for electoral and recall matters formed on the basis of the 1957 Election Statute. For the last few years, some of the councils started to constitute "atypical" committees, such as: maritime (Gdańsk PNC, Koszalin PNC, Szczecin PNC), administration and tenants' self-government (Warsaw city council), physical culture and tourism (Bialystok PNC and Bydgoszcz PNC) (Sokolewicz, *Przedstawicelstwo i Administracja*, 184).

140 The Statute of 1958, Art. 41.

141 Ibid., Art. 42.

142 Ibid., Arts. 43 and 44.

143 See for example Zygmunt Zell, "Funkcje Kontroli Społecznej Komisji Rad Narodowych," *Państwo i Prawo* 15 (June 1960): 967.

144 Gebert, *Komentarz do Ustawy o Radach Narodowych*, p. 122.

145 The college can employ fines of up to 4,500 *zlotys* and a term of imprisonment of up to three months. The official rate of exchange is $1 = 22.08 *zlotys*.

146 The Statute of December 15, 1951 on The Criminal-Administrative Colleges, *Dziennik Ustaw* (1959), no. 15, entry 79 and no. 69, entry 434 and *Dz.U.* (1961) no. 7, entry 46.

147 The elections to the Criminal-Administrative Colleges are regulated by the Regulation of the Minister of the Internal Affairs, 1959, *Dziennik Urzędowy*, no. 15, entries 80 & 81; and 1962, no. 16, entry 71.

148 In 1967 the colleges dealt with 505,500 cases as compared with 607,600 cases of the procuracy *(Rocznik Statystyczny* [1968], p. 586, table 4, and p. 587,

table 7). In 1970 the comparable figures were: 575,600 for the colleges and 424,200 for the procuracy (*Rocznik Statystyczny* [1971], p. 628, table 6 and p. 636, table 30). For more comprehensive discussion of the colleges see my "Polish Administrative Law" in W. W. Wagner, ed., *Polish Law Throughout the Ages* (Stanford, Cal., 1970).

3

POPULAR PARTICIPATION AND REPRESENTATION

The ideological and theoretical meaning of communist local government derives even more from popular participation and representation than from the structural organization and the distribution of functions. The councils are conceived to be the machinery of representation by which the true democracy—the socialist democracy—is realized. Through participation in the activities of the councils the people, the workers, peasants, and working intelligentsia, supposedly control their own social, political, and economic affairs.[1] Without this participation the whole socialist state becomes a meaningless shell. The people must be able to choose freely their representatives—the representatives whom they know, respect, and trust at the local level—if the state is not to become yet another machinery of oppression. Also, according to Marxist theory, the direct control by the people of their own local government is the only means by which the bureaucracy in a modern industrial society can be kept in its role as servant and not that of master. Furthermore, the participation of the masses in local government has a special educational meaning. It is cardinal for the creation of the new socialist man and for training him in socially oriented values. Involvement in the activities of the councils prepares the population for the future task of taking over the administration, when the state will start withering away in the transition to communism. The transformation from socialism to communism, the revolutionary movement from the administration of people to the administration of things, requires constant instruction of the people in the art of self-government.

True participation and representation is also necessary in order to maintain the free flow of information between the population and the leadership, and it should facilitate, from the point of view of immediate pragmatism, an easier acceptance by the population of the leadership's policies. The leadership's knowledge of the general mood of the population permits such adjustment of these policies as is necessary to insure that the population, instead of being unnecessarily aggravated, would cooperate willingly in their implementation.

Hence, the question fundamental to our study is: how representative is the system of the national councils? The answer should be found in the examination of electoral and recall procedure and practice and in the study of the membership of the councils returned by the elections. We must also look at the method of nomination of the candidates insofar as only those people whose names are printed on the ballot will be elected. The results of the elections will give us the composition of the councils and, in order to assess their representativeness, we must observe the councils in action. What does the council do? What kind of debates, diversity of views, are expressed on the floor? It would be unrealistic to assume that the interest of locality "x" must necessarily coincide with the interest of locality "y." Do these local diversities produce conflict in the councils' debates, and if so, how sharp is the exchange between different representatives?

We have learned from our study of the structure and the distribution of functions that the presidium tends to dominate local government affairs. How then is the presidium selected, and who are the members of this body? The standing committees can also add to the representative character of the council, and therefore it should be our task to consider the committees' selection. Finally, we ought to examine the committees in action; how effective are they in their contact with the population and in the transmission of the demands of the population to the council and the presidium? What notice do the two bodies take of the committees' recommendations? We hope that the examination of all these considerations will expand the image of the national councils in our study from the static position of structure and function to the dynamics of movement.

THE POLITICAL PARTIES

The electoral process cannot be comprehended without some knowledge of the party structure, and so we must start our discussion with its description. There are three political parties in

Poland: the Polish United Workers' Party (*Polska Zjednoczona Partia Robotnicza*), the United Peasant Party (*Zjednoczone Stronnictwo Ludowe*), and the Democratic Party (*Stronnictwo Demokratyczne*). In the Western understanding of the term, the name "party" in relation to the above political movements is misleading. They are not autonomous groups which contest elections in order to achieve and exercise control of the personnel and policies of the government. The Polish parties and all social and professional organizations are combined together in a superparty movement called The Front of National Unity (*Front Jedności Narodu*), and they present one single program and one list of candidates to the electorate.[2]

The Front has national and local organizations. This arrangement is officially considered to be a coalition of the parties of the working people. The leading role of the PUWP, which is the Communist party, is fully recognized by the other two parties of the coalition.[3] The existence of more than one party is explained by the structure of the society, which, in its present stage of development, still has vertical stratifications.[4] The parties, however, are not antagonistic, but are united in the common effort of building socialism.[5] They all represent the same class, that of working people. Accepting the Marxian definition of parties as groups of people representing the political aspirations of different social classes, the Polish parties, it is argued, cannot be hostile to one another. (Following the Polish Communists' argument to its logical conclusion, one sees that the Polish parties are not, in effect, real parties at all.) It is also acknowledged that the strong Polish tradition of peasant and social democratic movements, as well as the legacy of parliamentary multiparty traditions, play an important role in the political life of the country.[6]

The Communist leadership admits that the Polish masses are still under the influence of the centuries-old ideologies which have shaped their society and thinking. The Polish working people are not yet fully aware of the ultimate perfection of the communist dogma.[7] This statement, disrobed of its Marxist jargon, simply means that the Communist party could not muster the popular support necessary for the efficient functioning of an industrial state without the aid of the other two parties. These parties, though they follow closely the communist lead, present a somewhat different political image to the public, even if they are definitely only junior partners. In our estimation they play the role of Lenin's transmission belts, although this is specifically denied by the Polish communist literature. The final decisions are made exclusively by the communist leadership and are then passed on to the leadership of the two other parties. They incorporate them into their own specific programs and activities. The leadership of these two parties and, to a large extent, their membership as well was purged of any independent element. There is no organized political opposition, and the creation of any political movement which would challenge the communist hegemony (dictatorship of the proletariat) is expressly forbidden by law[8] and by a well-understood political reality in which such a challenge is regarded as treason to the state. Władysław Gomułka, in a speech to the IX Plenum of the Central Committee of the Party, underlined most clearly the limits of democracy in Poland:

> Each democracy has its own class base. Socialist democracy, which acts under the conditions of class war, should only consider the needs of building socialism, and it should operate within this framework. . . . Socialist democracy can only develop by eliminating the political and ideological influences of the bourgeoisie and by expanding the political and ideological influence of socialism. . . . The scope of democratic freedom in People's Poland will be wider; greater will be the unification of all forces of socialism and progress. . . . All who desire that democratic freedom be enlarged and deepened must fortify the position of our Party in the nation. . . .

This was reaffirmed by the new first secretary, Mr. Gierek, who stated at the VI Party Congress (Dec. 1971): "The basis of the program of our party transform themselves into reality, first of all, by means of the People's State, *which in our conditions performs the function of the dictatorship of the proletariat*" (emphasis added).[9] An individual is permitted to exercise his political "free will" in only one direction. He is allowed and encouraged to adopt of his own "free will" only one political solution, that of communist development as mapped out for him by the communist leadership. There is an assumption here that he would freely join the march of the faithful were he fully aware of the undisputable truth of communism, its blessings, and its historical necessity for human progress. Political opposition is not only an opposition to the government of the day, it is also a backward and criminal resistance to the enlightened and scientifically proven truth. Marxist philosophy excludes the possibility of any other political concept because it is based on the assumption that its own creed is undeniably superior. The political life of the country is directed by the Marxist-Leninist party, which "bases its activity on the knowledge of the objective laws of social development."[10] This stand leads to the logical deduction that the Communist party is the only really independent political movement in the country. It results from the theory of dictatorship of the proletariat, according to which the political power in the state belongs to the working people whose aspirations are expressed by their vanguard—the Communist party.

The political system in Poland is not a multiparty system because neither the role, the function, nor the place of the Communist party can be reconciled with the basic principle of such a system, namely that of competition for political power among different parties. It is a specific type of political system which is not much different in reality from the simple one-party state. The Communist party is in complete and perpetual control of the state machinery, and the leadership of the party, in its decision-making process, is superior to the Council of Ministers. Often the leadership of the party bypasses the formal state structure and acts directly through party lines of communication. The party is above the law because in fact the application of the law depends on the interpretation of the law by the party.

The dominant position of the PUWP is reflected in its membership, which is large in comparison with the other two parties. As of the end of 1970 the PUWP membership stood at 2,319,900 full and candidate members.[11] At the same time the UPP had only 413,500 members,[12] and the DP a mere 88,400.[13] Under different conditions one would expect a much larger membership of the UPP, as about 30% of the population are peasants and many more are of recent peasant origin.[14] The large membership of the PUWP results from the direct or indirect communist control of all communications media, the availability of large funds, and the definite attractiveness of membership in the party which is ruling Poland and which offers much greater opportunities for personal advancement.

Membership in the "upper class" of contemporary Polish society is determined by education and by Communist party affiliation.[15] Education coupled with outstanding ability may facilitate entry in some cases, especially if combined with active support of the system. Membership in the power elite of the two non-communist parties usually also leads to a privileged social position. In the last analysis only membership in the PUWP guarantees sure advancement. The PUWP members comprise the bulk of the power elite in all segments of society—political, cultural, medical, academic, military and police—and Communist party membership is almost a prerequisite for attaining any position of importance in terms of the decision-making process. The state regards educated nonparty people as not being fully qualified for positions of responsibility. There is much truth in this assumption, as only through the party can one bypass the complicated labyrinth of communist bureaucracy. The party is not only a political organization but also a managerial "country club" where administrative difficulties and economic bottlenecks are resolved. The nonparty manager can solve these problems only through the good graces of a colleague or even a subordinate who is a party member. A noted Polish jurist bears evidence to the above analysis by stating: "The deciding role in avoiding collisions and conflicts between state organs . . . must be played . . . by extra-legal factors and above all by the Party."[16]

The attractiveness and even necessity of membership in the PUWP for ambitious people is illustrated by the high percentage of white collar employees in the party ranks. In 1970 they were the largest single group in the PUWP composing 42.8% of membership, followed by 40.2% of workers, and only 11.4% of peasants (other 5.6%).[17] The low percentage of peasant membership reflects the weakness of the PUWP's influence and organization in the countryside. Despite constant organizational drives among the peasants, in 1970, for each one hundred private farms there were only about eight party members and candidates. The peasants formed only 39.6% of the total party membership in the countryside (the rest was composed of state employees, teachers, etc.).[18]

In its promotion of agricultural programs the PUWP has to depend on the United Peasant Party. The UPP is a socialist party, but devoid of Marxist materialism. This of course permits it to obtain at least some support from the deeply religious peasant population. Its program specifies that the party organizes peasants for the development of the Polish People's Republic and for the construction of a political system founded on social justice. The UPP recognizes the alliance of workers and peasants to be the basis for such a system, with the leadership firmly in the hands of the working class as represented by its party, the Polish United Workers' Party.[19] The UPP program does not differ from the PUWP platform, but the activities of the UPP aim specifically at the improvement of economic conditions in agriculture.[20] It attempts to provide leadership not only for its own members, but also for all peasants. It advocates the establishment of cooperatives, including Producers' Cooperatives, but only on a completely voluntary basis. The members of the UPP must be professionally connected with agriculture. This rule is loosely applied to intellectuals, but excludes industrial workers.[21]

The national leadership of the UPP is subservient to and cooperates closely with the leadership of the PUWP. The present National Chairman, Stanisław Gucwa, replaced at the end of 1971 the previous chairman, Czesław Wycech, since the latter was too closely identified with Gomułka's leadership.[22] The most influential member of the top leadership is a "Stalinist," one of the deputy chairmen, Józef Ozga-Michalski. He is assisted by another aggressive Stalinist, Ludomir Stasiak, a secretary of the UPP Secretariat and a former agent of the secret political police.[23] The general membership of the UPP is not as enthusiastic about close cooperation with the PUWP as the party leadership, and many rank-and-file members desire more independent policies which would represent the true interests of the peasants.[24]

The Democratic Party is a socialist, but non-Marxist party, which groups in its ranks intellectuals, craftsmen and other urban groups. Its program specifies cooperation with the PUWP leadership and recognizes the PUWP's dominance in People's Poland. The party promotes the participation of scientists, cultural leaders, and craftsmen in programs of economic and social development and in the cooperative movement. It stresses the necessity of increasing the degree of social self-government and the impact of society and public opinion on the activities of the state organs.[25] The membership consists of: 61.4% from the intellegentsia and others (employees of state administration, health service, teachers, lawyers, engineers, technicians, and economists); 30.0% of craftsmen; and 8.6% of small entrepreneurs.[26] During my stay in Poland I observed that the DP members of the national councils were more outspoken and critical of the local government's policies than their UPP colleagues. This was perhaps because of the relatively higher educational background of the average DP member. The party, however, is very small, its influence is limited, and it does not present any challenge to the communists.

All political parties cooperate on electoral and organizational matters in the Joint National Coordination Commission, which is composed of the leaders of the three parties and has similar bodies at all levels of local government. The national and local commissions decide on the list of candidates for election to the national councils and on the share of seats allocated to each party. They also prepare a common program and supervise its implementation by the national councils. The decisions of the National Coordination Commission are binding on the local commissions.[27] It is sufficient for the PUWP to control and influence the national leadership of the two other parties in order to achieve the docility of their lower echelons.

SOCIAL AND PROFESSIONAL ORGANIZATIONS

Apart from the three political parties, candidates to the national councils may also be nominated by social organizations. In most cases the organizations are closely controlled by the PUWP through an interlocking leadership and serve as "front organizations" for the communists. The social organizations, by their very functions, do not present a separate political program, and they do accept fully the political leadership of the PUWP.

One of the most influential and numerous of the social organizations are the trade unions, which in 1970 had a total membership of over ten million.[28] They are organized into twenty-three Craft Unions (e.g. The Union of Metal Workers, The Union of Railroad Workers and The Union of Health Service Employees), with offices at the enterprise, province and national levels. The officers of the unions are elected in theory by the general membership, but in fact are nominated by the top leadership of the union and of the party. There is only one slate of official candidates for all union elections. All employees of the same enterprise usually belong to the same union.

The unions are grouped together in the overall national organization called the Central Council of Trade Unions (*Centralna Rada Związków Zawodowych*), which also maintains offices at the province level. The trade unions do not bargain for pay increases but are in charge of the distribution of fringe benefits, such as very cheap or free holidays in the trade union resorts. They participate in decisions as to the allocation of bonuses and the setting up of work norms; organize credit unions, medical care, and sport activities; and perform other similar functions affecting the well-being of employees. Most of the employees regard it as wise to belong to and to participate in trade union activities. Their leadership is tightly controlled by the Communist party, and many trade union leaders are communists. The chairman of the Central Council of Trade Unions and, in fact, the trade union boss is customarily a member of the PUWP politburo, a top leadership body of the Communist party. Many of the other trade union leaders are full or candidate members of the central committee of the party.[29] This insures complete control by the PUWP of the top leadership of the trade unions and also indicates the importance which the PUWP attaches to the trade unions as a means of massive agitation.

The Polish youth is organized in three associations.[30] The Association of Socialist Youth (*Związek Młodzieży Socjalistycznej*), with a membership of about 1,300,000 is really the youth branch of the PUWP.[31] Members or the candidate members of the PUWP compose about 10% of the total membership of the ASY. The First Secretary of the ASY is, as a rule, a candidate member of the Central Committee of the PUWP. The association of Village Youth (*Związek Młodzieży Wiejskiej*) claims to be an independent socialist organization of agricultural youth. Its membership of about a million nearly matches that of the ASY.[32] It also follows the leadership of the PUWP and cooperates closely with the ASY (they were united up to 1956). The leadership at all levels includes many members of the PUWP and the UPP.[33] The third youth movement is the Association of Polish Students (*Zrzeszenie Studentów Polskich*), which professes acceptance of the general political program of the PUWP but often proves troublesome on specific political issues. It is, however, small in number in comparison to other youth movements (about 225,000 members).[34]

Polish women have their own organization, the Women's League (*Liga Kobiet*) with a membership of about 380,000.[35] The League propagates broad participation of women from all social groups in the fulfillment of the PUWP program; education of women in citizenship; stimulation of their share in economic production in cities and villages; organization of help for families; and rationalization of home economy and child care.[36] The members of the league are very active in the national councils, especially in matters concerning kindergartens, schools, housing, and supplies of consumer goods. My impression was that women council members were often more outspoken, critical, and daring than their male counterparts. But again, the leadership of the League shows a high percentage of PUWP members.[37] In addition to the above organizations, there are many smaller ones, social and professional groups which also put up candidates for elections to the national councils. All organizations, especially the leadership, with the exception of the religious associations, are infiltrated by members of the PUWP and are closely controlled by the Communist party.

ELECTIONS

Elections to the national councils are conducted every four years and are declared to be universal, equal, direct, and by secret ballot.[38] All citizens above the age of eighteen are entitled to vote and to be elected, with the exception of persons mentally ill or those deprived of their civil rights by verdict of the courts.[39] Persons under temporary arrest are also excluded from voting.[40] Election day is a national holiday. The election is supervised by the Electoral Commissions: the Central Electoral Commission,[41] established by the Council of State from the candidates proposed by the leadership of the social and political organizations, the Territorial Electoral Commissions (provincial, county, city and city-wards), and the Area Electoral Commissions (polling area). The Province Electoral Commissions are constituted by the Council of State; all other commissions are called together by the presidia of the council directly above. The selection of members of the Electoral Commissions by the presidia of the higher councils guarantees their political reliability and excludes the possibility of commissions at lower levels objecting to some of the electoral pressures from above. However, with only one list of candidates and no political contest between the parties, the commissions' function is limited to the actual organization of the mechanics of election, such as establishing polling stations and printing ballots.[42]

In theory, each organization legally permitted to submit candidates can do so on its own separate list. They may, however, agree to participate in the election on one joint list, and if the national leadership agrees to such a list, their decision is binding on all local units.[43] In practice a standing agreement is in operation, and only one single list of candidates is presented in the name of the Front of National Unity. The leadership of the Front is nominated at all levels by the Joint Coordination Commissions of the three parties. The commission in turn is controlled by the corresponding secretariat of the PUWP. The number of candidates on each electoral list should be greater than the number of councilmen to be elected, but not by more than half. If the polling district elects only one councilman, the list should include two candidates. The voters are given some choice, but only—to paraphrase Marx—with regard to which of the communist-sponsored candidates will represent them in the council.

During the period of construction of socialism the electoral system is not designed, according to the communist theory, to reflect mechanically all forces existing in the society, but "on the contrary, it clearly and openly endeavors to make the representative bodies (ideologically) best fitted to build socialism."[44] The system excludes from them all opposition groups. With only one electoral list, even though it includes a few more candidates than the number of councilmen to be elected, the function which determines the final results of the election is the selection of candidates. The National Coordination Commission of the political parties specifies in advance for all provinces the percentage of candidates for each party and each social organization. The Province Coordination Commissions divide the allotted quotas among the counties, and the County Commissions similarly divide them further among the communes. The generally applied key seems to be the following division: 50% for the PUWP, 30% for social organizations, and 20% for the UPP and DP.[45] At the commune level the number of candidates from the PUWP is often much lower, as there are not enough PUWP members to fill the allocation. In such a case the percentage of candidates from the UPP and social organizations is larger than that determined by the National Coordination Commission.

The Coordination Commission, acting as the leadership of the Front of National Unity, allocates places on the ballot to each party and each social organization. The parties and social organizations select and propose candidates to the Front. The leadership of the Front is entitled to cross out the names of candidates who meet with their disapproval. In such a case the organization which suggested the candidate must provide another name. After approval by the Front, the parties, social organizations, and the Front itself organize mass public meetings at which the candidates are formally proposed. Those who are strongly criticized at these meetings are sometimes crossed off the list and other names are substituted. Criticism is strongest at the commune level, as the peasants are in a position to be more independent of the government than are other social groups.[46] At the end of the meeting, the opposing vote only is taken by a show of hands. Characteristic of such meetings is the comment of one participant: "One does not have time to talk it over. They always organize it in such a way. . . . Why the people did not talk? People are afraid. If you talk too much you may have trouble."[47] Even if those at the meeting refuse to accept the official candidates, the proposing body is not forced to remove their names from the list. The following bears evidence to the truth of this statement: "There were some reservations regarding 289 candidates for councilmen of the commune national councils. The reservations as to 220 candidates were considered valid (by the PUWP)."[48]

The purpose of the meetings is not to nominate or to elect candidates, but to test the temper of the voters regarding the people already selected. If the opposition to a certain person is very strong, it may be considered wise to drop his name from the ballot and to substitute another who is less objectionable to the electors. The electors do not have the right to select candidates, but may be granted the privilege of expressing their opinion by the Communist party. This is not always the case, and in many counties there are only a few election meetings because, "There is a lack of efficient (Party) organization; too much conceit and self-confidence (within the Party) . . . . and there still exists a distrust of the broad masses of the population."[49] In this way, with some rather minimal participation and suggestions from the two non-communist parties and the social organizations, the Front presents the final list to the Electoral Commission. The Commission prints the ballot, placing at the top the names of the candidates whose election is most desired by the Front. The names on the bottom, those listed below the number of members to be elected, are called the nonmandate candidates and are placed there only to give an impression of "true" democracy and real choice. The men who run in the nonmandate places know themselves that their election is beyond the realm of possibility. By their candidacy, however, they serve the party.[50]

The whole selection process is designed to nominate the people who are unquestioning advocates of the communist regime and who can, at the same time, muster enough popular support among the population to be effective sponsors of the government's policies. It is possible that some candidates opposed to the regime and yet willing to serve for a variety of reasons might squeeze through the elimination net. Nevertheless, the selection method falls short of being truly representative. The voters may be allowed to make suggestions which are in no way binding on the communist leadership. They may occasionally persuade the leadership to drop one or two candidates, but they are not permitted to choose or to support candidates who present alternative political programs.

The election itself is only a formality. During the election period the whole blast of official propaganda is turned on in order to exhort the citizens to perform "their duty" by participating in the voting. The atmosphere which the government tries to create is best illustrated by the description of Election Day 1961:

> The day of the elections, a warm truly spring-like Sunday, April 16, passed in the whole of Poland in a festive, serious and dignified atmosphere. The people of our country, in their general participation in the ballot, have once again confirmed their confidence in, and their support

for the leading force of the nation, the PUWP, and for all political parties and organizations which form the Front of National Unity. . . . Whole peasant families and social organizations came in droves to the polling stations. In Baków Górny (Łowicz powiat) 150 members of the agricultural circles arrived singing in decorated carts and tractors.[51]

The description of the 1965 election also produces the same image:

The country assumes a holiday look. It is enough to look at the streets decorated in flags and banners. Look at the houses which are elevated to the position of the headquarters of the regional electoral commissions. Here it is especially beautiful and elegant, plenty of flowers, clever decorations.[52]

Members of the local units of political and social organizations, factory workers, and office employees march together to the polls with flags flying and bands playing. In many polling districts the voting is concluded several hours before the legal closing time. Inside the polling station names are checked against the electoral roster, after identification by an internal passport or other proof of identity. This procedure is, of course, necessary in order to prevent multiple voting. However, with one government-sponsored list the possibility is not that important.

The marking of the electoral list is an effective way by which the government is informed of an individual's participation. The very fact that their names are checked intimidates the citizens into attendance at the polls. The propaganda, the large organizational effort, and the various pressures applied pay high dividends. Attendance at all Polish elections is unbelievably large by Western standards. It is usually well above 90% of the citizens entitled to vote.[53] While we cannot entirely disregard the possibility of falsification of the results as there is no opposition party to challenge the count of the ballots, all observers bear witness to high participation.

Voters indicate their preference for candidates by crossing out all other names on the ballot. The candidates with the largest number of votes are elected. An unmarked ballot is considered to be a vote for the candidates appearing at the top of the list. This place is reserved for the names of the government "preferred" candidates, among them well-known communist leaders, and an unmarked ballot is regarded as an unconditional act of allegiance. In theory the election is secret, and the law requires that curtained booths be placed at the polling stations, but voters are not obliged to use them.[54] The political parties and social organizations have the right to decide that their members shall vote openly.[55] The law allows them to place observers at the polls, supposedly to insure fairness in the elections, but actually to supervise the electoral behavior of their members. The lack of insistence on secret balloting further reduces the possibility of dissent.[56]

The success of the above-mentioned practice is evident in the election results, in which about 98% of the valid votes are cast for the Front of National Unity.[57] But it has to be admitted that many Poles voted willingly for the Gomułka government. Some supported the communist social reforms and industrialization of the country; others viewed the alliance with the Soviet Union as a political necessity required to prevent yet another German aggression. The majority regarded Gomułka's rule as the lesser of two evils. They preferred to follow his "sophisticated" communism and "the Polish road to socialism" rather than to allow the political power to fall into the hands of the hard-core Stalinists. But this was less and less true in the late sixties, especially after the March, 1968, students' "revolt" and the participation in the invasion of Czechoslovakia. Gomułka had lost most of the goodwill he acquired in the 1956 revolution for Poland's "independence" from the Soviet Union. By 1970 any major upheaval was bound to topple him from power. The Workers Revolt of December 1970 provided such a stimulus and Gomułka was replaced by Gierek.[58]

Finally some Poles vote for the government because their own social and economic status and advancement depend on its political survival. They owe their present position to the communist revolution. The placid electoral behavior is at the same time a result of the psychological effect of the habit of political conformity and a reflection of political apathy.

> After long acquaintance with his role, a man grows into it so closely
> that he can no longer differentiate his true self from the self he simu-

lates, so that even the most intimate of individuals speak to each other in Party slogans.[59]

All these attitudes are reflected in the local elections, since everybody recognizes that the support or rejection of local candidates is in effect a judgment on the national leadership. One of the Polish scientists calls the Polish elections "the consent elections," the function of which is not to elect but to give consent to the communist rule.[60] The elections are not a solution to political strife between the contesting parties but an expression of unity. Of course a boycott of the elections by a substantial part of the population would indicate popular opposition to the PUWP domination and would be considered as a serious political defeat. It would challenge the party's claim that its program has wide support. The appearance of validity for this claim is needed for propaganda reasons and because the implementation of the communist social and economic program requires active participation of at least a strong minority.

By winning of the meaningless elections by an overwhelming majority, the communists confuse their opponents, who are unable to ascertain the degree of opposition which may exist and who may finally end by believing that almost the whole nation is unanimous in its approval of communist rule. Such a belief has an extremely important psychological effect. The elections are designed to generate mass psychosis, which clouds reasonable judgment and plays on the human urge to belong to and to participate in what seems to be a popular movement. The opposition is not given a chance to stand up and be counted. For these reasons the government exercises all possible pressures in order to induce mass participation in the elections. One's absence from the polling stations is regarded as a hostile act and is most probably noted as such in the citizen's personal file. This may have highly unpleasant repercussions in a state in which the government, apart from having complete political control, directs almost all the economic activities of the nation. A citizen must be desperate to risk the displeasure of an omnipotent state. Most people regard it as folly to attract attention by not participating in the elections. As the results are decided well in advance, it would seem to be a completely futile act of defiance.

WHO IS ELECTED?

"Consent" elections with so many control devices practically eliminate the possibility of surprises to the communist leadership, and their results correspond very closely to the selection key discussed above. This is evident from the percentages of party affiliation of the councilman elected to all national councils in the previous four elections as shown in table 1.[61]

Table 1

Party Affiliation of Elected Councilmen
(%)

	1958	1961	1965	1969
PUWP	40.5	45.3	46.8	46.5
UPP	21.2	21.5	21.6	20.9
DP	1.7	2.0	2.5	2.6
None	36.6	31.2	29.1	30.0

As discussed previously the total percentage of the PUWP does not come to the 50% designated by the key because of the party weakness in the countryside. The 1965 increase resulted mostly from an aggressive recruitment campaign in the villages.[62] The lower number of the PUWP members elected in 1958 was due to comparatively freer elections when voters, just two years after the limited revolution of 1956, were less afraid to exercise their preference for candidates without party affiliation. Also the communist leadership in 1958 was more confident when it had a large and genuine popular support, and it could rule comfortably with a relatively smaller majority. The increasing percentages through 1961 and 1965 indicate the gradual erosion of popular support for the PUWP. The party thought it necessary to pack the councils with a larger number of its members in order to insure an absolute majority. Apparently the docility of the councils could not be assured any longer without the numerical superiority of the communists.[63]

The examination of the results of four previous elections with a breakdown for each level of local government is even more revealing (see table 2):[64]

Table 2

Party Affiliation of Councilmen at Three Levels
(%)

	Provinces				Counties				Communes			
	1958	1961	1965	1969	1958	1961	1965	1969	1958	1961	1965	1969
PUWP	52.6	51.2	50.4	50.0	51.5	50.8	49.9	48.7	36.5	42.7	44.8	44.7
UPP	21.4	20.2	19.6	19.2	27.3	26.1	25.4	24.2	22.7	23.6	24.2	23.8
DP	9.3	9.5	9.3	9.2	4.1	4.1	4.5	4.4	.3	.3	.5	.4
None	16.7	19.0	20.7	21.6	17.1	19.0	20.2	22.7	40.5	33.4	30.5	31.1

The strength of the three parties at the province and county level remained relatively the same, with only a slight decrease in the percentage of PUWP and UPP members. The increase in the number of councilmen without party affiliation at province and county level can be interpreted as an attempt to draw more social and professional organizations into the work of the councils. The PUWP control of these organizations is quite conclusive at the province level. The county organizations may be less reliable from the PUWP point of view, but certainly not to such a degree that they would present some challenge to the communist leadership. It could be that at these two levels the councilmen without party affiliation are easier to control than the members of the UPP and DP. They enter the councils as individuals representing many different organizations and varied interests. Members of the two minor parties form blocks of votes, and in recent years there has been a growing spirit of independence from PUWP domination among them, especially at the county level. The small growth of the DP membership in the county councils reflects the communist leadership's concern with the services of craftsmen and the drive of the government to stimulate individual crafts, especially in small towns and settlements.[65]

The significant development happened, however, at the commune level. Through a vigorous campaign and through manipulation of the nominations for the elections, PUWP strength in the commune councils increased by 8 percent. Also UPP and even DP experienced small increases. All these were at the expense of the councilmen without political affiliation, whose percentage dropped by over 9 percent. As pointed out before, the majority of the non-party councilmen at the commune level do not represent the social and professional organizations, but rather speak for the individual peasants. The communist decision to decrease their number indicates the PUWP concern that it may be losing its grip on the Polish countryside. The party popularity among the peasants was definitely declining and hence the necessity to increase the percentage of the communists in the commune councils. The party members in the countryside seldom come from the individual peasantry, but rather are recruited from the state and cooperative employees (agricultural experts, teachers, medical personnel, managers, etc.) and the workers of the state farms.

It is important to note that the PUWP constantly maintains close to 50% majority in the province and county councils. PUWP members control the province councils because of their dominant function in the decision-making process. The county councils, which perform the bulk of the administrative duties, must also have an absolute majority of communists. The reluctance to shift more responsibility to the communes—responsibility delegated to them by the spirit of the communist local government theory and even by the letter of the 1958 Statute—was no doubt the result of the Communist party's weakness at the commune level. The PUWP was not prepared to allocate even a small segment of power to these "unreliable" bodies, which, without an absolute communist majority, might have become an independent factor outside the communist dominance. Recent transfers of power to these bodies could have been the result of the growing strength of the communists (44.7%).

Further analysis of the previous four elections indicates a growing tendency to retain in the councils individuals who have proven themselves in their political reliability. In the 1958 elections 31.6% of the elected councilmen had served already during the previous term. Their number increased to 42.6% in the 1961 elections, to 44.3% in the 1965, and to 50.4% in the 1969 elections. In addition, councilmen who have been reelected for the third time and more constituted as much as 34.5% of the total number of the councilmen.[66] Apparently, the communist leadership is less and less inclined to risk new "blood" in the councils and prefers to rely on the tested quality of what one Polish author calls the "iron councilmen."[67]

Connected with the above process is the growing number of

older men and women in the councils' membership. The emphasis today is definitely not on "youth" but on "maturity." In the 1961 election councilmen up to 29 years of age constituted 16% of the total number of councilmen. In the 1965 election their number dropped to only 12% and in 1969 increased slightly to 12.5%. In the 30–39 age bracket the decrease was from 31.6% in 1961 to 27.6% in 1965 and further to 24.5% by 1969. At the same time the participation of councilmen over 50 years old increased from 25.4% in 1961 to 29.8% in 1965 and then dropped a little to 28.3% by 1969.[68] It is hard to say if this inclination for the councils to "grow old" can be interpreted as evidence of the general movement of young people away from communism in search of their own dynamism.[69] But what is certain is that the communist leadership prefers older, well-established individuals in the local government structure to younger men and women who might become the councils' "Young Turks." The older men, with families to support and with careers painfully built over the long years, are not likely to engage in "revolution" and risk their lifelong achievements. Also these people have more at stake in the existing system. Many of them belong to the managerial class and identify themselves much more closely with People's Poland as it is. The "revolution" might upset their comfortable, if not perfect, lives. This of course reflects the normal process in all societies; division between the "conservative" older generation and a "revolutionary" impatient youth.

The movement toward the consolidation of communist power in the councils is also evident from the increase in the number of councilmen with white-collar occupations, most of them employees either directly of the state or of communist-controlled institutions. They increased their share of the membership in the councils from a low of 28.4% in 1958, through 35% in 1961, to the impressive figure of 37.1% in the 1965–1969 term. In 1969 their share dropped slightly to 36.5 percent.[70] The internal composition of this group includes administration employees, who form the largest single element, followed in decreasing order by teachers, engineers, agricultural and forestry specialists, and finally doctors.[71] This tendency is true at all levels of the councils including the communes, which show a decreasing number of farmers. The percentage of farmers is diminishing constantly in all councils: 53.2% in 1958, 47.4% in 1961, 44.9% in 1965, and 43.0% in 1969.[72] Yet another proof that the peasants are considered politically unreliable, but also an indication of industrialization and urbanization. On the other hand, the white-collar workers, or "intelligentsia," as pointed out before, are for the most part dependent on the government for their livelihood and are therefore more likely to respond positively to communist pressure. They form the privileged class and enjoy a standard of living generally superior to that of the workers and peasants. They may be annoyed by the general economic mismanagement, bureaucratic stupidity, and delays in administrative process and by the lack of response to their views on the part of the Communist leadership, but they are not likely to endanger their relatively secure and privileged positions in open revolt against the establishment of which they are —in the last analysis—part and parcel. Their lives are full of petty annoyances, but they are not desperate to the degree to which the worker trying to support his family on 2,500 *zlotys* a month might be. They are also not as independent economically as the individual peasants.

On ideological grounds the Polish Marxists can find consolation in the fact that despite changes in the composition of the councils, the peasants and workers counted together are still the dominant group within the national councils, composing 58.4% of the total membership (workers 15.4%).[73] The worker-peasant alliance is as strong as ever. Under closer analysis, however, this figure indicating worker-peasant domination has no political significance, although it may be used to prove ideological purity. In the first place the interests of the urban workers and even the agricultural workers are vastly different from the desires of the peasants who own and operate their own farms on an individual basis. Even in view of Marxist theory itself the peasants are nothing less than small capitalists. How can their interests be equalized with those of the urban proletariat? For example, it seems only reasonable that the urban dwellers would want low prices on food products, while the peasants, producers of food, would naturally desire the highest prices possible. In the councils themselves these two groups are bound to clash on the issue of investment in agricultural services versus urban improvements. Only the dire misery of both groups could unite them together in unusual common front against the existing government.

The percentage figure does not tell us anything of the political affiliation of the workers and peasant councilmen. How many of them belong to the PUWP and are therefore disciplined party members rather than representatives of their class? The high percentage of the PUWP membership indicates that indeed many councilmen classified professionally as workers or peasants are in fact also communists. Even those who are now professional party cadre, but were once workers or peasants, are still listed in the category of their original profession.

Partially resulting from the increasing number of white-collar workers on the councils, but even more from the general uplifting of the educational level in the country is the constant increase in the educational level of the councilmen. This is illustrated quite dramatically by table 3:[74]

Table 3

Educational Level of Councilmen
(%)

	No Primary	High School or University
1949	38.2	16.7
1955	43.9	15.9
1958	42.6	20.4
1961	27.6	25.0
1965	19.1	28.2
1969	10.3	30.9

What is the political significance of this development? Are better-educated councilmen more or less likely to support the communist rule? In view of the lack of enthusiasm for Marxism-Leninism among the university students, their cynical political apathy, and, in some cases their more or less active opposition to the status quo and admiration for Western cultural values, it seems that education has failed completely as a means of indoctrination in the communist faith. On the other hand studies conducted among Warsaw students indicate their passive acceptance of the communist rule and their great concern with material benefits rather than with political questions. A Polish sociologist, Stefan Nowak, thus summarizes his findings:

> When analyzing other items of our questionnaire we may observe a distinct increase of political indifference, along with a decreased interest in political affairs and ideology. We can also see a diminished need for involvement in anything which overpasses the narrow limits of arranging one's own private life. . . . In general it seems to be more correct to speak of the increased adaptation of students to socialism than of their increased active acceptance of socialism and greater involvement in socialist values.[75]

Assuming that the attitude of the Warsaw students was characteristic then of all Polish students and assuming again that the students continue this approach to politics after their graduation, we could have expected an increased number of the councilmen with university degrees to be more easily managed by the communist leadership. This also supports our previous assessment of the political role of the intelligentsia and explains to a degree why the councils continue "to grow old." The apolitical inclination of the students and the young people in general prevents them from engaging in any political activity within the system, including that of a councilman.

How then can Nowak's findings be evaluated in view of the March 1968 students' riots? The answer is simply that the new Polish generation, as do many students in other countries, considers itself outside the political system. They do not attempt to reform the system, but to destroy it. A riot is not a political act within the framework of the system, but rather a political act in *the field*, which lies outside the system. In a way, the students' attitude, and here may lie the difference between the students of 1962 and 1968, is the result of the affluent life. Many of the leaders of the Polish riots were sons and daughters of prominent individuals (politicians and scientists). They did not have to strive hard to climb the social ladder, but were ready for a search for new and more idealistic goals. The riots, which were as much antigovernment as anti-Russian, were the result of constant communist indoctrination in Polish nationalism directed against West Germany. Intense nationalism and patriotism can, however, work both ways. In 1968, students were much more insensed by the actual Soviet domination, than by the distant dangers of "German revanchonism," which could still have disturbed their fathers.

The decreasing number of councilmen without primary education is of course most evident in the rural commune councils. In 1958 every second commune councilman lacked the primary schooling. In 1961 every third councilman had not finished primary school, in 1965, every fourth, and, in 1969 only every seventh.[76] In our opinion there is no evidence that the increased educational level at the commune level basically changed the peasants' political attitudes. It has been our contention that between 1958 and 1969 there has been a growing opposition among the peasants to the communist rule. This opposition, however, cannot be attributed to the increased educational level of the councilmen, but rather to political factors, specifically, the reversal of certain goals and expectations of the 1956 "revolution." On the other hand, there may be a correlation between the increasing educational level and the increasing percentages of PUWP members in the commune councils.

Finally, there is one more important implication of the growing educational level of the commune councilmen. The communist leadership argument that the communes cannot be allocated more responsibility because of the lack of "preparation" of their membership becomes less and less valid. Better-educated commune councilmen should be able to cope more adequately with their problems, and there is less real need for delaying the "deconcentration" of decision-making and administrative functions to the communes.

The data available on the councils' political behavior does not permit much meaningful generalization regarding the attitudes of the increased numbers of councilmen with a completed high school education. There are two possibilities of logical analysis of this development. First of all, high school education is often thought of in Poland as a stepping stone to a university degree. Individuals matriculating from the high schools who, although ambitious enough to aim for the university degree, fail to gain entrance to the university, either through inability to pass a stiff examination or inability to obtain a state scholarship, are likely to blame the communist rule for their failure. If they were to become councilmen, which is not very probable, they would probably have a negative attitude toward the communist leadership. Secondly, persons with a high school education may enter the lower ranks of state administration. Realizing that their advancement, hindered by the lack of the university degree, depends on their political shrewdness, they will vigorously support the establishment and even attempt to join the PUWP. Such people in the council membership will be willing tools in the hands of the communist leadership. There is also a greater possibility that this group, "half educated," without the more sophisticated critical ability which the university degree is supposed to give, will embrace Marxism in its primitive form as their true faith. They will be much more "conservative" communists than their counterparts with university degrees, who often tend toward a more "liberal" and flexible ideological position.

All in all, any discussion of the impact of the increased educational level of the councilmen on their political behavior is highly speculative and can be answered with a degree of certainty only by the actual sampling of their opinions. We do not feel, however, that the educational factor in the period studied changed the basic political attitudes of the councils' membership. We are inclined to give much more weight to political and economic considerations.

The manipulation of the nomination process, combined with the consent elections with the single list presented in the name of the Front of National Unity, produces a council membership under the firm control of the PUWP. The communists, on the average, maintain their absolute majority at the province and the county level. There is a tendency to retain in the councils people who have already served for one, two or even three terms. The proportion of councilmen with white-collar occupations and of those more advanced in age is increasing. At the same time the percentage of peasants is constantly diminishing. Workers and peasants combined still form a majority today, but this has only ideological and not political significance. There is a marked increase in the educational level of the councilmen, without, however, a significant change in their political outlook. This development could show more dynamism over a longer period of time. All the changes observed, apart from the educational factor, were instituted by the conscious management by the communist leadership and were designed to increase the PUWP hold on the councils as the general popularity of the Gomułka government decreased.

DEPRIVATION OF THE MANDATE

Much of the communist theoretical claim to democracy and representativeness in their local government structure is based on the right of the voters to recall their elected representatives at any time and for any reason. Marx admires the Paris Commune for its emphasis on this rule. Lenin reasserts the value and necessity of recall to the socialist democracy.[77] And indeed the freedom of deprivation of the mandate by the voters allocates to them a powerful weapon of control over their representatives. In view of our previous discussion of elections in Poland and the PUWP control and manipulation of the nomination process, it is not surprising to learn that the deprivation of the mandate is also within the realm of communist dominance.

Legally, the electors have the right to petition the council through the local committee of the Front of National Unity for the revocation of the mandate of their councilman. After its approval of the petition the committee transmits it to the council together with proof that the councilman has failed the trust of his electors. The petition is in turn examined by the mandate committee of the council, which permits the councilman to offer his explanation. Then the mandate committee submits the petition to the whole council in session. The decision of the council requires a two-thirds majority and the approval of the higher council (with the exception of the province council). If the petition fails to receive the necessary majority, the committee of the Front can submit it directly to the higher council. In this case the higher council has the right of final decision with a simple majority. After the approval of the petition the presidium of the province national council calls within the two-week limit for the referendum in the council's electoral district. A simple majority of votes against the petition permits the councilman to retain his seat at least for the rest of his term.

The recall procedure is too cumbersome to have any practical meaning. At no time does the PUWP relinquish its control. The petition, to be successful, has to achieve concurrence of the committee of the Front as well as the approval of the mandate committee. Both bodies are under full domination by the communists. Furthermore, the petition has to pass by a two-thirds majority in the council itself. With the PUWP members in opposition such a majority is impossible even at the commune level (where the communists have an average 45% of the total vote). If, on the other hand, the PUWP desires the petition to succeed but for some reason fails to achieve the required majority in the lower council, the communist-controlled committee of the Front can still submit the petition to a higher council. Here the PUWP is in the majority and, with a simple majority required, can approve the petition without any difficulty. Actual practice proves this evaluation of the futility of the recall system. To quote one of the outstanding Polish specialists, "The lack of even one example [between 1961 and 1963] of the recall of the councilman by his electors seems to indicate that the present regulations in this matter are lifeless."[78] This must also be the official position, since the government did not even establish a format for ballots for a referendum concerning recall, although it was delegated to do so by the 1957 Electoral Statute.[79] The theory of recall, on which a substantial part of the claim of popular representation rests, does not have any application in actual practice.

There is, however, an effective machinery by which the communist leadership can deprive a councilman of his mandate. It is effected by the rule of responsibility of a councilman to his own council. The council is empowered to revoke the seat for four distinct reasons: if a councilman absents himself from his duties for at least six months; if he is convicted by court verdict of a crime committed for "dishonorable motives";[80] if he violates his oath; and, finally, if by his activity he plainly damages the good name of the councilman. The first two rules are normal disciplinary procedures practiced by most elected bodies and as such have no specific political significance. The last two are means of political control. Both cases permit the council a broad degree of interpretation. It can decide itself what constitutes action damaging to the good name of its member. Activity against the program of the Front of National Unity is interpreted as a violation of the councilman's oath.[81] The program of the Front is equal to the goals of the PUWP.

Revocation under this provision requires a two-thirds majority which in most cases the communists can muster easily at the county and the province level. The decision of the commune council, the level in which the communists do not have complete confidence, requires the concurrence of the county national council, no doubt in order to prevent the possibility of loss of mandates by councilmen who support the government. The machinery for the revocation of a mandate does, in fact, permit the communist leadership to cleanse the local government bodies of any active opposition, but does not in practice allocate to the electors the right to change by recall their representatives chosen in the communist-staged elections.

THE COUNCIL—REPRESENTATIVES IN ACTION

A session of a national council is of one day's duration. The law requires a minimum of one session per quarter for the province council, one session every two months for the county council, and one session a month but at least eight sessions a year for the commune council.[82] In practice the province councils exceed the minimum and have an average of about seven sessions. The county councils have slightly more than the legal minimum, and the commune councils meet about seven to ten times a year.[83] Hence the representatives of the public in the province council, which is the most important unit of local government in the decision-making process, meet only about seven days a year. The commune councils virtually cease their activity during the intensive agricultural work in summer, especially during harvest.

The first yearly session of each council, but especially the province councils, has a festive atmosphere. Many long ostentatious speeches are delivered by local Communist party and state dignitaries. Apart from the election of the chairman and the secretary of the session, no other real business is conducted. Another ceremonial session is organized on July 22, again with state and political personages in attendance, to commemorate the birth of People's Poland. One more session is required to pass the yearly economic plan and budget, and yet another is needed for the report by the presidium on the fulfillment of the plan and the budget of the previous year.[84] The province and county are left with only about three days and the commune council three to six days a year in which to conduct all other business. As a result the normal sessions are crowded with the variety of matters, and there is little time for a meaningful debate on each issue. Table 4[85] showing sessions and resolutions of selected councils at each level illustrates this point:

Table 4

Sessions and Resolutions of Selected Councils, 1962

	Sessions	Resolutions
Province		
Lublin	5	22
Kraków City	7	32
County		
Chełmno (Lublin Prov.)	7	26
Nowy Sącz (Kraków Prov.)	8	21
Jelenia Góra (Wrocław Prov.)	7	65
City		
Kazimierz (Lublin Prov.)	9	6
Nowy Targ (Kraków Prov.)	9	21
Kowary (Wrocław Prov.)	8	13
Lublin	8	20
Commune		
Rejowiec (Lublin Prov.)	10	19
Karpniki (Wrocław Prov.)	12	25
Stara Kamienica (Wrocław Prov.)	11	48

Deducting the two ceremonial sessions, the Lublin province council passed twenty-two resolutions in three working sessions, or an average of seven resolutions a day. The Kraków city council managed six to seven resolutions per working session. At the county level, Nowy Sącz had only three to four resolutions a meeting, while Jelenia Góra marathoned thirteen resolutions each session. The city councils showed more moderation, with less than one resolution per session in Kazimierz and three to four in Lublin. Stara Kamienica Commune was more prolific, with five to six resolutions a session, while the other two communes confined themselves to two to three resolutions. All the studied councils passed on the average about four resolutions per working session. Other studies confirm that the sessions of the councils are overcrowded with business.[86] Many sessions merely succeed in passing, practically without any discussion, the proposals introduced by the presidium. In these circumstances the presidium, the executive branch, acquires most of the powers vested in the council, the local parliament.

The councilmen are entitled to demand convocation of a special session on a specific topic by a request addressed to the presidium and signed by at least one quarter of their total number. The presidium is obliged to call a special session within ten days from the date of such a request.[87] There is no evidence that a special session has ever been instituted by the demand of the councilmen in any of the councils.[88] This law does not seem to have any application in practice.

Within the council, the members (and candidate members) of the three political parties are organized in separate party clubs.[89] In some communes the councilmen from the PUWP and the UPP form a common club. The club elects a secretary (PUWP "troupe") or a chairman (other two parties) and a presidium of three to seven people to manage its business and to provide the leadership. The club is not formally a party organization, but it cooperates closely with the local party headquarters. The directives of the party leadership are binding on the club. This collaboration is especially evident in the PUWP and is thus described by one of the Polish theoreticians:

> In practice, the harmonization of the activity of the troupe with the Party executive committee is facilitated by the personnel connections (the secretary of the troupe as a rule is a secretary of the committee). Within the framework of the resolutions of the committee the troupe has full independence. Its task is to insure the realization of the policies of the Party by the national council, deepen influence and authority of the Party among the non-party people, strengthen party and state discipline, fight against bureaucracy and for the development of social activeness in the fulfillment of tasks set by the Party.[90]

The clubs discuss in advance the issues to be considered, decide on their speakers, and agree on the final vote. The party discipline requires the councilmen to submit to the decisions of their clubs. The chairmen consult together and formulate their common policies under the leadership of the secretary of the PUWP troupe. The clubs also accept the leadership of the local committee of the Front of National Unity. The result is that during debates on important issues there is almost always a complete unity among the members of all three parties. Here again the characteristics of a one-party state are in evidence.

Most of the councils form a Convent of Seniors composed of the chairmen of the party clubs, the chairmen of the standing committees, and, as exofficio members, the secretary of the presidium of the national council and the chairman of the session, if he is appointed for more than one session. Generally, the convent, together with the presidium of the council, prepares the yearly plan of work and the agenda for each session. It organizes support within the council for the official proposals and musters the debate through the membership of the clubs. The real power within the council, therefore, belongs to a few individuals grouped together in the Convent of Seniors. They command the debates and the votes. The convents "sometime become 'little national councils' examining the merit of matters, which will constitute the subject of the sessions of the councils. After the analysis of these matters by the convent, the debates of the session become a ceremonial . . . formality."[91] The majority of the convent members are communists. The members from the two other parties take their orders from their party leadership, which in turn follows the lead of the PUWP. Communist control is facilitated by the convent device, and the party does not necessarily have to maintain its absolute majority in order to be master of the debate. Some of the councils do not institute convents, and then the power lies with the meeting of the club chairmen.

The machinery of control of the behavior of the councilmen is especially well organized and efficient at the province level, where the PUWP has an absolute majority of militant supporters and where it takes care to exercise the full weight of its pressure. The county councils are slightly more independent, and the commune councilmen sometimes manage to stage a lively debate, but the results of these debates are insignificant, as the commune plays only a minor role in the structure of Polish local government.

Lively debates even at the commune level are rather an exception. Typical sessions of the commune councils are described by a Polish author in this manner: "Those who come are often not prepared. Some of them grumble a little; propose this or that measure; are informed that there is no money, that those on top do not want to give more, and so the discussion is ended."[92] The session of the province council attended by the author was an extremely dull affair. Most of the time was taken by long-winded speeches prepared well in advance by the presidium members and other political leaders. During the speeches the councilmen talked freely among themselves; walked from the chamber to the buffet, where coffee, beer, and excellent food were served; and generally paid no attention whatever to the proceedings. The atmosphere was that of a large gathering of acquaintances who seldom meet and so have much to tell one another. The chairman of the session periodically called for order, but to no avail. His voice sank in the muffling fog of cigarette smoke. The only true participants were the principal actors (and this author taking copious notes). It was anything but a serious meeting of the "local parliament." From a description of other sessions, one concludes that this type of debate is quite characteristic of the national councils.

A session of a city council witnessed by the author was, however, much more lively. Perhaps the subject of the session, kindergartens, and the active participation of the women members added the needed spark. The official speeches were shorter and more to the point than those of the province council.[93] The debate from the floor was quite heated, and it produced three different proposals. However, after a speech by the chairman of the session, who was in favor of one of the solutions, that particular proposal was accepted by a unanimous vote. The unanimity of votes is always insisted upon by the communists as an expression of unity, the merger of an individual with the "common will." Cases of abstention or dissenting votes are extremely rare, although we admit their possibility, especially at the commune or county level.

In the majority of cases the sessions are dominated by the presidium, and the role of the councilmen is limited to unanimous approval of the proposals presented by the presidium. The council, in practice, abdicates its superior position as the representative of the people and quite realistically regards the presidium not only as the leader of local government, but also as the true authority representing the omnipotent state. Individual councilmen almost never dare to challenge the executive branch, no doubt realizing that in the last analysis they are powerless. In any conflict between the administration and the people there is always an assumption of the superiority of the government. "Simply the authority (council) cannot imagine, that in the dispute between administration and society, the administration would not always be correct."[94] The role of the councilman as the protector of society against bureaucratic abuses is highly limited by this attitude and by the unwillingness to question the action of the presidium or of the administration.

The docility of the councilmen is also a result of what one Polish newspaperman calls the "schooling" of councilmen by the presidium:

> More and more often department heads, members of the presidium and other representatives of the administration teach councilmen in what way they should, as the representatives of the people, delineate direction of activity of the administrative organs and how they should control them.[95]

The effectiveness of such a schooling is illustrated by the following description of a council session, which is very similar to the author's own experience:

> Here is the picture of the traveling session of the province national council in Ustrzyki in September of the last year [1965]. The realization of the government resolutions regarding economic development of Bieszczady is discussed and the general directions of the development of the South-East region of the province is being determined. The appropriate resolution was prepared on the basis of the previous specific discussions in the [standing] committees of the province national council. In spite of it during the session itself a change in the wording of the tourist section of the proposal of the resolution is being made; a major change cancelling the previous decisions and introducing completely new ones. The matter involves millions of *zlotys*, new tourists locations. Nobody from the Presidium justifies these changes, *no councilman* asks for the reason of these changes![96]

The councilmen accepted the alteration like sheep because the chairmen of the clubs, perhaps themselves not informed of the change, did not instruct them as to what position they should take. It is not the practice for a councilman on his own to dispute the decision of the presidium.

Legally the presidium must report on its activity to the council and periodically such a report, especially on budgetary matters, is presented. But the result is nothing more than a formality. The councilmen listen to the report in complete passivity. The presidium does not even consider it necessary to organize a "debate":

> It never happened to me on any session, and I sat through a multitude, to hear some discussion on the subject of the presidium work between the sessions, evaluation of its activity, questions by the councilmen.[97]

In theory the council has to approve the nomination and the recall of the heads of departments of the local government. But:

> Nothing of it! This point of order passes without a discussion; the chief bows and smiles, because he already has in his pocket the nomination by the presidium; the council approves him formally, in reality he does not depend on the council, but on the presidium.[98]

The Director of the Office of the National Councils of the Chancellery of the Council of State, Kazimierz Kucner, offers many examples of the abuse heaped by high state officials on the councils which dared to criticize the administration. When admonished publicly the officials become offended, claiming damage of their authority. "How many Kazimierz Kucners there must be for the high officials to understand whose authority is more important. . . ."[99] The timidity of the councilmen and their evaluation of their own position in relation to the presidium and the state power in general is succinctly expressed by one of the old councilmen: "In councils you aren't supposed to think, in councils you're supposed to vote."[100]

And yet the generally characteristic lack of criticism of the administration by the councils and the councilmen's want of self-confidence is the result more of the spirit of the communist political system than the conscious desire of the top leadership. The leadership recognizes the necessity for public debate if the councils are to perform their functions.

> The importance of sessions should be improved. Although in recent years raising of the level of debates and matters prepared for sessions took place—still there is yet a lot of formalistic elements in the methods of work; and the participation of councilmen in the critical illumination of different parts of the activity of the executive apparatus is insufficient. Many a time the proposals for the councils resolutions are prepared by the executive apparatus without the consultation with the interested groups and committees.[101]

There are sporadic cases of councils' "revolts" against the administration. Out of four events known to the author three involved budgetary matters. In 1966, the committee on retail trade of the national council of the city of Wrocław, after examination of the city's budget for the retail trade recommended to its council refusal of the proposed budget and economic plan. In a rather unusual manner the council rejected the budget and the plan, instructing its presidium to submit new proposals based on the criticism of the retail trade committee. This example stands out as totally un-characteristic. Normally the council would have approved the budget asking at the same time its presidium to introduce the suggested corrections during the implementation of the budget.[102] This procedure was followed in the "revolt" in the Lublin City Council. After the rejection of the budget by the committee on cul-ture, the council nevertheless approved the budget, instructing the presidium to make representation for change to the province coun-cil and to search for additional funds for cultural affairs from the council's own income.[103] Do these two examples indicate freedom of the councils to challenge the administration? This hardly seems to be the case. The "revolts" are so rare that they must be regarded as exceptional events, rather proving than disproving the rule of the councils' submission to their presidia. They occur in highly specific circumstances, and they do not indicate a loss of control by the party. This was emphasized by the first secretary of the PUWP in the city of Gorzów Wielkopolski in his explanation of the city council's refusal to accept the five-year economic plan (1961–1965) voted on by the province council. The secretary stated: "Were we prepared to give the Party order . . . that the plan must be accepted without amendments, obviously it would have been accepted. . . . However such a Party order . . . would have been a political flop.[104] The fourth "revolt" was of most recent vintage (1971) and concerned a serious matter of the recall of the chairman of the presidium of the County National Council (Strzelin, prov-ince of Wrocław) by his own councilmen. The act, by admission of the Polish press, was extremely unusual for the practices of Polish local government. It was a result of the continuous incom-petence of the chairman, evident for at least eight of his fourteen years in office. The recall took place at the session visited by the secretary of the presidium of the province council, who himself berated the county administration for the low level of general development of the county. His presence indicated approval of the recall by the higher levels of local government and the party leadership. Even so, twenty-eight councilmen voted for recall, while sixteen cast ballots against it. The question which could be asked, and indeed which was raised by one of the Warsaw news-papers, was why the chairman stopped being good after sixteen years in office? One could assume that the "revolt" succeeded be-cause of the general wave which resulted from the workers up-rising in December of 1971 and the change in the top party leader-ship.[105] The "revolts" occur not because they are the normal result of vigorous debate in the councils, but rather for reason of poor presession coordination between the administration and the party and between the different levels of the administration and the party hierarchy. The "revolt" is permitted and indeed perhaps even encouraged by the local party and state leadership. We can-not exclude the possibility of a clash of personalities between the different leaders, although the hard-core data on this matter is very difficult to come by.[106]

Polish writers point with pride to the sporadic cases of the coun-cils' independence from administrative dominance. They do not, however, claim such free action to be a common pattern of be-havior. They admonish the councilmen for their sheepishness and claim that more vitality is possible in the councils' scrutiny of the administration's proposals and activities. But is it? Do the ex-amples of Wrocław, Lublin, Gorzów Wielkopolski and Strzelin point to the conclusion that the councilmen are to blame for their own inactivity? This is hardly the case. A leading Polish local government theoretician acknowledges that there is a need for "the creation of an atmosphere of free criticism during the ses-sion."[107] Such free criticism is not possible as long as there exists a complete political monopoly of the PUWP, with its mastery of the Polish economy and the state repressive agencies, and with its insistence on the principle of complete national and social unity.

A councilman is intimidated in the expression of his real opin-ion by the knowledge that the minutes of each session, including a summary of all his speeches, must be submitted to the presidium of the higher council, or, in the case of the province council, to the office of the Council of Ministers (see chapter 2). The state's power in the use of physical or economic repression is practically unlimited. Admittedly, many councilmen follow the communist lead not out of fear but simply because they are supporters of the regime. They accept the internal discipline of the three parties, are grateful for the honor of being selected to the council, and do not want to lose that privileged position. In our discussion we must remember that the councilmen are handpicked by the communists during the elections.

The practice of crowding the few working sessions of the councils with a large number of resolutions prevents meaningful debate. It is true that some of the resolutions, by their limited and technical nature, do not need much time in passing, but others require thorough discussion by the council of at least one day's duration. Some should be referred back to the committees for further investigation and reported at the next session—a procedure virtually unknown to Polish local government practice. The debate itself cannot have much meaning in view of the complete regimentation of the councilmen by the PUWP troupe and the clubs of the other parties, which slavishly submit to the unquestionable PUWP leadership. Party discipline is, of course, not unknown in other political systems, and the American lack of it is an exception. But party discipline in Western democracies operates within the framework of a multiparty system in which the recognized function of the opposition is not to submit to but to question and attack the government in power. In the Polish national councils the discipline does not bring together the ranks of the two sides of the aisle in attack and defense, but it insures the complete hegemony of the PUWP and permits a perfect prearranged orchestration of the debates.[108] The arguments, if any, are settled and the compromise is achieved outside of the chamber, not by an open and free debate, but by secret discussion at the PUWP headquarters and negotiations between different levels of the PUWP leadership, the bosses of the presidia of the national councils and the leaders of the minority parties. Again, secret negotiations between the leaders of different parties and among the leaders at different levels of the party hierarchy are quite normal in Western democracies, especially in the multiparty systems, but the individuals involved in these talks can always back their demands by the threat of opposition in free and full parliamentary debate. In Poland the leaders can bargain only with the help of their own wits and, if they have them, with strong connections at the top of the party-state structure. In the last analysis the orders sent down from Warsaw must be executed, and the leeway lies not in their outright rejection, but in their skillful modification.

The manipulation by the PUWP, effected with the willing co-operation of the presidium and the minor parties' leadership, results in dull debates—prerehearsed shows in which the actors play their roles, make speeches, and present their arguments in accordance with the well-defined script. The work of the council is dominated by the presidium, which in turn receives its cues from the PUWP headquarters. There is very little possibility indeed for the independence of individual councilmen and, hence, little opportunity for a true representation of their electorate.

RESOLUTIONS AND DEBATES

The formal will of the councils is expressed by their resolutions. Despite the passivity of the councilmen in the activities of the councils, the subject matter of the resolutions offers some insight, if not into the representative character of the national council structure, at least into its responsiveness to the needs and wishes of the local population. What problems, as indicated by the resolutions, occupy most of the councils' time? Do they, in practice, concern themselves with all the functions allocated to them by law? What legislative product emerges from "local parliaments?"

The extensive analysis of the subject matter of the resolutions of the councils still awaits a systematic year-by-year investigation, although there is voluminous source material available for the researcher in the offices of the state procurators, who, in their role as the watchdogs of general legality, gather data on and scrutinize all resolutions of the national councils and their presidia. The first attempt at analysis of the resolutions was made by a group of researchers under the aegis of the Institute of Legal Sciences of the Polish Academy of Sciences.[109] Our own analysis is based on this pioneering work and permits only a bare minimum of generalization, which may yet be proven groundless by further, more substantial investigation. Nevertheless this partial analysis should be helpful in our investigation of the role of the national councils. It is substantiated to a degree by scattered remarks of various Polish authors commenting on the resolutions, but, unfortunately, not offering any hard-core statistical data. Table 5[110] lists the subject matter breakdown of the resolutions passed in one year (1962) by selected national councils at the five levels:

(% given in italics)

Subject	Province			County			City				Commune			Total resolutions & % of Totals
	Lublin	Wrocław	Kraków City	Chełmno	Nowy Sącz	Jelenia Góra	Lublin	Kazimierz	Nowy Targ	Kowary	Rejowiec	Karpniki	Stara Kamienica	
Agriculture/Forestry	3 *13.7*	0	0	2 *7.8*	2 *9.5*	2 *3.1*	0	0	0	0	2 *10.5*	0	3 *6.3*	14 *4.0*
Industry/Trade	0	0	2 *6.3*	1 *7.8*	0	0	3 *15*	0	0	0	0	0	1 *2.1*	7 *2.0*
Building/Spatial Planning	1 *4.5*	0	0	1 *3.8*	0	0	1 *5*	0	0	0	0	0	0	3 *.9*
Communal Economy	0	3 *9.1*	1 *3.1*	0	0	1 *1.5*	1 *5*	0	3 *14.2*	2 *15.4*	2 *10.5*	1 *4.0*	0	14 *4.0*
Communication/Transport.	0	1 *3.0*	0	1 *3.8*	0	0	1 *5*	0	0	0	0	0	0	3 *.9*
Education	0	1 *3.0*	0	1 *3.8*	0	1 *1.5*	1 *5*	0	1 *4.8*	2 *15.4*	0	0	0	7 *2.0*
Culture	0	0	2 *6.3*	0	0	0	0	0	0	1 *7.7*	0	0	1 *2.1*	4 *1.1*
Health/Welfare/Employ.	0	0	0	0	0	1 *1.5*	2 *10*	0	1 *4.8*	1 *7.7*	0	0	0	5 *1.4*
Internal Affairs	1 *4.5*	0	0	1 *3.8*	0	1 *1.5*	1 *5*	1 *16.7*	1 *4.8*	0	1 *5.3*	0	0	7 *2.0*
Finances/Economy	6 *27.3*	4 *12.2*	11 *34.4*	5 *19.3*	8 *38.0*	4 *6.2*	4 *20*	3 *50*	6 *28.6*	1 *7.7*	6 *31.6*	9 *36.0*	19 *39.5*	86 *24.5*
Prices/Fees	11 *50*	0	2 *6.3*	0	1 *4.8*	0	3 *15*	1 *16.7*	0	0	2 *10.5*	0	0	20 *5.7*
Organization	0	24 *72.7*	13 *40.5*	14 *53.9*	9 *42.9*	55 *84.7*	3 *15*	1 *16.7*	9 *42.8*	6 *46.1*	6 *31.6*	15 *60.0*	24 *50.0*	179 *51.0*
Others	0	0	1 *3.1*	0	1 *4.8*	0	0	0	0	0	0	0	0	2 *.5*
Total	22 *100*	33 *100*	32 *100*	26 *100*	21 *100*	65 *100*	20 *100*	6 *100*	21 *100*	13 *100*	19 *100*	25 *100*	48 *100*	351 *100*

Most striking is the large number of resolutions in the organizational matters. With exception of two councils, the Lublin city council and the Kazimierz city council, this category accounted for one-third to two-thirds of all the resolutions, with the Jelenia Góra county council passing as many as fifty-five organizational resolutions out of a total of sixty-five. The organizational resolutions deal with the internal organization of the councils, such as changes in the membership of the presidia and committees, regulation of the work of the committees, recall of councilmen, councilmen's leaves of absence, approval of department heads, structural changes, and supervision of lower councils. Although important to the efficient functioning of the councils, the organizational resolutions have little representative character. They are also usually passed with little or no debate and, in terms of the time factor, constitute a minor part of the councils' work.

The second large block of resolutions in the councils was passed in the category of finance and economic planning, with the exception of the Kowary city council, which passed only one resolution in this field. Two of the economic resolutions are the yearly economic plan and the budget. The remaining resolutions usually deal with changes in the approved budget and plan. The importance of the finance and economic resolutions cannot be overstressed, but, as indicated above, there is usually very little real debate on these matters, and the "revolts" against the presidia proposals are so sporadic as to be insignificant. Practically without exception, changes in the budget and economic plan are passed *without any debate.*

Most of the councils investigated occupied themselves with the discussion of agricultural and forestry matters, passing from two to three resolutions in these categories, with the logical exception of the city councils. The lack of resolutions on agriculture in the activity of the Wrocław province council cannot be justified, since agriculture is one of the most important economic activities of this province.

Wrocław province rehabilitated itself, at least in the eyes of this writer, by passing one resolution in the important field of education. Conspicuous was a lack of concern with education in the activity of the two large cities, Kraków and Lublin, while, at the same time, there was a relatively good record in this category at the smaller cities level. It could be that the smaller units find it more difficult to muster funds for the physical maintenance of their schools and that this requires more of their attention. Such an hypothesis may be disproved, however, by the lack of concern with education in two out of three communes investigated. It is the commune which finds financing of education the most difficult. Is it that communes resign themselves to their dire position and wait for the higher levels to make the decisions on education for them? The passivity of the communes is well established, but their lack of concern with education may also be due to the lesser sophistication of the rural councilmen in comparison to their urban brethren.

Two large cities, Kraków and Lublin, passed resolutions on industry and trade. They were also joined in this category by the Chełmno county council and the Stara Kamienica commune council. It is disheartening to note that neither the two provinces (Lublin and Wrocław) nor the three smaller cities (Kazimierz, Nowy Targ, and Kowary) found it necessary to concern themselves with trade, in which there is in Poland such a great need for drastic improvement. In this important respect the above councils failed to represent their constituencies. Even worse was the situation in building and city planning, where, among the selected councils of the study, only the province and city of Lublin and the county of Chełmno each passed one resolution. A poor record was also shown in communication and transportation, with only the province of Wrocław, the city of Lublin, and the county of Chełmno enacting one resolution apiece. Both housing and transportation as will be discussed in chapter 5 are in short supply, and they should be a subject of discussion and resolutions for all the councils in the country, at least once a year, perhaps with the exception of the commune councils, which have only little authority in these matters. Communal economy, which is also a neglected and vital question, especially in the cities, was paid somewhat more attention by the councils. Nearly all the cities, with the "shameful" exception of Kazimierz, addressed themselves to the problem. Most concerned were again the province of Wrocław and the city of Lublin.

Culture was not under serious consideration, with only the city of Kraków, the city of Kowary, and the commune of Stara Kamienica putting themselves on record. Kraków's interest, with the city's many historical monuments[111] and its aspiration to the title of most cultural of Polish cities, is easily understood. The concern of Kowary and Stara Kamienica is commendable. Only the city of Lublin showed itself to be preoccupied with health, social welfare, and employment (2 resolutions), and it was followed to a lesser degree by one county (Jelenia Góra) and two smaller cities (Nowy Targ and Kowary). The communes, where the problems of health and welfare were most pressing, did not produce any health and welfare resolutions.

More than half of the councils studied passed resolutions regarding internal affairs, which include matters of population registration, policing, fire prevention, and the like. The number of resolutions and the number of councils enacting them seems reasonable, especially since most councils expressing involvement with these activities were at the county and city level. Many of the Polish urban centers have serious problems with petty crime and hooliganism.

On balance, the city of Lublin had the most even distribution of resolutions classified by subject matter. This indicates to us a relatively good organization of work in the Lublin council and a more successful attempt to concern itself with the large diversification of the national councils' functions and prerogatives. Also, even if indirectly, the Lublin council represented the varied interests of its population better than any other of the studied units of the local government. The other councils' record in overall performance in terms of the legislative output considered by subject matter was much poorer, with great concentration in the fields of internal organization, finance, and economic planning. Out of the total number of resolutions of all the councils under investigation, as much as 51% was devoted to matters of internal organization and 24.5% to finance and economic planning (see also table 5). The councils under investigation paid little attention to the vital questions of housing, communal facilities, communication and transportation, and health, social welfare, and employment. Building and city planning accounted for only .9% of the total number of resolutions; communal economy, as little as 4.0%; communication and transportation, .9%; health, social welfare, and employment, 1.4%.

The study of the debates in the province councils shows an interesting trend toward broader involvement in a variety of problems (see table 6): [112]

Table 6

Subjects of Debate in the Province National Councils

Subject	1961		1962		1963	
	Sessions	Councils	Sessions	Councils	Sessions	Councils
Agriculture/Forestry	11	8	14	9	21	15
Industry/Trade	5	5	14	14	10	14
Building/Communal and Housing Economy	11	7	21	15	20	15
Communication/ Transportation	1	1	8	8	5	6
Education/Culture	5	4	14	13	10	10
Health/Welfare	4	4	17	12	16	17
Security/Public Order	1	1	7	7	7	7
Budget/Finances	61	22	40	22	45	22
Other	94	22	39	13	24	17

NOTES: Sessions total 129 in 1961, 126 in 1962, and 100 in 1963. Figures exclude budget sessions in 1962.

Unfortunately the two studies are not comparable in absolute terms. Table 5 dealt with the number of resolutions passed, or, in other words, with the legislative output, while the above study concerns itself with the number of debates on certain topics, and the number of councils engaged in these debates. Also, the previous study involved selected councils at all levels. The latter table deals exclusively with the twenty-two province councils. Nevertheless some comparison may be illustrative.

Over the period studied (1961, 1962, 1963), all the province councils naturally debated the subject of budget planning and finances. Interesting is the decline in the preoccupation with economic and budgetary planning between 1962 and 1963. The year 1962 in table 6 does not include the budget sessions. If we add the budget sessions to the total of forty sessions spent in debate on finances and economics, assuming one budget session a year for each council, we obtain the total of sixty-two debates, one more than in 1961. This is nearly three finance-economic debates a year per council. As indicated above, one session a year must be devoted to economic planning and one to the budget. Hence in the years

1961 and 1962 most of the province councils spent only one session more than the minimum required on economic-budget matters. In 1963 most of the councils just fulfilled the minimum of two debates. We cannot accuse the province councils of assigning undue importance to their budgets or economic plans in the period studied. This does not mean, however, that the yearly economic and budget plans, once made, were not altered. It rather indicates to us the freedom which the presidia exercised in making the necessary changes without prior formal consultation with the councils.

Between 1961 and 1962 there is a considerable decline in debates on matters classified as "other." It is reasonable to assume this classification to include mostly questions of internal organization. In 1961 all twenty-two councils debated these matters as many as ninety-four times. In 1962 and 1963 thirteen and seventeen councils engaged in a total of thirty-nine and twenty-four debates, respectively, on internal organization. It seems to be a healthy development, especially since the province councils used the time previously spent on organizational matters for discussion of all other problems under their jurisdiction. There was a marked increase in debates on industry, trade, and services, (one hopes with emphasis on trade and services); on building, communal and housing economy; on roads and communication; on education and culture; and on health, social welfare and rest—all vital matters which required considerable improvement and, therefore, attention by the councils at all levels. And yet even with the generally increased involvement in socioeconomic problems, not all the province councils thought it necessary to consider these questions. For example, only fifteen councils out of a total of twenty-two debated building and communal and housing economy in 1962 and 1963. On balance, the study of the debates of the province councils between 1961 and 1963 indicates a trend toward broader involvement in diversified problems, which in turn suggests growth of the representative character of the province councils. Again it has to be stressed that the term "representative" does not mean here a direct participation of the voters in the decision-making process. This participation is limited by the nature of Polish elections and by the organization of the debates of the councils. The term, rather, indicates the degree to which the councils reflect the assumed wishes of the population. In this discussion this behavior will be called the responsiveness of the councils.

The third study available to us deals with the debates in the county national councils in the province of Wrocław over a two-year period (1961–1962).

Table 7

Main Issues of Debates in the County National Councils, Wrocław Province

	Councils		% of Total Councils	
Issues	1961	1962	1961	1962
Yearly economic plan/Budget	31	31	18.45	14.41
The resolutions of the VIII Plenum of the C.C. PUWP	12	2	7.14	.93
Realization of the election program and of the suggestions by the voters	31	15	18.45	6.98
The subordinate national councils	3	15	1.79	6.98
The work of national councils and their organs	25	24	14.88	11.16
Health	7	16	4.17	7.44
Education/Culture	9	26	5.36	12.09
Public Order/Security	12	13	7.14	6.05
Supplies for the population/Trade	10	9	5.95	4.19
Crafts/Services	5	10	2.98	4.65
Agriculture	13	22	7.74	10.23
Communal, housing and building economy	7	24	4.17	11.16
Roads and bridges	2	5	1.18	2.33
The "social deeds"	1	3	.60	1.40
Total	168	215	100.00	100.00

NOTE: A total of 31 Councils, 27 County and 4 City.

The study reflects the same general pattern as the two previous investigations. Again this data is not easily comparable with that provided in the two previous studies, because table 7[113] does not indicate how many times each council debated a specific issue. All the thirty-one councils devoted some time to discussion of the yearly economic plan and budget—in 1961, 18.45% and in 1962, 14.41% of the total number of councils debating the listed issues. The second major bloc of time was used for debates on organizational matters, listed as "the subordinate national councils" and "the work of national councils and their organs." Altogether, twenty-eight councils discussed organizational matters in 1961 (16.67%), and thirty-nine councils in 1962 (18.14%). Interesting is the concern of some councils with the resolutions of the VIII Plenum of the Central Committee of the PUWP. The plenum, which took place in June of 1961, stimulated discussion in twelve councils in that year and in two councils in 1962. These debates illustrate the direct impact of the higher organs of the party on local government (to be fully discussed in chapter 4), and, at least in the Wrocław province, the majority of the county councils failed to debate the guidelines of the party's august body. More attention was paid to the evaluation of the election program (of the 1961 elections) and to the suggestions of the voters. All the councils debated these issues in 1961 and fifteen councils did so again in 1962, indicating that at least immediately after the election the electoral program is used as a guideline for local government activity, and that voters' suggestions constitute an important line of communication between the councils and the general public.

Relatively low priority was given to the debates on supplies for the population (ten councils in 1961 and nine in 1962) and the related subject of the development of crafts and services (five and ten councils, respectively). Little attention was paid also to the construction and maintenance of roads and bridges, perhaps because the first issue had already been delineated in detail in the seven-year plan and because maintenance is considered to be a normal administrative function, not directly involving the legislative process. There was a considerable increase between 1961 and 1962 in the concern over the problems of education and culture (from nine councils to twenty-six councils), and of communal, housing and building economy (from seven to twenty-four); and a smaller increase in the number of councils debating public health and health services. Generally speaking, in the year 1962 there was increased involvement by the Wrocław county councils in the issues which may be termed as "service to the population." The data of the study suggest that while in 1961 the councils sifted through their own electoral programs and through the considerable maze of voters' suggestions to formulate the priorities, in 1962 they started the implementation of their own electoral promises and of the more pressing, and yet politically and economically acceptable, voters' demands.

An analysis of debates of all the province councils for 1966–1968 confirms our previous findings (see table 8): [114]

Table 8

Subjects of Debate in Province National Councils, 1966–1968

Subject	Debates	% of Total Debates
Supervision over own organs	628	40.0
Planning/Finances	400	25.2
Building/Communal and housing economy	82	5.2
Health/Welfare/Recreation/Tourism	53	3.4
Agriculture	50	3.2
Education/Culture	49	3.2
Industry/Trade/Services	48	3.2
Supervision of lower councils	39	2.4
Security/Public order	38	2.4
Highway/Transportation	23	1.5
Other	159	10.1

Again the most dominant subject was of an organizational nature, classified here as supervision over own organs and supervision of lower councils. As before the planning, budgeting and financing claimed second place. Together these three categories accounted for 67.6% of all the debates in all the province councils.

A comparison of all four studies indicates considerable pre-occupation of the national councils with organizational matters. This is especially evident in the years 1961 and 1962. The source of the high concern lies in the impact exercised on the councils by the debates and resolutions of the VIII Plenum of the Central Committee of the PUWP. The plenum set the guidelines for the change in the system of local government transferring, in agreement with the 1958 statute, many functions retained up to this time by the province councils to the prerogatives of the county councils. In turn, the county councils were pressed to delegate some of their powers to the communes, especially in planning and directing agricultural production. The councils at the province and county level were forced to debate the party's instruction, but, generally speaking, they were successful in slowing down the process of deconcentration and in effectively sabotaging the decisions of the top party leadership.

The relatively high degree of concern with the economic planning and budget evidenced in the frequency of debates and volume of legislation dealing with these matters can be easily attributed, no doubt with some justification, to the overriding Marxist stress on the importance of the economic base. On the other hand, Polish local government has to search for funds just as any Western local authority must, and its success or failure depends on its ability to obtain maximum grant-in-aid from the central government as well as on its efficiency in mastering its own financial resources. Of course Polish local government involvement in the economy is that much greater due to its ownership of small industries and practically all the services. The legislation on the economic plans and budgets is no different in technical nature than local government planning in the West, and it requires the same amount of the councils' time. What is, of course, characteristic of communist local government and lacking in democracies is the centralization of planning at the national level and, hence, the much smaller freedom of planning at the local level.

An evaluation of all the councils together in terms of their legislative output and debates shows that they payed little attention to the vital issues of housing, communal economy, public health, transportation, and supplies for the population. One has the feeling that in these spheres of activity the councils performed only the minimum and therefore did little in considering the most appropriate means for alleviating the pressing needs of their communities. It could be argued that the concentration on economic and organizational matters—local government business for which there is considerable pressure from above—and the lack of involvement in the social services output results from the councils' realization of their own impotence. No doubt this is true in many cases, but yet some councils have shown a more balanced approach, evenly combining, in their debates and their legislative output, functions resulting from the demands of the centralized economic planning and from the needs of their own communities (for example: the cities of Lublin, Nowy Targ, and Kowary and the county of Jelenia Góra). The passivity or activity of councils in the realm of social services and, therefore, the degree of their responsiveness to local demands is a function of pressure from above for meeting quotas determined by the national party and administrative leadership and of the public service spirit of the local councilmen and their leaders. The lethargy of the local councils manifested in their lack of aggressiveness in the social services field is not necessarily an inherent characteristic of the system, but rather is caused by the passive attitude of the local councils, which are satisfied in meeting the demands of the center of power and not willing to risk any activity on their own initiative. The system no doubt enforces the passivity by assigning priority to the prompt and exact fulfillment of the central commands, at the same time punishing local initiative, which in many ways interferes with the general guidelines of performance. To be active, the local council, and especially its leadership, must be brave enough to accept responsibility to the point of defiance of the national authorities. The reward is often only the satisfaction of work well done; the penalty, the destruction of the personal career. The challenge to the central power, which effectively controls all political and economic life of the country does not come easily, and it is often much more effective and safe for the individual administrator to execute efficiently the center's orders.

ELECTION OF THE PRESIDIUM

The structural arrangement of Polish local government, the allocation of many special functions to the executive, the short and infrequent sessions of the council, and the practical ability to control debates and legislative output concentrates effective power of local government in the hands of the presidium, and in the presidium, in the person of its leader, the chairman. The representativeness of the whole system relies to a very large degree on the manner of selection of the membership of the presidium and especially on the manner of selection of its chairman. The presidium is not elected by popular vote as are ordinary councilmen. The local community does not choose directly the leadership of its local government, but the presidium is elected by the council at its first session. Individual candidates are not proposed by individual councilmen, but a single slate is offered to the council jointly by all the clubs. The PUWP naturally attaches special importance to the selection of candidates, and its strict control of the clubs' membership means, in practice, that the only list proposed to the council originates with the local party secretariat and not with the body of councilmen. The election itself is only a formality. There is no debate, there are no competing proposals from the floor, and although the vote is by secret ballot, the candidates are almost always elected by unanimous affirmation.[115] Two leading Polish authorities on local administration casually remark that it is advisable before the election to give some description of the candidates.[116] Apparently the councilmen are not always even familiar with the individuals whom they are required to elect as their leaders. The candidates do not have to inhabit the locality which they are to lead.

Added control by the central government of the election of the leaders of the national councils is provided by the legal requirement that the choice of the chairman must be approved by a higher authority. This safeguard against the remote possibility of manipulated elections' going astray is always located in a higher level of government. In practice, the choice of the chairman is already agreed upon by the central and local leadership before his election, and the approval is an automatic formality.

Who is then elected? Those nominated by the PUWP. Most likely some bargaining takes place between the local and national leaders of the PUWP and between the local Party leaders and the heads of the clubs in the councils. All this negotiation is carried on in the best spirit of "democratic centralism," and the ordinary mortal is not privy to the struggle between different leaders in their attempts to build their own personal following and to enlarge their own control and power. Normally the presidium and its chairman are in accord with the local party bosses, but in some places the local government leader manages to run a wrangle with the local secretary and yet be continuously reelected to his office.[117] This indicates a high degree of control by the national party leadership, which is capable of "planting" an undesirable local government leader on the local party bosses.

The chairmen of five province councils belong to the UPP (in the provinces of: Białystok, Bydgoszcz, Koszalin, Łódź, and Rzeszów). All the remaining chairmen are members of the PUWP.[118] Such a ratio of UPP chairmen to PUWP chairmen would reflect the ratio between the total memberships of the two parties, in which the PUWP is roughly five times larger than UPP. The five chairmen from the UPP are all members of that party's Supreme Committee and, as such, are guaranteed supporters of the government. In the presidia headed by chairmen who are not PUWP members, the real power often lies with a communist vice-chairman or secretary. The election of noncommunist chairmen in about a quarter of the councils is an effective propaganda measure which attempts to prove that the system of local government is based on the free cooperation of all political parties, but it does not challenge in any way the preponderant influence and control of the PUWP.

The position of the province chairman is relatively stable, and in most cases, he is reelected time and again by his "grateful" council. In 1961 only four chairmanships changed hands; in 1965 six provinces got new bosses. Over the whole period investigated (1958–1969), twelve chairmen (55% of the total twenty-two) have served the total of eleven years each. The rest have retained their jobs for two terms (seven or eight years),[119] with the exception in the province of Rzeszów, which apparently had more than the normal share of troubles and had its chairman changed every election.[120] What is significant is that the five UPP provinces remained over this period in the UPP hands, although Białystok and Rzeszów substituted new personalities. One wonders if Rzeszów's troubles did not originate because of the UPP leadership in the province. Perhaps Rzeszów was showing more independence than desired by Warsaw, although plain incompetence cannot be ruled out and might be an equally plausible explanation.

PRESIDIUM IN ACTION—MEETINGS AND RESOLUTIONS

Whatever real power the system locates in the national councils is concentrated in the presidium and in practice the presidium, not the council, "represents" the locality and creates the link between the local interest and the directives and demands of the central authorities. The presidium acts formally in its meetings, the frequency of which depends on the plan and volume of work. A study of the presidia of selected councils in 1962 indicates on the average a meeting every ten days (see table 9).[121] The meet-

Table 9

Resolutions of the Presidia of Selected Councils (1962)

	Sessions	Resolutions
Province		
Lublin	30	424
County		
Chełmno (Lublin Prov.)	33	154
Jelenia Góra (Wrocław Prov.)	54	302
City		
Kazimierz (Lublin Prov.)	27	41
Kowary (Wrocław Prov.)	28	40
Lublin	39	359
Commune		
Rejowiec (Lublin Prov.)	25	24
Karpniki (Wrocław Prov.)	30	34
Stara Kamienica (Wrocław Prov.)	42	48

ings have a much more informal and working character than the sessions of the council. Generally speaking, they are not open to the public, although in some special cases the presidium holds a public meeting in order to ascertain the feelings of the population and to advertise its own activity, especially when it is advisable to mobilize the locality for a specific action.

The presidium of the province council is obliged to invite to its meetings the representatives of the ministries or the commissions of the central government appropriate to the discussion. All other presidia communicate to the higher presidia the proposed subject matter of their meetings and the higher presidia are always free to send representatives. The presidium also invites the directors of the enterprises and institutions which are not under the supervision of the council, notifying the higher council of the invitation. The practice of inclusion of individuals other than the members of the presidium, on one hand, permits the presidium to exercise its role as the coordinator of *all* activities on its territory and, on the other hand, to facilitate control and insight by the higher authorities (ministries, higher presidia) into the presidium's deliberation. The chairman must insure that the resolutions are of a concrete nature, specifying clearly the action to be undertaken and indicating the means and the dateline for the execution. Often the meeting sets up only a general framework, charging the chairman with the final wording, which is normally edited by him with the assistance of the professional employees of the departments.[123] This practice, although reasonable from the point of view of effective utilization of the meeting's time, especially in cases of resolutions requiring technical or legal expertise, does nevertheless allocate undue power to the chairman.

The nature of the agenda for each individual meeting is usually predetermined to a large degree by the yearly and monthly plan of operation of the presidium for the period in question, determining datelines, means of execution, control of fulfillments, and reports of performance. It is not supposed to be simply a calendar of meetings.[124] Most of the matters discussed at the meetings of the presidium concern the direct or indirect policy determinants of the central government or the top party leadership—direct, by specific instructions or policy statements; indirect, through the economic plan and budget. Of course, the presidium is also occupied with the questions of efficiency of operation of the existing projects and what may be termed the day-to-day administration. The presidium's own initiative takes place within this general framework, and it becomes less and less significant as the decision-making process descends the national council ladder of authority and the instructions of all the higher levels become more and more detailed and narrower in scope.

The activity of the presidium is increasingly dominated by economic problems because of the continuous deconcentration of the execution of economic policies (see chapter 5). This means, in reality, that although the presidium is still subject to the specific directives of the central authority, it is charged more and more with the execution of the centrally determined plans. It often has to find its own financial means for implementing these projects, as a progressively larger degree of financial responsibility is being transferred from the central ministries and the higher councils to the lower levels of the unified state administration. An example of its high degree of concern with economic matters is evidenced by a study of the resolutions of the selected presidia (see table 10).[125] At the province level, the Lublin presidium passed 28.1% of its resolutions in that year (1962) in the category of finances and economic planning. The presidium of Wrocław was even more

Table 10

Resolutions of Selected Presidia by Subject (1962)
(% given in italics)

Subject	Province Lublin	Province Wrocław	County Chełmno	County Nowy Sącz	City Jelenia Góra	City Kazimierz	City Lublin	City Kowary	Commune Rejowiec	Commune Karpniki	Commune Stara Kamienica	Total Resolutions & % of Totals
Agriculture/Forestry	21 *5.0*	26 *2.4*	23 *14.9*	21 *8.2*	26 *8.6*	12 *29.4*	3 *.8*	4 *10.0*	2 *8.3*	20 *58.9*	18 *37.5*	176 *6.4*
Industry/Trade	19 *4.5*	3 *.3*	0 *0*	4 *1.6*	5 *1.7*	1 *2.4*	18 *5.0*	0 *0*	0 *0*	0 *0*	0 *0*	50 *1.8*
Building/Spatial Planning	17 *4.0*	33 *3.1*	5 *3.2*	6 *2.3*	2 *.7*	0 *0*	9 *2.5*	0 *0*	2 *8.3*	0 *0*	0 *0*	74 *2.7*
Communal Economy	59 *13.9*	43 *4.1*	4 *2.6*	73 *28.4*	3 *1.0*	11 *26.8*	159 *44.3*	4 *10.0*	2 *8.3*	0 *0*	0 *0*	358 *13.1*
Communication/Transport.	9 *2.1*	3 *.3*	0 *0*	1 *.4*	0 *0*	1 *2.4*	4 *1.1*	0 *0*	0 *0*	0 *0*	0 *0*	18 *.7*
Education	12 *2.8*	1 *.7*	1 *.6*	6 *2.3*	2 *.7*	1 *2.4*	2 *1.1*	3 *7.5*	1 *4.2*	1 *2.9*	1 *2.1*	31 *1.1*
Culture	8 *1.9*	0 *0*	0 *0*	0 *0*	0 *0*	0 *0*	3 *.8*	0 *0*	0 *0*	0 *0*	0 *0*	11 *.4*
Health/Welfare/Employ.	18 *4.2*	0 *0*	2 *1.3*	2 *.8*	4 *1.3*	1 *2.4*	4 *1.1*	1 *2.5*	0 *0*	1 *2.9*	1 *2.1*	34 *1.2*
Internal Affairs	14 *3.3*	2 *.2*	1 *.6*	2 *.8*	3 *1.0*	1 *2.4*	5 *1.4*	0 *0*	0 *0*	0 *0*	0 *0*	28 *1.0*
Finances/Economy	119 *28.1*	376 *35.6*	39 *25.4*	101 *39.2*	84 *27.8*	6 *14.7*	67 *18.6*	15 *37.5*	6 *25.0*	0 *0*	2 *4.2*	815 *29.8*
Prices/Fees	6 *1.4*	0 *0*	4 *2.6*	2 *.8*	1 *.3*	1 *2.4*	4 *1.1*	1 *2.5*	0 *0*	0 *0*	0 *0*	19 *.7*
Organization	98 *23.1*	546 *51.7*	75 *48.8*	39 *15.2*	172 *56.9*	6 *14.7*	81 *22.7*	12 *30.0*	11 *45.9*	12 *35.3*	26 *54.1*	1,078 *39.4*
Other	24 *5.7*	23 *2.2*	0 *0*	0 *0*	0 *0*	0 *0*	0 *0*	0 *0*	0 *0*	0 *0*	0 *0*	47 *1.7*
Total	424 *100*	1,056 *100*	154 *100*	257 *100*	302 *100*	41 *100*	359 *100*	40 *100*	24 *100*	34 *100*	48 *100*	2,739 *100*

occupied with these matters (35.6% of all its resolutions). The presidia of the three counties examined adhered to the pattern: 25.4% in Chełmno, 39.2% in Nowy Sącz, and 27.8% in Jelenia Góra. The communes show a varied behavior with one following the same pattern as the provinces and counties (Rejowiec, 25.0%), and two suggesting lack of concern, especially the commune of Karpniki, which, astonishingly, did not pass any resolution of finances or economics at all; Stara Kamienica at least had some activity in this field with 4.2%. The cities lie somewhat in the middle with Kowary following the example of the higher presidia (37.5%), and Kazimierz and Lublin trailing behind (14.7% and 18.6%, respectively).

The relatively high number of resolutions on finances and economic planning is more than justifiable as it is the presidium which must coordinate the various components of the economic plan, achieve some balance between the instruction of the central authorities and the local needs and popular demands, and, often, find financial means for the local projects. It is surprising that the presidia of the two communes (Karpniki and Stara Kamienica) could function the whole year with either no resolution or only two resolutions in economic matters. Apparently both councils blindly accepted the directives from above and mechanically prepared the required proposal for the yearly economic plan without any discussion. Other evidence indicates that this is the practice in many communes which are not yet touched by the drive for deconcentration. And yet the example of Rejowiec indicates the possibility of much greater involvement by the communes in their own financing and economic planning.

In discussing the concern of the presidia with purely economic matters, as distinguished from the socioeconomic, we recognize at the same time that such a distinction must be made on more or less arbitrary grounds, and that we should include in this category the resolutions passed in the categories of: industry and trade, agriculture and forestry, communication and transportation, and, finally, prices and fees. Generally speaking, the presidia's involvement with industrial and trade activities was less than one would expect, considering the assignment to the councils by the 1958 statute of the role of local initiator and coordinator of total economic development. The two provinces, Lublin and Wrocław, occupied themselves with industry and trade for only 4.5% and .3%, respectively, of their total number of resolutions. The city presidia followed suit: with Lublin, 5.0%; Kazimierz, 2.4%; and Kowary not bothering to pass any resolution at all. The counties did not show any enthusiasm for industry and trade, limiting themselves to no resolution for Chełmno, 1.6% for Nowy Sącz, and 1.7% for Jelenia Góra. None of the three communes acted in these matters at all. While we would not expect a high degree of involvement with industry at the rural commune level, the general trade situation in the countryside required considerable improvement, and the performance of the three presidia showed indeed a lack of responsiveness to local needs.

The central government's pressure for an increase in agricultural production was reflected in the number of resolutions passed on agriculture and forestry at the commune and, to a lesser degree, the county level. The commune of Karpniki devoted more than half of its time (58.9%) to agriculture and forestry, and Stara Kamienica more than one-third (37.5%). Rejowiec was an exception, with only 8.3%, but the overall performance of the Rejowiec presidium (see below) strongly suggests to us that the commune has more of an urban character, although it does not seem to be industrialized. The counties passed resolutions on agriculture and forestry totaling from 8.2% (Nowy Sącz) to 14.9% (Chełmno) of all the resolutions. Amazing was the behavior of the presidium of the city of Kazimierz, which involved itself in agriculture and forestry in as much as 29.4% of its activity. The other two cities subscribed more to the expected pattern of the urban communities, with Lublin being the more typical with only .8% and Kowary still showing a relatively high degree of involvement with 10.0%.

The category of communication and transportation languished in all the presidia. Even at the province level, where planning for and development of transportation and communication networks one supposes would be of considerable concern, Lublin passed only 9 resolutions (2.1%) and Wrocław only 3 resolutions (.3%). The three cities, where again transportation and communication was of vital importance, were at the same level of performance: Kazimierz passing one resolution (2.4%); Lublin 4 resolutions (1.1%); and Kowary none at all. It is easy to analyze the commune presidia, since none produced anything on transportation and communication, notwithstanding the fact that local roads demand considerable overall improvement. The counties must have taken the cue from the communes; the presidia of Chełmno and Jelenia Góra passing no resolutions, and Nowy Sącz only one resolution (.4%).

Fixing prices and fees was apparently not very popular with the presidia in 1962, since the highest involvement was at 2.6% (Chełmno). The three communes and, surprisingly, the province of Wrocław, passed no resolutions in this field at all, while the rest of the presidia ranged between 0% and 2.6%. The second sphere of operation in which all the presidia manifested similarity of behavior was in the large number of resolutions on matters of organization. The standard procedure was to have from approximately 25% to 50% of all resolutions passed in this field. Only two councils (the county of Nowy Sącz and the city of Kazimierz) fell short of the normal average, but both still devoted a considerable portion of their time (15.2% and 14.7%, respectively) to organization. The presidium is involved in day-to-day administration and, naturally, has to make new appointments, organize new agencies, and shift personnel.

In other functions the presidia investigated showed a marked degree of diversification. Some indicated more responsiveness to the needs of the local population by a high degree of involvement in the issues of communal economy: the city of Lubin leading, with 44.3%; followed by the county of Nowy Sącz (28.4%); and the city of Kazimierz (26.8%). Others concerned themselves very little with this basic need, the most negligent being the communes of Karpniki and Stara Kamienica with no resolutions at all. The dormant position of the communes, which, in theory, should have been the most representative as the members were in direct contact with their electors, was more than obvious. Again the commune of Rejowiec challenged this general proposition by passing two resolutions (8.3%) on the issues of communal economy. On the other hand, Rejowiec fell behind the two other communes in the equally important matter of health, social welfare and employment: Rejowiec had no resolution; Karpniki and Stara Kamienica had one apiece (2.9% and 2.1%, respectively). It could, of course, be that the general situation of public health and social welfare was that much better in Rejowiec and thus did not require special attention by the presidium in that particular year. Generally speaking, all presidia were only mildly interested in public health, social welfare and employment. Once more the leadership went to the province of Lublin (4.2%), while the province of Wrocław did not show any interest in this matter. The counties and cities devoted, on an average, about one to two percent of all their resolutions to health, social welfare and employment. A vigorous campaign and local government action is needed in this field, and no doubt the rural population desires considerable improvement. Here the presidia of the national councils seem to fail, with some commendable exceptions, their assumed representative character.

The analysis of the resolutions does not imply that the presidia were culturally oriented. Only two presidia, Lublin province and Lublin city, passed any resolutions on culture (1.9% and .8%). All others ignored the matter entirely. We cannot judge if the population of these localities wanted to be more "cultural." An intellectual would argue that more culture is always desired. Probably, other more pressing needs justly demanded the priority of the presidia.

The involvement in building, city and country planning was at the average level of two to four percent with the city of Kamimierz lowest, with no resolutions, and the commune of Rejowiec with 8.3%. The two other communes did not pass any resolutions in this subject either, but most of the building in the rural areas is done by private farmers so that the role of the rural communes is limited to enforcement of building regulations and overall, often sporadic, planning. The councils provide only the physical facilities for schools and institutions of higher learning though they also have a vaguely defined role of general supervision (see chapter 2). It is not surprising, then, that the record of involvement of the presidia in education does not indicate extensive activity. Most of the presidia passed resolutions in this field averaging between a high of 2.9% (commune of Karpniki) and a low of .1% (province of Wrocław). The marked exceptions were the presidium of Kowary, with 7.5%, and the less significant presidium of Rejowiec, with 4.2%. Many schools in rural areas were in dire need of modernization of their buildings and upgrading of their faculty. Also distances to school from the villages served by it were often great, demanding the establishment of new schools. The presidia of the three communes investigated showed relatively more concern with education than some of the other presidia (Rejowiec, 4.2%; Karpniki, 2.9%; Stara Kamienica, 2.1%), suggesting that they were aware of the problem. It is also possible that their relatively higher degree of involvement resulted because the communes found it more difficult to obtain financial resources for the upkeep of their schools (see chapter 2).

The accumulation by subject matter of all the resolutions of all the presidia (see totals, table 10) shows marked concern with matters of organization (39.4%) and with finances and economic planning (29.8%). Together these two categories required more than two-thirds of all the resolutions (69.2%). The third significant group of resolutions fell in the category of communal economy (13.1%). Also relatively important in quantity was the group classified as agriculture and forestry (6.4%). Surprising in the rapidly industrializing country, and rather unusual from the point of view of the bias of communist ideology, was the presidia behavior in the field of industry and trade, with only 1.8% of the total. Health, social welfare and employment; education; internal affairs; prices and fees; and communication and transportation were all given a definite low priority. Culture obviously was given only passing attention and, but for the province of Lublin (city of Lublin and province of Lublin), there would have been no resolutions in that particular year.

Judging all the presidia by the degree of their responsiveness to the population of their localities, the large amount of involvement in organizational matters is justifiable, as argued above, by the executive character of the presidia. The concern with finances and economic planning also requires high priority in the presidia activities, although a large part of their behavior in these matters is the result of the impulses from above. The improvement of communal economy at all levels of local government is no doubt deeply desired by the population, and the presidia show here a considerable degree of responsiveness. However, in those spheres which may be called *society directed services* and which, on the basis of our field research, have a high degree of priority in terms of popular wants, the presidia fail to be responsive. Especially critical in view of the housing shortage in the cities is the low concern with building and city planning. The shortcomings of health services, social welfare and education in the rural areas and the growing problem of finding employment in the cities require more attention. Communication and transportation need improvement everywhere, but the aggressive program in the cities would be more than welcomed by the urban population, who have to suffer an overcrowdedness of their streetcars and buses perhaps only comparable to New York and Tokyo.

Grouping the resolutions of the selected presidia together according to the four levels of national council investigated, we obtain a clearer picture (see table 11). The presidia of the provinces

Table 11

Resolutions of Selected Presidia of the Four Levels of the
National Council by Subject (1962)
(% given in italics)

Subject	Councils			
	Province	County	City	Commune
Agriculture/Forestry	47	70	19	40
	3.2	*9.8*	*4.3*	*37.7*
Industry/Trade	22	9	19	0
	1.5	*1.3*	*4.3*	*0*
Building/Spatial Planning	50	13	9	2
	3.4	*1.8*	*2.0*	*1.9*
Communal Economy	102	80	174	2
	6.9	*11.2*	*39.5*	*1.9*
Communication/Transportation	12	1	5	0
	.8	*.1*	*1.1*	*0*
Education	13	9	6	3
	.9	*1.3*	*1.4*	*2.8*
Culture	8	0	3	0
	.5	*0*	*.7*	*0*
Health/Welfare/Employment	18	8	6	2
	1.2	*1.1*	*1.4*	*1.9*
Internal Affairs	16	6	6	0
	1.1	*.9*	*1.4*	*0*
Finances/Economy	495	224	88	8
	33.4	*31.4*	*20.0*	*7.6*
Prices/Fees	6	7	6	0
	.4	*1.0*	*1.4*	*0*
Organization	644	286	99	49
	43.5	*40.1*	*22.5*	*46.2*
Other	47	0	0	0
	3.2	*0*	*0*	*0*
Total	1,480	713	440	106
	100	*100*	*100*	*100*

were highly diversified in their activity and had resolutions on all the subjects. The largest amount was passed on organizational matters (43.5%), followed closely by finances and economic planning (33.4%). Together these two groups of subjects claimed 76.9% of all the resolutions, leaving only 23.1% for all other subjects. Far down the line, the province presidia dealt with communal economy, with 6.9%. Building and city planning (3.4%) competed closely with agriculture and forestry (3.2%). The smallest amount of resolutions was passed on culture (.5%) and prices/fees (.4%). The presidia of the counties followed the general pattern set by the province presidia. Organizational matters took 40.1%, finances and economic planning, 31.4%—together they represented a hefty share of 71.5%. There was an increase at this level in concern with communal economy (11.2%) and with agriculture and forestry (9.8%). Culture again was at the bottom, with no resolution at all. Cities showed a healthy involvement in the affairs of communal economy (39.5%), only then following the pattern of provinces and counties, with 22.5% for organizational matters and 20.0% for finances and economic planning. Surprising was the cities' involvement in agriculture and forestry (4.3%). Culture did a bit better than at the county level, but still occupied the lowest position, with only .7%.

There is significant change, in comparison to the other levels, in the behavior of the commune presidia, which show much less subject matter diversification in their resolutions. It is understandable that communes did not pass anything on industry, but there was no explanation for lack of interest in trade. Lacking also were resolutions on communication and transportation, culture, internal affairs, and prices and fees. By far, organization occupied the most prominent position (46.2%), followed closely by agriculture and forestry (37.7%). The commune presidia's concern with agriculture is explainable, since their political life often depends on their ability to fulfill the demands of norms of agricultural production set up by the higher councils. Finance and economic planning did not occupy such a dominant position as at the higher levels. All in all, the activity of the commune presidia supports the previously stated assertion that they follow orders from above and do not dare to express their own initiative. Once again we have to draw the following conclusion: the communes, which are in the position of the most direct representation of the population and are the logical pivot of the whole system of national councils, show the least amount of vitality and independence.

Presidia of provinces, counties, and cities show predominant concern with planning and financing and with organizational matters —spheres of activity in which they have the least degree of independence. Their action here is more than often predetermined by the directives from above: the economic plans and budgets of the higher councils and the state, the instructions and regulations of the central government, and the politico-economic directives of the party. Generally speaking, the presidia are much less involved with matters of direct services to the population, the weakest situation existing at the commune level. On this basis the representative character of the presidia may be questioned, although the somewhat larger involvement in these fields of at least some of the presidia suggests to us that the presidia's responsiveness to popular demands depends only so much on the structural organization of the national councils system. Equally important are the initiative and, perhaps, the political daring of the local leadership. The fact remains, however, that the political survival of the presidium, and especially of its chairman, does not depend on the approval or disapproval of the local population, but on the evaluation of their performance by the central government and the leadership of the party.

THE RELATIONSHIP BETWEEN PRESIDIA AND COUNCILS

The presidia are in a strong position to control the activities of the councils. As noted above, the presidium prepares the agenda for the session and controls the debates. It is reasonable to assume that the output of the council, as exemplified by the council's resolutions, would follow closely the directive of the presidium. Assuming that these directives are expressed in overt manner by the resolutions of the presidia, we can now attempt to examine the response of the council to the presidia's leadership by measuring the correlation between the resolutions of the presidia—presidia's directives—and the resolutions of the councils—councils' responses —as ranked by the subject matter of both sets of the resolutions.

The coefficient of linear correlation [126] (see table 12) for each set

Table 12

Coefficients of Linear Correlation of Subject of Resolutions by Selected Presidia
and Councils (1962)

National Council	Correlation Coefficient
Province of Lublin	.1
City of Kazimierz	.2
Commune of Karpniki	.3
City of Lublin	.5
City of Kowary	.6
County of Nowy Sącz	.6
Commune of Stara Kamienica	.7
Province of Wrocław	.8
County of Chełmno	.9
Commune of Rejowiec	.9
County of Jelenia Góra	.9

of presidia and councils indicates a very high degree of correlation
in the province of Wrocław, the county of Chełmno, the county
of Jelenia Góra and the commune of Rejowiec. Still significant
correlation exists for the county of Nowy Sącz, the cities of Lublin
and Kowary, and the commune of Stara Kamienica. In three national councils—the province of Lublin, the city of Kazimierz,
and the commune of Karpniki—the coefficients manifest lack of
direct correlation. In other words, in the eight national councils
with high correlation coefficients the output of the presidium
correlates closely with the output of the councils, indicating that
the presidia exercise a high degree of control over the activities of
the councils. What is equally significant in terms of the normal
simplistic view of the communist system as a highly coordinated
monolith is the low correlation of the three remaining councils,
indicating a relative lack of control by the presidia of the output
of these three councils.

Further evidence of the diversification in the controls is also
presented by the city of Lublin, which has the lowest correlation
coefficient among those councils classified by us as having a significant correlation. The author had the good fortune of attending
one of the sessions of the Lublin city council in 1962 (the year of
the study on which the calculation is based), and he was struck, as
mentioned before, by the relative vitality and forcefulness of the
debate. The final outcome however, was close to the original
program proposed by the presidium, but the nature of the debate

and our calculation indicates that the Lublin city council was not always prepared to accept passively the dominant control of the presidium and, by implication of the party.

Somewhat surprising is the coefficient for the province of Lublin, by measure of which the council shows a high degree of independence from the directives of the presidium. One of the meetings of this council in the same period was also attended by the author, and it was a totally dull, fully orchestrated performance. The author did not get the impression that it was an uncharacteristic session. It could very well be that our figures do not tell the whole story. It is possible that in the councils with low correlation coefficients the presidia themselves were careless in coordinating their own activities with the output of the councils. Perhaps this was not a lack of control, but rather a lack of proper organization of work. Whatever the case, the fact remains that there is more variability in the relationship between presidia and councils than is generally assumed by the proponents of the monolithic theory of communist systems. Again we suggest the impact of the human factor. The degree of control is as much a factor of the institutional framework as of the behavior of the individuals who make the framework operational. The attitudes and daring of the councilmen and of the members of the presidia must be taken into consideration in our evaluation of the degree of control and leadership, and even in our assessment of the responsiveness of the various councils to public demands and pressure. Let us see to what degree this hypothesis is verified by our study of the relationships between councils and presidia of different levels.

THE RELATIONSHIP BETWEEN PRESIDIA OF DIFFERENT LEVELS

Again we assume the directions of the province presidium to be expressed in its resolutions and the impact of these directions on the subordinate presidia to be measured by their resolutions. The correlation coefficients for these two sets of resolutions (see table 13) indicate a considerable similarity of behavior. Subjects treated by the province presidium are also dealt with by the presidia of the counties, cities, and communes. Does this indicate a high degree of control of the province presidium of the behavior of all other presidia, and hence, logically a relatively small degree of responsiveness of the presidia to their own councils and, in turn, through the councils to the public? As far as we can judge from our limited sample, this is indeed the case and the objective data reenforce the theory argued before on the basis of more subjective data.

The explanation of the relatively servile behavior of the lower presidia no doubt lies in their role as part and parcel of the *unified state administration*, by which most of their acts have the routine administrative character. The behavior of the presidia in our sample does not vary significantly from the behavior of any other normal state bureaucracy, and we can seriously question their representative character in relationship to the community which they theoretically are supposed to represent.

Table 13

Coefficients of Linear Correlation of the Subject of Resolutions of the Presidia & Councils of Lublin & Wrocław Provinces and the Subordinate Presidia & Councils within those Provinces (1962)

	Correlation Coefficient	
	Presidium	Council
Lublin		
County of Chełmno	.8	−.3
City of Kazimierz	.5	.5
City of Lublin	.6	.4
Commune of Rejowiec	.8	.3
Wrocław		
County of Jelenia Góra	.9	.9
City of Kowary	.9	.9
Commune of Karpniki	.3	.9
Commune of Stara Kamienica	.6	.8

Looking at table 13 which represents correlations for the province of Lublin and the province of Wrocław, we notice once more an element of variability indicating dynamism not evident with a superficial investigation. The degree of correlation is lower in some presidia than in others. The commune of Karpniki in the Wrocław province has the lowest correlation, so low that it is doubtful if it has any significance at all. The city of Kazimierz in the province of Lublin follows, with a correlation indicating a considerable independence from the province. On the other hand, the presidia of the county of Jelenia Góra and the city of Kowary, both in the Wrocław province, follow the province directives in a near perfect way. This diversification of performance is spread over the whole sample, and in our comparison of the two provinces and the different levels we cannot rank the performance in any orderly manner. At first glance at the tables it appears that the higher presidia are more responsive to the directives from above. But further scrutiny reveals that the commune of Rejowiec also has a high correlation (.8). In the final analysis the presidia behave in a highly individualistic way, some closely following directives from above, some exercising a more independent stand. Once more we are tempted to stress the role played by human behavior and to explain the variety of performance in terms of the personalities of the presidia membership.

THE RELATIONSHIP OF THE COUNCILS OF DIFFERENT LEVELS

A scrutiny of the relationship between the councils in the Lublin province and the councils in the Wrocław province (table 13) shows little correlation of behavior in Lublin and a strong correlation in Wrocław. The Lublin councils are so diversified in terms of their output that one of them, the county of Chełmno, has an adverse correlation. We are not accusing the good councilmen of Chełmno of being antagonistic to their province council and consciously avoiding passing resolutions on the same subjects as the province council, but the correlation coefficient indicates without doubt that the Chełmno council has its own mind and acts as it seems fit. Other councils in the Lublin province, while perhaps not as bold as Chełmno, also show a degree of independence, with the city of Kazimierz coming closest (.5) to the position of following the province's directives.

The councils in Wrocław province follow closely the initiative of the province council and do not show any degree of independence. The final question is whether the higher degree of independence also means a higher responsiveness to the demands of the local population. If our assumption that each community has different interests is right, then a more varied behavior does indicate more sensivity to popular pressures. But even if our assumption is wrong, a council's independence as expressed by a legislative output not closely correlated with the output of the province council gives a strong indication of that council's independence in at least one of its fields of behavior and, therefore, of the potential of responsiveness to the interests of the locality. In this sense the Lublin councils seem to us to be more viable organizations of the local population, more likely to challenge the directives from above. As the reader remembers, the same could not be attributed to the Lublin presidia, and as the presidia in many ways exercise the dominant functions in the local government structure, the more independent character of the Lublin councils may not be of great practical significance.

STANDING COMMITTEES

Theoretically, the standing committees of the national councils form yet another important link between the population and the administration, by means of which the population can transmit its demands in a more informal and less organized way than through the system of representation based on the elected councilmen. The committees have two functions: one, to mobilize population for local programs and tasks and persuade them to accept the goals of the local government; and, second, to create conditions by which the population can communicate their wishes and criticism to the leadership, especially on the narrower specific issues which escape formulation in the broader spectrum of formal representation. We will address ourselves to the function of mobilization by the committees in our next chapter and concern ourselves here with their representative character.

There is no doubt that the committees have a potential for performing an important addition to the representative character of the councils. The inclusion in their ranks of members from outside the council—members who, theoretically, should not have direct vested interest in the activity of the councils—should broaden the social base of the committees and permit them to extend their lines of communication down to the level of the ordinary citizen. Their legal obligation to control all the activities of the departments corresponding to them in functional terms, and the requirement that their opinion be consulted before any important decision is taken by the department's head, allocates to them the real power of supervision of the administration and the right of safeguarding the interests of the individual. The allocation of this power to the committees, which was increased by the 1963 amendment to the Statute of 1958, indicates the realization of the possibility of a conflict of interest between the population and bureaucracy, and, by implication, a conflict of interest between the rulers and the ruled.

Their cooperation, through their chairmen, in the preparation of the agenda of sessions and in the organization of the debates, as well as their right to suggest legislation, gives the committees a channel of translating into action, as expressed in the council's output, those pressures of the population so specific and localized as to escape the normal avenue of representation. The committees also introduce into the Council's output a necessary degree of technical expertise.

The evaluation of the behavior of the committees and, therefore, their practical effectiveness as an important avenue of informal representation must start with the committees' composition, as their membership will be the first indication of their ability to perform their assigned legal functions. The election of the councilmen to the committees follows the pattern of the election of the presidium. The slate for each committee is submitted jointly by all the clubs and a vote is taken by a show of hands. Seldom is there any debate on the candidates, and there are never any candidacies from the floor. The election is only a formality, and the PUWP, after some consultation with the council's leadership, is in full control. The committees co-opt the noncouncil members from the list of candidates provided by the coordination committee of the political parties. There is practically no possibility of anybody's being elected or co-opted without prior approval of the PUWP. The co-option procedure has not been utilized to the degree permitted by the law (half of the membership must be councilmen). In the term of 1961–1965 the councils elected to their committees 254,000 members, of which 168,000 were councilmen (66.1%) and about 86,000 were noncouncilmen (33.9%). In the 1965 election the proportion increased slightly in favor of the noncouncilmen, when, out of a total of 245,000 members, the committees had the same number of noncouncilmen 86,000

(35.2%)—and this after the specific instruction by the Bureau of National Councils of the Office of the Council of State to increase substantially the percentage of noncouncilmen. The proportion again increased after the 1969 election. Out of a total of 246,000, the noncouncilmen numbered 94,000 (38%).[127] The obvious domination (2–1) of the committees by the councilmen limits their effectiveness as an additional channel of representation.

More serious, however, is the common practice of including in the composition of the committees the state functionaries, both councilmen and noncouncilmen. They are often employed by the departments, which are subject to the committees' control. In their presence on the committees the function of the controlled is unified with the function of the controller, and one would naturally suspect that the effectiveness of the control must approximate zero. The committees' membership also includes large numbers of the presidium members; not only the ordinary members, but also the vice-chairmen. After the 1961 election 14,500 presidium members served on the committees, with 9,000 of them occupying the chairmanships of the committees. The same practice continued after the 1965 election, with 12,700 presidium members in the committees, and out of that number 1,956 presidium vice-chairmen; and 5,069 presidium members were committee chairmen, among them 700 presidium vice-chairmen.[128] Here is a definite conflict of interest. The man who is supposed to defend the citizens against the abuses of power is himself the top representative of that power. Both practices, the inclusion of state functionaries and members of the presidium, lead to serious doubt concerning the effectiveness of the committees as a channel of representation and a clearing house for individual grievances. The plaintiffs cannot be effective judges in their own cases. In many instances the committees become instruments of the presidia or the departments by which these bodies can assess the performance of the subordinate organs and of the public.

Generally speaking, the membership of the committees includes a smaller percentage than the councils of nonparty and younger people, women and new members.[129] It includes few individuals who are not connected to the existing alignment of power and who would be capable, because of their detachment, of representing the consumer, the individual, and the social groups which do not fit nicely into the established social and political structure. The committees are staffed by "professional" politicians and social workers and, as such, do not provide a real challenge to the bureaucracy.

Polish writers vary in their assessment of the actual work of the committees. They divide along a spectrum ranging from the enthusiastic analysis of Dr. Jan Szreniawski[130] to the more pessimistic evaluation of Professor J. Wróblewski.[131] It could be that this diversity of opinion stems from observations of different bodies in two different councils (Lublin and Łódź). There is no doubt that some committees are more active than others, and that some committeemen are serious about their function of representing the "lost" individual. On balance, the committees are not as influential as the letter and the spirit of the law suggest. Most of them are timid, and their lack of valid impact is recognized even by the Polish political leaders. The leadership would like to see the committees grow more agressive, perhaps not so much in their representative aspect but in their function of public control, at least to the extent of preventing the worst abuses of bureaucratic behavior as well as bribery and corruption.

The 1963 amendment of the 1958 statute was intended to put more teeth in the committees' bite, obliging the department heads to consult with the committees in important matters and empowering the committees to issue binding opinions and even instructions. The amendment did not, however, relieve the department heads of complete responsibility for the actions of their departments, and, indeed, any such arrangement would have violated the rudimental principle of public administration, in effect depriving the administrative branches of their unified, responsible command. The situation created by the amendment established an ambiguous relationship between the committees and the department heads. The department head has to take notice of the committees' recommendations or instructions, but he may appeal for the final decision to the presidium. It is only natural to expect the department head to attempt to tame the committee and to alter its purpose from that of controlling the department's actual performance to that of reviewing the reports submitted for this purpose to the committee by the department. These reports are far from reflecting the real failures and difficulties. One of the Polish journalists thus describes the situation:

> The institution of binding recommendations and opinions imparted to the department heads by the committees . . . still waits for somebody to breathe life into it. The heads are not anxious to ask for binding opinions, presidia do not consider it to be of their concern, and the committees themselves very timidly try 'to bind' with their recommendations. This is to a large degree the result of the fact that the general form of control of the department by the committee is not a direct control in the department itself, but the evaluation of the performance on the basis of a report by the head of the department. The smoothed over reports of the departments, without confrontation with reality, do not provide opportunity for the demonstration of the committee's authority over the department.[132]

The above statement supports strongly our own argument of the limited effectiveness of the committee as a factor of popular representation.

The councils themselves do not respect their own standing committees. A study by Dr. Witold Zakrzewski of the legislative behavior of the councils in the Kraków province in 1955 and 1962, and a study by Dr. Marian Surmaczyński of the behavior of the councilmen in the Wrocław province between 1961 and 1965 showed the councils only sporadically reviewing the reports of their committees.[133] In all the analyzed councils there was a complete dearth of resolutions setting directions for the work of the committees and attempting to integrate that work with the activities of the councils. There was no evidence of the utilization of the committees as sources of information, which the authors of the two studies felt would have permitted "creative and fruitful deliberations"[134] by the councils.

Thus, the representative character of the committees is made nonfunctional by the strict control of the elections by the PUWP, by the dominance of their membership by the councilmen themselves, and by the practice of inclusion of the state functionaries and presidium members. These practices lead to the "tame" character of the committees' control of the departments and to a lack of independent influence on the work of the council. The committees do not provide a viable channel of representation and cannot be considered as even a limited substitute for the formal representation by the councils.

PUBLIC OPINION

It is extremely difficult to assess public opinion in the communist countries. In view of the prevailing dogmatism of political and social doctrine, the local social scientists are unwilling to undertake broad surveys which would give the true picture of the popular attitudes and mentality. Visiting social scientists have to consider the general political atmosphere, and, in our opinion, would risk expulsion or confiscation of their material were they to undertake a public opinion poll based on a broadly distributed questionnaire. Such a study would probably be possibly only in a narrower, more technical sphere, as for example, agriculture,[135] than in the broader social or political sphere. In Poland there are only a few attitude studies—all concerning narrow groups as, for instance, the study of attitudes among Warsaw students referred to above—which may be categorized as public opinion surveys. There are also some assessments of attitudes arrived at in a semi-scientific manner by the more enterprising journalists, whose work we have tried to use in this study.

Our own survey is far from adequate, measured by the rigorous standards of Western political science. The results should, however, be evaluated in relationship to the circumstances of the research and to the available literature on the subject. This study cannot in any way claim to give a well-proven and conclusive answer. The data obtained is no more than an indication of tentative directions, of meaningful validity only when paired together with other evidence and argumentation in this book.[136]

There was one question in our survey pertinent to the problem of the representativeness of the national council system. The question asked: "Is the national council: (1) state administration or (2) self-government or (3) both?"[137] The responders were advised that the choice of "state administration" would completely exclude the representative character of local councils. The "self-government" choice would indicate a strong feeling of representative character, and the third alternative would mean a combination of representativeness and administrative character. Of course from the theoretical point of view the third answer was the correct one, and the whole purpose of this question was to test, even if only in this small sample, to what degree the theory was reflected in the actual behavior of the national councils as seen by the population. From our sample of 80, 75 gave meaningful answers: 46 (61%) decided for state administration, 5 (7%) for self-government and 24 (32%), for both. Two-thirds then supported our thesis concerning the limited representative character of national councils and thought that the theoretical combination of administration and representation was lacking in practice. Five respondents repudiated the theory by claiming the system to be representative to the point of exclusion of its administrative aspect. One-third of the group, however, stuck with the theory and gave rebuttal to our own arguments. The negative vote (for state administration) came from very young or older people, women rather than men, people with very little or a technical education, independent peasants, craftsmen, workers, housewives, and clerks and those with inferior economic status, nonparty affiliation, and from a rural-agricultural rather than city-industrial location. The list can be summarized as follows: the negative vote came from groups least involved in the actual operation of the system and least aggregate with it.

Before we push our analysis to a final conclusion, let us yet examine the answers to the second question of the survey, also focusing on the subject of representation. The question was: "Does the activity of your national council express the will and wishes of the inhabitants of the territory under the council's authority?"[138] The idea was to measure the degree of the councils' responsiveness as distinguished from their representative character. The assumption was that even if the population regarded councils as not representative in the absolute sense, they might have viewed the system as closely reflecting their wishes. In such an instance the system of Polish local government, while not representing the population physically, would represent it indirectly and, therefore, would still fulfill at least in part the role assigned to it by the theory of communist local government.

What do the figures tell? The group divided more evenly between the two possibilities than it had in the responses to the question discussed above; 47% answered "yes," and 53% "no." Still a majority felt the councils to be not only nonrepresentative, but also nonresponsive. But the majority was much smaller than in the previous case, indicating that more people regarded the system as responsive even if not necessarily representative. It indicates to us that the contact between the population and the local administration is greater than that argued on the basis of the analysis of the structure, the press reports, and the election and economic statistics. Apparently the local officials are more attuned to the pressures of their locality and more solicitous of the local needs than we were willing to grant them. The system is least responsive, in their own estimation, to certain definite groups of the population: very young or older people, those with primary or technical education, farmers, craftsmen, and workers, individuals of intelligentsia origin, individuals with bad or average economic status, nonparty members, and the inhabitants of villages and agricultural districts.

Considering the two tables, our survey shows the feeling of nonrepresentative and nonresponsive character of the local government to be predominant among the groups least integrated with the political system of Poland: young and old, least educated, farmers, craftsmen, workers, poor economic-status groups, and nonparty people. The national council system is responsive, and it may even appear representative to those who, by virtue of their advantageous economic, educational, or political position, or a combination of all three, can exercise meaningful pressure on local bureaucracy. It can be argued that this is true of any society in any political system. While this may be correct, the lack of meaningful formal representation in the Polish system of national councils limits the responsiveness of government to the extent that only those who are influential can exert pressure. The informal avenue of pressure is the quickest and, in many cases, the only way by which the citizens can readily have the ear of a public official. Pressure by ballot box has no application, and the officials need not satisfy the public in order to retain their offices.

We have argued the true meaning of the socialist state to be expressed through direct representation of the population at the local level. The system of national councils falls short of this theoretical ideal. The dominant position of the Communist party, enforced by the monistic character of its ideology, precludes meaningful representation. Indeed, the party boldly admits that the electoral systems during the period of construction of socialism is not designed to reflect mechanically all forces existing in the society.

Because of the use of one exclusive list and the legal provision for the validity of the unmarked ballot which permits effective intimidation of the voters, the key to election lies in the nomination procedure. The nomination is beyond doubt the prerogative of the Communist party, which decides who should "represent" the people. The elections are not even "consent elections" but a grandiose fraud, hardly designed to deceive anybody. The existence of the key delineating the percentages of party, minor party, and nonparty councilmen is clearly evident from the election results and illustrates the effectiveness of control by the PUWP. The absolute majority of communists at the two decisive levels of local government, the provinces and the counties, guards effectively against revolt from below as long as the party maintains its internal discipline.

An analysis of the past four elections indicates decreasing popularity of the communist leadership. (This was proven by the fall of that leadership in 1971.) The growing emphasis on reelecting an "old guard" tested in previous performance and the growing percentage of older, well-established councilmen point toward the conservatism of the leadership and its distrust of "new faces" and youth. Our own survey suggests the younger group to be highly critical of the existing system. The election results also show an increasing reliance on white-collar employees and people with at least a high school education. No doubt the regime is most capable of manipulating those who are most dependent on the system: those who are so advanced economically as not to be willing to risk their advantageous position. Our own survey supports the communist leadership's evaluation by suggesting that the most outspoken opposition comes from individual peasants, workers, craftsmen, and women, and, generally, from those with a bad economic status. The greatest opposition comes not from the upper classes, who tend to support the government or permit the communists to manipulate them, but from the classes who, in the Marxist terminology, are defined as the "masses."

The electors' right to recall their elected representatives, thought by Marx to be an essential prerequisite of "socialist democracy," is as meaningless in its practical application as the elections. The process is too cumbersome to have applicability. It is also completely controlled by the communists through their domination of the committees of the Front of National Unity, the mandate committees of the councils and their ability to muster a two-thirds majority within the councils. Recalls are extremely rare and can be used, not by the electors, but by the PUWP to cleanse the councils of its opponents on grounds that they violated the councilman's oath or damaged the good name of the council—as defined by the communist majority.

The best evidence of the lack of the representative and working legislative character of the councils is the one day duration and the infrequency (a few times a year) of their sessions. The session itself, managed to perfection by the clubs, with the PUWP troupe in full command produces the output as conceived by the local political leadership, in most cases not even the presidium but the Communist party's first secretary and its executive committee. In most councils, the real power in terms of the presession bargaining lies with the Convent of Seniors. The communists' insistence on the unanimity of vote, nearly always met in practice, tints the whole system with totalitarian paint, in which the individual completely merges his individuality with the "general will," the only modification being that the "will" is not "general," but is that of the communist leadership.

Without any doubt, whatever actual power the councils have is allocated to the presidium and, especially, to its chairman. The presidium "schools" its own councilmen in the art of conducted representation. The reports of the presidium to the council—in theory the superior body—on presidium activity are always accepted unanimously and without any discussion. The presidium, not the council, appoints the departments' heads, and the council's approval is only a mere formality. Revolts of councils against the sovereignty of the presidia are so sporadic (a few cases for the whole country over a several years period) that they reinforce our arguments by the very fact of being so unusual. In no instance were they combined with loss of control by the party, but resulted because of the poor coordination between party and state leadership. Nevertheless, they point to the possibility of more independence by the councils, were the councilmen a little bit braver and less manipulable. Even the election of the presidium by the council has no practical meaning in terms of popular, or even indirect, representation. The single slate of candidates, decided upon by the party leadership, is accepted without debate, with no competing slates from the floor and again by unanimous vote. The chairmen, as well as other important members of the presidia, generally stay in office for eight to twelve years and leave their position not because they are defeated in councils' election, but because they are promoted or demoted by the party.

The standing committees, hailed by legal provisions as the most direct link between the population and the administration, are nothing more than tame and, generally, ineffective tools of internal control. The two-to-one domination of their membership by the councilmen insures the same party control to which the councilmen are already subject within the council proper. The inclusion in their membership of large numbers of state functionaries and presidium members diminishes whatever minute role they might have in protecting the citizen against abuses by the bureaucracy. The smaller percentage in their membership of nonparty, younger people, women, and the "new faces" than in the membership of the councils suggests an even tighter control of their performance by the party; although another explanation may be that the individuals from the groups mentioned above couldn't be bothered to participate in the work of such insignificant bodies. The common practice of evaluating the work of the administration on the basis of reports prepared by the departments themselves reduces the control function of the standing committees to a mere formality, without any impact on the actual behavior of the bureaucracy. All in all, the system of national councils does not, in practice, show even a small degree of the true, independent character of popular representation. This conclusion is substantiated by our limited survey of public opinion in which 61% of the respondents claimed the system to be a straightforward state administration, without any representative character whatsoever.

The picture of the councils' responsiveness to the wishes of the population is a little bit brighter. In our survey 47% claimed the councils to be responsive. The investigation of the councils' responsiveness, however, shows the resolutions of the selected councils and presidia to be predominantly concentrated in organizational matters (51% of all resolutions in all councils) and in the subjects of finance and economic planning (24.5%). The presidia and the councils mostly deal with matters imposed on them by the higher levels of the administrative hierarchy, which stresses their position as administrative rather than representative bodies and which limits their ability to respond to the needs of their own localities. Judging by their resolutions, the presidia, as well as the councils, pay much less attention to such public-oriented services as: housing, communal facilities, communication and transportation, and health, social welfare and employment. All these services are in short supply in Poland and evidence of more involvement by the councils in these spheres of activity would increase the measure of their responsiveness. The exceptions to this general rule, councils and presidia which show more concern with the services for the public, suggest that, despite the institutional counterweights, braver and more socially conscious local government officials can be responsive to the well-being of their locality. The risks encountered in taking the initiative, discussed above, deter all but the boldest.

The relationship between the resolutions of the councils and the resolutions of the presidia generally correlates highly, proving a large degree of control by the presidia of the performance of the councils. The same is true of the relationship between the higher and lower presidia. The relationship between the higher and lower councils, as judged by their output, varies—one of the provinces examined having a high correlation and another a low correlation. It would appear that the system is controlled from the top down through the structure of presidia, rather than through the pyramid of councils, the presidia in turn dominating their own councils. The communes, and especially the commune councils, are the weakest link in the control chain. Their functions are limited, however, and of little significance to the operation of the whole system. The slowness of the deconcentration of the decision-making process to the communes proves the higher-level administrators' awareness of the unreliability of the communes.

Generally speaking the national councils are slightly more responsive than representative. However, the evidence indicates that they respond most readily and effectively to those individuals who are fully integrated with the system and who can exercise direct pressure on the local officials, and to those who occupy positions of such significance as to make overt pressure unnecessary. The responsiveness of the local council is directed toward the upper classes, with considerably less regard for the young, those least educated, the manual laborers and those of the lowest economic status.

The system of the national councils has within itself such a maze of interwoven controls that not only the representativeness of the system, but even its responsiveness is effectively denied. The logical question then is why the communists bother with the whole confusing labyrinth, which is no doubt highly expensive and much less efficient than a straightforward centralized administrative structure. The answer lies in the political rather than in the administrative role of the councils, which we propose to examine in the next chapter.

NOTES TO CHAPTER III

[1] The Constitution takes full account of this by declaring: "The working people exercise their political power through representatives elected to Parliament of the Polish People's Republic and to the National Councils" (Art. 2).

[2] The same political arrangement exists in other "people's republics." In addition to the Communist party (often appearing under a different name) there are in the German Democratic Republic, the Peasant Party, The German Liberal-Democratic Party, the Christian Democratic League, and the German National Democratic Party; in Czechoslovakia, the Czechoslovak Socialist Party and the Czechoslovak Populist Party; in Slovakia, the Party of Slovak Regeneration and the Freedom Party; in Bulgaria, the Bulgarian Agricultural Alliance.

[3] "The political system of our state is based on an alliance. . . . This is mirrored in the Front of National Unity; in the cooperation between the P.U.W.P., the U.P.P., the D.P., the social and professional organizations and the non-party citizens under the general political leadership of the P.U.W.P." (VI Congress of the Polish United Workers' Party, *Uchwała O Dalszy* [Warszawa, 1971], p. 26. See also Sylwester Zawadzki, *Rozwój Więzi Rad Narodowych z Masami Pracującemi w Polsce Ludowej* [Warszawa, 1955] p. 67, and Zygmunt Rybicki, *System Rad Narodowych w PRL* [Warszawa, 1971], pp. 20, 32, 36).

[4] Workers, peasants, and working intelligentsia. Of course, calling these

social groups "vertical stratifications" and not classes is a matter of pure semantics.

5 Rybicki, *System*, p. 48.

6 Wiesław Skrzydło, "System Partyjny PRL i Jego Wyraz w Ustroju Politycznym Państwa," *Państwo i Prawo* 14, no. 7 (1959): 11.

7 Władysław Gomułka, "Speech to the IX Plenum of the Central Committee of the PUWP (Przemówienie do IX go Plenum Komitetu Centralnego PZPR) *Nowe Drogi* 13, no. 6 (1959): 8.

8 Poland, *Constitution*, Art. 72, par. 3.

9 Gomułka, "Speech to the IX Plenum," p. 8; and *VI Zjazd Polskiej Zjednoczonej Partii Robotniczej* (Warszawa, 1972), p. 135.

10 Zawadzki, *Rozwój Więzi*, p. 248. Dr. Wiatr classifies the Polish system as belonging to the type of the hegemonic party systems (*Społeczeństwo*, p. 325).

11 *Rocznik Statystyczny* (1971), table 8, p. 61. At the time of the Fifth Congress (Nov. 1968) the party claimed over 2 million members. There was a far-reaching purge, mostly of intellectuals and scientists, between March and summer of 1968. Since in 1964, the party membership stood at 1.6 million full and candidate members (*Rocznik Polityczny* [1965], p. 130), and 700 thousand new members were admitted between 1964 and the Fifth Party Congress, the purge involved approximately 300 thousand (data on the 1968 membership and the new admissions from *Uchwała V Zjazdu*, p. 81).

12 *Rocznik Statystyczny* (1971), table 7, p. 60.

13 Ibid.

14 It can be argued, however, that peasants are relatively less active politically than the urban population and that a smaller percentage among them would join any party. This perhaps explains, but only partially, the small membership of the UPP. What is significant is that in the opinion polls quoted previously "close to 90 percent of the peasants participating in the poll believed that the peasants should be represented by a single party" (Korbonski, *Socialist Agriculture*, p. 303, 61n). This seems to indicate that the peasants, at least those polled, did not quite regard the UPP as their own party and that they resented the PUWP recruitment in the countryside.

15 The "upper class" in this context is meant to include: higher party, industrial, and state bureaucracy; higher officers of the armed forces and the police; and the top intellectuals and professional people.

16 Jaroszyński, *Zagadnienia Rad Narodowych*, p. 296.

17 *Rocznik Polityczny* (1970), p. 171. In 1964, the comparable figures were: 43%, 40.2%, and 11.4% (others 5.4%) *Rocznik Polityczny* (1965), p. 130. The white collar employees remained the largest membership group over the whole period.

18 *Rocznik Polityczny* (1970), p. 171 and the percentage of peasants calculated from: *Rocznik Statystyczny* (1971), table 8, p. 61.

19 In 1964, the Chairman of the UPP Czesław Wycech, stated: "The United Peasant Party stands on the foundation of the workers-peasant alliance and the fraternal cooperation with the Polish United Workers' Party, which we recognize as the leading force of the nation" ("Owocnych Obrad—Dla Dobra Robotników, Chłopów i Całego Narodu—Przemówienie Powitalne Prezesa NK ZSL Czesława Wycecha Na IV Zjeździe PZPR," *Trybuna Ludu*, June 16 1964; also see: Rybicki, *System*, p. 48).

20 The UPP chairman of the province organization kept repeating to my questioning as to his party's program that it is exactly the same as that of the

PUWP. The minor status of the UPP is accentuated by the fact that the Minister of Agriculture is traditionally a PUWP, and not a UPP member. Professor Korbonski comments with some well-taken sarcasm: "The fact that . . . ZSL (UPP) did not obtain the Ministry of Agriculture implied that the Communists did not intend to tolerate any outside interference in matters as vital as agriculture." (Socialist Agriculture, p. 277).

21 Interviews.

22 The chairmanship of the UPP was, between October 1956 (the Polish Revolution) and July 1962, in the hands of a liberal, Stefan Ignar. He was removed, and replaced by Wycech, most likely because of pressure exercised by the leadership of the PUWP. The change coincided with the return of some "Stalinists" to the PUWP leadership.

23 "New Peasant Party Leadership," *East Europe* 11, no. 7 (July 1962): 46. In my conversations in Poland I often came across the opinion that a previous connection with the secret political police was quite common among the members of the present UPP leadership. This may not be true, but it reflects the low regard of my informers, many of them members of the UPP—some with close association with the top leadership—for the present UPP top echelon. The fact is that in 1948, after the escape abroad of the Peasant Party chairman Mikołajczyk, the chief opponent of the complete communist takeover, those leaders who remained were extremely viable to blackmail.

24 Interviews; and Władysław Gomułka, *Przemówienia, 1959*, p. 379.

25 *Rocznik Polityczny* (1965), p. 149.

26 Ibid. (1970), p. 186.

27 Wiesław Skrzydło, "Partie Polityczne w Systemie Przedstawicielskim PRL," *Ruch Prawniczy i Ekonomiczny* 21 (1959): 37.

28 *Rocznik Statystyczny* (1971), table 9, p. 62.

29 The Trade Union's leadership is relatively stable and most of the same persons continued in the top positions between 1956 and 1971. That year those trade union leaders closely identified with Gomułka were replaced with the Gierek men.

30 The splitting of the youth movement into three separate groups occurred in 1956.

31 *Rocznik Statystyczny* (1971), table 7, p. 60.

32 Ibid.

33 The chairman of the National Secretariat is, as a rule, a member of the Central Committee of the PUWP, and the vice-chairman a member of the National Committee of the UPP.

34 *Rocznik Statystyczny* (1971), table 7, p. 60. Children and youth up to the age of sixteen are organized in the Polish Scout Association (*Związek Harcerstwa Polskiego*), a social-educational movement based on the ideas represented by the PUWP and having an important indoctrination function, but playing no part, because of the age group, in national council politics.

35 *Rocznik Statystyczny* (1971), table 7, p. 60.

36 *Rocznik Polityczny* (1965), p. 186.

37 The League's national chairman as a rule is a member of the Central Committee of the PUWP.

38 Poland, *Constitution*, Art. 2; the Election Statute of 1957, Arts. 1, 2, 5, 6, and 7.

39 The courts are obliged by the circular No. 7/NS/57 of the Minister of Justice to search their reports, starting with 1944, for names of persons de-

prived of their civil rights and to send the list of such persons to the presidia. The date 1944 is significant because the period includes the 1945-1949 civil war, the time of elimination by the communists of all the opposition, and also the era of "Stalinism," when many political suspects were sentenced and imprisoned. Starting in 1953, there was amnesty for political prisoners, but we can expect that a number of people are still without their electoral rights. The statistics on this subject are not available.

40 This provision legally permits the government to eliminate its most active opponents from elections by placing them in temporary custody. Today there is no need for this practice and it is not employed. It was widely used in the 1947 elections (see, for example, Stanisław Mikołajczyk, *The Rape of Poland: Pattern of Soviet Aggression* (New York, 1948), pp. 180-202.

41 With the simultaneous elections to the national parliament (*Sejm*) and to the national councils, the Central Electoral Commission is not formed, but its duties are performed by the State Electoral Commission constituted by the Council of State on the basis of the Parliamentary Electoral Law.

42 A polling area includes from 1,000 to 3,000 inhabitants.

43 The Election Statute of 1957, Art. 39.

44 Maurycy Jaroszyński, *Zagadnienia Rad Narodowych*, pp. 43-44. See also Jarosz, *System Wyborczy*, p. 61 and *VI Zjazd Polskiej*, p. 104.

45 Interviews. The percentage key of allocation is never mentioned in the professional literature, though one journalist refers to it in his discussion of the elections to the standing committees (Tadeusz Kołodziejczyk, "Nowy Garnitur," *Polityka* 10, no. 14 [1966]: 3). Instead it is claimed that the allocation is made on the basis of the number of members in each of the organizations. The latter method would give a much larger representation to some social organizations, especially the trade unions with 10 million members as against 2.3 in the PUWP. Of course, again, it could be argued that the member of the trade union who is also a PUWP member is representing the union and not the communists.

46 Marian Miśkiewicz, "Z Krytyki Wyciągamy Wnioski," and also Edward Babiuch, "Szczera Rozmowa Na Wsi," both in *Nowe Drogi* 15, no. 6 (1961).

47 Jiri Kolaja, *A Polish Factory* (Lexington, 1960), p. 67. My own experience verifies Mr. Kolaja's quotation.

48 Miśkiewicz, "Z Krytyki," p. 45. In 1961, election consultations in 20,000 villages lead to a change of about 8,000 candidates out of the 133,776 councilmen elected to all rural commune councils (Wybory do Sejmu i Rad Narodowych Oraz Zadania Organizacji Partyjnych—Referat Biura Politycznego na III Plenum KC PZPR," *Plenum KC PZPR*, p. 95; and *Rocznik Statystyczny*, 1971, p. 58, table 4). In the 1965 elections in the province of Kielce, 720 candidates were changed as the result of meetings with the electors, out of a total of over 16,000 candidates (Franciszek Wachowicz, First Secretary of PUWP for the province of Kielce, "Rady oglądane z bliska, "*Trybuna Ludu*, May 28, 1965).

49 Ibid., Wachowicz.

50 Kołodziejczyk, "Nowy Garnitur," p. 3.

51 *Trybuna Ludu*, April 17, 1961, p. 1.

52 "Jak głosujemy," ibid., May 29, 1965.

53 In the 1961 elections it ranged from the high of 95.37% in the elections to the municipal councils to the low of 94.19% in those to the commune councils ("Communique from the National Electoral Commission on the Re-

sults of the Elections to the National Councils," *Trybuna Ludu*, April 20, 1961). In the 1965 elections the highest percentage of participation was at the county level (96.92%) and the lowest in the city wards (93.58%) ("The Results of Elections to the National Councils—Communique of the State Electoral Commission," *Trybuna Ludu*, June 3, 1965). In the 1969 elections the participation was 97.61% for the whole country (*Rocznik Polityczny* [1970], p. 94). In the 1972 elections to the Sejm it was about 97% (*Trybuna Ludu*, March 21, 1972, p. 1).

54 Wiesław Skrzydło and Kazimierz Sand, *Wybory do Sejmu i do Rad Narodowych* (Rzeszów 1961), p. 15 and Jarosz, *System Wyborczy*, pp. 174–76. The parliamentary electoral law of 1956 required use of the booths. This provision was abolished by the 1957 electoral law.

55 Interviews.

56 For a description of a similar practice in the Soviet Union see John N. Hazard, *The Soviet System of Government* (Chicago, 1960), p. 49. A Polish acquaintance of mine, a prominent scientist, votes by placing the ballot in the envelope without even a casual glance at the candidates and dropping it in the box—his own method of protest. The author's own observation of the 1972 parliamentary elections leads him to conclusion that only very old and some young voters use the booths and presumably vote against the official list of candidates.

57 The results in the 1961 elections were 99.46% for the Front out of the total number of valid votes cast in the elections to the municipal councils and 98.43% in the elections to the province councils ("Communiques," *Trybuna Ludu*, April 20, 1961). In the 1965 elections, the municipal districts were again best with 99.46%, but this time the counties performed worse with "only" 98.80% ("Results," ibid., June 3, 1965). In the 1969 elections 99.22% voted for the Front (*Rocznik Polityczny* [1970], p. 95).

58 The author visited Poland in 1968 and 1969.

59 Czeslaw Milosz, *The Captive Mind* (New York, 1953), p. 55. This is ironic in view of Engel's argument that the low participation is indicative of political apathy.

60 Jerzy J. Wiatr, "Elections and Voting Behavior in Poland," paper delivered at the International Political Science Conference, September 1960, p. 4.

61 *Radni Rad Narodowych, 1958–1969* (Warszawa, 1970), table 9, p. 15.

62 Tadeusz Kołodziejczyk, "Nowy Garnitur," p. 3.

63 It is amusing to reflect that the Communist party's popularity in the communist countries may be in adverse proportion to the number of communists "elected" to the representative bodies. With the decreasing general support, the party is forced to rely more and more on direct dictatorship and less and less on rule by means of the "transmission belts"—indirect domination of the social and political organizations. The Polish scientists are also aware of this development as witnessed by the following comment: "In the light of the data above (on the increased number of the party members in the Councils—J.P.) the question should be investigated if we do not have here a somewhat twisted concept of the leading role of the Party" (Barbara Zawadzka and Sylwester Zawadzki, "Ewolucja Składu Rad Narodowych," *Problemy Rad Narodowych, Studia i Materiały*, no. 10 [Warszawa, 1967], p. 19). In view of this argumentation, the drop in the party's strength in 1969 would indicate the more secure position of the party.

64 *Radni, 1958–1969*, table 9, p. 15.

65 Similarly to the failure in agriculture, "socialization" of services resulted in a drastic decline in their supply. By 1964 the party leadership realized that the lack of repair and personal services had become a major economic problem. It was decided to stimulate the growth of individual crafts and to facilitate the training of new craftsmen. The necessity of finding additional employment for the rapidly growing population also contributed to the party decision.

66 *Radni, 1958–1969*, table 17, p. 35.

67 Tadeusz Kołodziejczyk, "Nowy Garnitur," p. 3.

68 Ibid., p. 3; and for the 1969 figures: *Radni, 1958–1969*, table 2, p. 45.

69 For an excellent, if brief, discussion of this process, see: Edmund Stillman, "A Thaw in East Europe's Ice Age," *The New York Times Magazine*, August 21, 1966, p. 108. The author quotes a liberal Czech Marxist as saying: "But what is odd is that the young people today are not really afraid of the party people. They do not hate them either. You see, the young people . . . they think the Communists are square."

70 Kołodziejczyk, "Nowy Garnitur," p. 3; and for the 1969 figure: *Radni, 1958–1969*, table 12, p. 23. In this number about 5% are direct employees of the departments of the Councils (Zawadzka and Zawadzki, "Ewolucja," p. 20).

71 *Radni, 1958–1969*, table 12, p. 23.

72 Ibid.

73 Ibid., pp. 22 and 23.

74 Kołodziejczyk, "Nowy Garnitur," p. 3; and for the 1969 figure: *Radni, 1958–1969*, table 7, p. 10.

75 Stefan Nowak, "Social Attitudes of Warsaw Students," *The Polish Sociological Bulletin*, nos. 1–2 (January–June 1962): 102.

76 *Radni, 1958–1969*, table 7, p. 11.

77 See chapter 1.

78 Gebert, *Komentarz do Ustawy o Radach Narodowych*, p. 299. By 1971 the situation had not changed, see: Wendel and Zell, *Rady Narodowe W PRL*, p. 103; and also T. Bocheński, S. Gebert, J. Starościak, *Rady Narodowe, Ustrój i Działalność* (Warszawa, 1971), p. 271.

79 Gebert, *Komentarz*, p. 299.

80 This is understood to be the crime committed for material profit (see Gebert, p. 298).

81 Ibid., p. 298. During the 1961–1965 term, 3,886 councilmen (2.1% of the total number of councilmen) were deprived of their mandates by the councils (Wendel and Zell, *Rady Narodowe W PRL*, p. 105).

82 The Statute of 1958, Art. 30.

83 Interviews.

84 Franciszek Szczerbal, "Usprawniać Pracę Rad," *Nowe Drogi* 15, no. 2 (February 1961): 127.

85 Derived from Instytut Nauk Prawnych Polskiej Adademii Nauk, *Problemy Rad Narodowych—Studia i Materiały*, no. 3 (Warszawa, 1965).

86 For example: in 1960 all county councils of the Rzeszów province passed a total of 471 resolutions, or about 3–4 resolutions a meeting, including in the calculation the two ceremonial sessions. The then secretary of the presidium of the Rzeszów province national council, Franciszek Kiełbicki, complained that it was difficult to implement such a large number of resolutions (Skrzydło, "Zasady Ustawodawstwa," p. 156).

87 The Statute of 1958, Art. 31.

88 Szczerbal, "Usprawniać," p. 128.

89 The PUWP statute calls the communist clubs "party troupes." The communists always try to distinguish their own organizational devices from those of the other two parties by allocating to them special names. See the PUWP statute, Art. 60 in *Nowe Drogi* 13 (1959): 759 as quoted by Gebert, *Komentarz do Ustawy o Radach Narodowych*, p. 248, note 9.

90 Ibid., p. 249. Also on the same subject see: Sokolewicz, *Przedstawicielstwo I Administracja*, p. 129.

91 Bronisław Ostapczuk, "Nowe Aspekty Sytuacji Prawnej Prezydiów Rad Narodowych" (New Aspects of the Legal Situation of the Presidia of National Councils), *Państwo i Prawo* 18, no. 10 (October 1963): 501. In note 27 Ostapczuk states: "Such a situation exists among others in the functioning of the Convent of Seniors of the National Council of the capital city of Warsaw." According to a more recent study nearly all decisions are formulated at the meetings of the clubs, which instruct their members as to the final votes (Marian Surmaczyński, "Aktywność Radnych i Ich Satysfakcja Z Pracy Społecznej," *Problemy Rad Narodowych*, no. 14 [Warszawa, 1969], p. 13).

92 Dusza, *Budżety i Gospodarka*, p. 84.

93 The study conducted by Dr. Surmaczyński ("Aktywność Radnych," p. 20) shows the verbal activity of the councilmen to be greatest at the commune level with each council member addressing the council on an average 11.8 times during his term of office, followed by the settlement councils (11.3), the city councils (10.1), and finally the county councils with only 3.2 times (no figures for the province council).

94 J.F., "Nabijanie w kaloryfer," *Trybuna Ludu*, March 3, 1964.

95 Tadeusz Kołodziejczyk, "Wysoka Rada Podlegać Raczy" (The High Council be kind enough to submit), *Polityka* 10, no. 16 (April 16, 1966).

96 "Nabijanie," *Trybuna Ludu*, March 3, 1964.

97 Ibid.

98 Ibid.

99 Ibid.

100 As quoted in ibid.

101 "Wybory do sejmu i rad narodowych oraz zadania organizacji partyjnych," *Referat Biura Politycznego na III Plenum KC PZPR* (The Report of the Political Bureau to the III Plenum of the Central Committee of the PUWP), *Plenum KC PZPR* (Warszawa, March 16–17, 1965), p. 85.

102 Kołodziejczyk, "Wysoka," p. 4.

103 Ibid.

104 Jerzy Szperkowicz, "Wniosek Nie Uzyska Większości," *Świat* (November, 1961): 9.

105 Ryszard Świerkowski, "Rada Odwołała Przewodniczącego," *Perspektywy* (January 7, 1972): 22–23. I admit the possibility of a few more "revolts" in the period 1958–1972, and indeed I heard of two or three other cases. This does not, however, make the "revolts" a common occurrence.

106 It was a common "secret" that a longstanding feud existed between the first secretary of the Lublin province PUWP, Franciszek Kozdra, and the chairman of the province national council, Paweł Dąbek, both no doubt with good connections in Warsaw. Finally, Dąbek lost in 1968.

107 Sylwester Zawadzki, "Kierunek Pogłębienia Demokratyzmu Systemu Rad Narodowych," *Nowe Drogi* 15, no. 7 (August 1961): 80.

108 For the domination of the council by the presidium see: Jan Szreniawski, "Prezydium Rady Narodowej—Model I Dewiacje" (The Presidium of Na-

COMMUNIST LOCAL GOVERNMENT

tional Councils—Model and Deviations) *Annales Universitatis Mariae Curie-Skłodowska* 14, no. 6 (Lublin, 1967).

109 The group consisted of Witold Zakrzewski, Henryk Rot, Wiesław Skrzydło, Wojciech Sokolewicz, and Sylwester Zawadzki. The first results of their research were published in 1965 under the title *Problemy Rad Narodowych—Studia i Materiały* (Warszawa, 1965).

110 Compiled from ibid.

111 Kraków was the medieval capitol of Poland. It is also the seat of the oldest Polish university, the Jagiellonian University, est. 1364.

112 Rybicki, *Działalność I Organizacja*, p. 321.

113 Adopted from ibid., p. 322.

114 Zygmunt Zell, "Analiza Tematów Sesji Ubiegłej Kadencji," no. 9 (September 1969): 13.

115 In his own interviews and in the Polish literature the author never came across any evidence of negative votes; however, sporadic cases are possible and no doubt have taken place. There is also no evidence that the official slate has ever been defeated. The election procedure is clearly described in: Tadeusz Szymczak, "System Powoływania I Skład Prezydium Rady Narodowej," *Problemy Rad Narodowych*, no. 9 (Warszawa, 1967), pp. 14–16. See also Sokolewicz, *Przedstawicielstwo I Administracja*, pp. 137–40.

116 Tadeusz Bocheński and Stanisław Gebert, *Zadania i Organizacja Pracy Rad Narodowych* (Warszawa, 1966), p. 278.

117 The best example was the open animosity between Paweł Dąbek, chairman of the Lublin province council, and Franciszek Kozdra, first secretary of the Lublin province committee of the PUWP.

118 Generally speaking, the Polish statistics avoid publicizing the political affiliation of public officials. *Rocznik Polityczny i Gospodarczy* dropped the party identification from its 1965 list of the members of the *Sejm*. After the 1965 elections, 57.7% of all presidium members were members of the PUWP and 76.8% among the salaried members (Mieczysław Wentlandt, "Structura Osobowa PRN W Latach 1944–1965," *Problemy Rad Narodowych*, no. 10 [Warszawa, 1967], p. 73), and after the 1969 elections 56.4% were PUWP (*Rocznik Polityczny*, p. 132).

119 The difference is due to the change in the frequency of elections from three to four years. In fact, the salaried members of the presidia are a professional group of "permanent social activists" (Janusz Borkowski, "Formy Działania Prezydiów Rad Narodowych," *Problemy Rad Narodowych*, no. 9 (Warszawa, 1967), pp. 34–35, and also Sokolewicz, *Przedstawicielstwo I Administracja*, p. 137, and Rybicki, *System*, pp. 311–12). 55.3% of all the presidium members (salaried and nonsalaried) elected in 1969 performed this function in the previous term (*Rocznik Polityczny*, p. 132).

120 Aside from the chairman, the "purge" extended to the whole leadership. We leave to the reader to decide whether this high turnover means more or less representativeness.

121 Compiled from *Problemy Rad Narodowych—Studia i Materiały*, no. 3 (1965).

122 Bocheński, et al., *Rady Narodowe*, p. 343.

123 Bocheński, et al., *Rady Narodowe*, pp. 345–46.

124 Ibid., p. 341.

125 Compiled from *Problemy Rad Narodowych—Studia i Materiały*, no. 3 (1965).

126 For our reader who is not familiar with statistics, the value of "r" (correlation coefficient) measures the degree of predictability of a series of events "y" by a series of events "x." In our calculation the "y" stands for the number of council resolutions in each category, and the "x" represents the number of presidia resolutions in each category. In other words, the value of "r" indicates the degree of predictability of the number of council resolutions in each category by the number of presidia resolutions in each category. The maximum value of "r" is +1, which indicates perfect predictability or that the number of council resolutions in each category corresponds exactly to the same proportional number (2, 3, 4 times as many) of presidium resolutions in the same category. The minimum value of "r" is 0, meaning a complete lack of positive relationship between the two sets of events. Any value lower than +1 indicates the relationship less than perfect, becoming less and less meaningful as it approaches 0. The value of "r" which lies between 0 and −1 indicates a negative relationship in which, in our example, the high number of presidium resolutions in any given category corresponds to the low number of council resolutions in the same category, and the low number of presidium resolutions corresponds to the high number of council resolutions.

127 Bocheński, et al., *Rady Narodowe*, p. 297, *Rocznik Statystyczny* (1968), table 6, p. 15, and *Rocznik Statystyczny* (1971), table 5, p. 59.

128 Bocheński, et. al., *Rady Narodowe*, p. 297.

129 Kołodziejczyk, "Nowy Garnitur," and *Rocznik Statystyczny* (1968), table 6, p. 15. See also Tadeusz Bigo, Jan Jendrośka, Józef Wołoch, *Pozycja Ustrojowa Komisji Rady Narodowej* (Warszawa, 1966), pp. 23–24; and Sokolewicz, *Przedstawicielstwo I Administracja*, p. 191.

130 Jan Szreniawski, "Komisje Rad Narodowych w Systemie Terenowych Organów Władzy PRL," *Annales Universitatis Mariae Curie-Skłodowska* 6 (1960).

131 Jan Wróblewski, "Formy Pracy Rady Narodowej m. Łodzi," *Zeszyty Naukowe Universytetu Łódzkiego, Prawo*, no. 17 (Łódź, 1960).

132 Kołodziejczyk, "Wysoka." Yet another study supports this opinion (Bigo et. al., *Pozycja Ustrojowa*, pp. 41–42. The most recent study argues that the opinions are only of a vague and general form at the province level. In the counties they take the form of more precise recommendations, even involvement in specific cases—matters of individual citizens—Józef Chwistek, "Wpływ Instytucji Wiążących Zaleceń I Opinii Na Prawną Pozycję Komisji Rad Narodowych," *Problemy Rad Narodowych*, no. 12 (Warszawa, 1968), p. 64.

133 Witold Zakrzewski, "Z Zagadnień Działalności Uchwałodawczej Rad Narodowych i Ich Prezydiów w. Woj. Krakowskim w Latach 1955 i 1962," in *Problemy Rad Narodowych—Studia i Materiały*, no. 3, (Warszawa, 1965), and Surmaczyński, *Aktywność Radnych*. Also see Bigo, et al., *Pozycja Ustrojowa*, p. 46 and Sokolewicz, *Przedstawicielstwo i Administracja*, pp. 199–201.

134 Zakrzewski, "Z Zagadnień Działalności," p. 70.

135 A very successful, widely based study of agricultural organization was done in Poland and Yugoslavia in 1967 by my colleague at the University of Kansas, Professor Roy Laird. This was indeed a pioneering work matched only by Professor Kolaja's study of attitudes among Polish factory workers conducted in 1956, see Jiri Kolaja, *A Polish Factory*. The only exception to this pattern is Czechoslovakia, where twenty very extensive public opinion polls were taken between April 1968 and March 1969 (see my *Public Opinion Polling in Czechoslovakia, 1968–69* [New York, 1972]).

[136] See the note on the survey on the public attitudes regarding the national councils, table 1, appendix 2.

[137] See table 1, appendix 2.

[138] See table 2, appendix 3.

4

THE ROLE IN THE POLITICAL STRUCTURE

In many ways it is fatuous to ask why something exists, the reason for its existence being its very existence. Every political system falls short of perfection if exclusively measured by the rigorous standards of absolute efficiency. The payoff is not its perfect efficiency, but its capability to work in terms of the set of goals determined by the society and by the political leadership. In many cases improvement of the technical efficiency imperils the effectiveness of the system. It changes the well-established and slowly evolved customs of procedure which the society accepts and which are a reflection of the mores and values of that society. The communist system of government, wasteful even if only by the existence of the extremely expensive method of representation which really does not represent, is the result of the ideological commitment of the leadership to the political philosophy of Marx, Engels, and Lenin. Of course it could be argued that the communist leaders use their ideology in a cynical manner in order to perpetuate their rule. If this is the case, they could have devised a much more effective system of controls and ideology, which, on the one hand, would have permitted a higher degree of technical efficiency, and, on the other hand, would have prevented the dangers resulting from even a highly controlled system of deconcentration and representation. The periodic elections, apart from their enormous costs, require constant and skillful manipulation and can, under specific circumstances, get out of hand. The communists' justification of their rule on the basis of the "scientifically proven" doctrine of Marxism—Leninism and their adherence to the complicated machinery of government by which this rule is exercised gives evidence of the basic "morality" of man. The use of physical force is seldom justified by the possession of that force alone, but is explained by higher motives of ethical sublimation. The system of national councils is also a result of the evolutionary development of historical precedence; first the Paris Commune and second, and even more important, the experiences of the Russian Revolution. The viability of the national councils derives, furthermore, from the role which these institutions played during the period of the German occupation of Poland (1939–1945) and later on during the postwar struggle between the nationalist underground and the newly established communist administration (1945–1948). During the war the dominant anti-German political force, with its fully developed conspiratorial state and administration, was, without any doubt, the nationalist Home Army (A.K.). The communists came to the scene late, not until after the German attack on the Soviet Union, and for various reasons, the Polish hatred of Russia being no less valid than the others, were never able to create a truly large and popular movement. They were, however, consciously concentrating on the lower levels of society and, in their underground administrative efforts, on the construction of a network of conspiratorial local councils, starting from the commune up.[1] Through their councils structure and also through their underground armed forces they were able to draw into their movement many individuals who, although not communists themselves, were searching for an alternative to German administration and terror. During the war the councils proved to be an effective base for partisan operation.[2] After the war they were skillfully utilized in the communist bid for absolute political domination. With the retreat of the Germans, the councils provided in some localities the new Communist-sponsored Provisional Government with a loyal local government.[3] Thus the councils grew not only out of the theoretical speculations of Marx and Engles and out of the experience of the Russian Revolution, but also out of the indigenous struggle of Polish communists during the German occupation and the postwar fight for political power.

Today, apart from the gratification of ideological commitment and reasons of historical precedence, the system of national councils plays an important practical role within the dynamics of Polish politics.

COUNCILS AS THE METHOD OF RULE

To govern, in any political system and in any society, does not imply simply the issuance of orders, regulations, and laws. Equally important from the point of view of governmental effectiveness is the transmission of these expressions of the will of authority from the government to the population in such a way that the orders are widely disseminated, enforced, and obeyed. In communist states the top leadership of the Communist party is the source of all major decisions. The party's decisions are then transferred into the legal norms by the Council of Ministers and the local councils at different levels, with the most important acts passed first by the National Parliament. Responsibility for the dissemination of the will of the party's leadership, the persuasion of the people as to its validity, and the enforcement of compliance with it lies with the party itself, the social and professional organizations, and with the councils—the last playing, at least formally, the most important role. The structure of the councils is the medium by which the leadership's will is communicated to the population and transferred into action. The party rules, not directly, but through the government and, therefore, through the pyramid of the local councils with their executive committees and departments. The councils are, to use Lenin's famous phrase once again, "the transmission belts," by means of which the party transfers its decisions to the masses; they connect the party, active and aggressive, but relatively small in numbers in relation to the total population, with the nation; and they can perform this function effectively because they form a unified state administration with a strictly defined relationship of authority and subordination based on the principle of democratic centralism.

In the modern state, the efficiency of the government depends also on the constant flow of information up to the leadership about the performance of the state machinery at all levels and, what is perhaps even more vital, about the attitudes of the population. Theoretically, the leadership can rule without this flow of information, or it may disregard public opinion even if it has the means of assessing it. In that case it has to rely on brutal force, demanding compliance to its will by fear of severe punishment. In the long run, however, the reliance on force alone always proves wasteful, and it seldom insures a smooth achievement of the intended goals. Communists, by their very belief in the superiority of their political doctrine and by their commitment to the education of the masses, have always admitted the superiority of persuasion over force, although in the history of their rule they have never shunned application of physical violence if they judged it to be more expedient.

Persuasion, then, can be fully effective only when the government is aware of the moods of population and can adjust its propaganda machine and its program to the attitudes of the people; and indeed the political success of the leaders depends much on their ability to understand public opinion. The cold fact of politics is that every program has to be implemented through human beings and, therefore, requires their active support. In that respect communism is no different from democracy, but its channels of information are not as open or as spontaneous as in a free society, in which every act of government is widely commented upon by varied sectors of the population.

The communist leadership, controlling completely all media of communication, must rely for its information on the moods and trends of public attitudes on the official lines of communication. One of the most important channels is provided by the councils through their semidemocratic discussions, which are centered around the sessions and the meetings between councilmen and their electors. Also important are the public's suggestions on the activities of local government and press criticism of local bodies. The meetings of the councils serve as a sounding board for the people's acceptance or rejection of the party's policies, especially at the lower levels, where discussion and criticism are freer. They also provide the platform from which the state and party officials can explain and justify these policies. Some localities are used for trial purposes before the leadership attempts to employ certain decisions on the national scale (as assessment of taxes by the commune, see chapter 2). Today, the communists realize that the modern industrial society—especially a society wholly committed to rapid economic development—requires for its smooth operation the active participation of the population, since the tasks performed by individuals and groups are often so complicated and technical as to escape effective control by the government. This enthusiastic cooperation by citizens is especially vital for the communist government, which, in addition to its political and welfare functions, owns, controls, and directs by far the largest part of the country's economic enterprises. It would be impossible to devise means of effective police control of every worker, engineer, technician, and scientist. Thus, if the system is to function with some degree of efficiency, it must effect the willing cooperation and participation of at least the majority of individuals involved in production:

> All kinds of willful decisions and rule by fiat are alien to the nature of the socialist state of the entire people. These are the wrong methods. The abuse of them leads to serious mistakes and miscalculations, fetters the initiative of the masses and reduces the sense of civic responsibility in the 'people.'[4]

Before we attempt an evaluation of the national councils system as the successful method of rule in a modern industrial society, we have to embark on the perilous undertaking of analyzing the decision-making process in Poland. This understanding of the process of public policy formulation explains the role of the councils within the political system.

PUBLIC POLICY FORMULATION

Most of the Western students of the communist system assign the decision-making authority to the First Secretary, claiming, at the same time, a more precise evaluation to be impossible for lack of available data. Our own model assumes the First Secretary to be the source of *all* major decisions, but at the same time tries to place him within the operational structure of the whole political system. Appendix 4, diagram 2, "Input-Output Analysis—Polish Political System" traces the outputs and inputs of public policy starting from the center, through the circles of the Polish United Workers' Party, the general administration, the economic administration, the minor parties (the UPP and the DP), the social and professional mass organizations, and the media of communication. The closer the circle is to the center, the more influential the organization in terms of inputs and the more relied upon on the output side. It is not quite clear if the minor parties placed on the fourth circles from the middle are more important than the social and professional organizations. They are in a more respectable position than, let us say, the Polish Hunting Association, but in an overall evaluation show less impact on public policies than some other social and professional bodies, such as the trade unions. For simplicity in the diagram the minor parties were placed closer to the center of power. The reader is well-advised to remember that the fifth circle is the aggregate of all social and professional organizations. Some of them play only a minute role, some are extremely important. Also, the minor parties represent broad sectors of society, the UPP the peasants and the DP some of the urban intelligentsia and craftsmen, while the social and professional organizations are vocal in the narrow matters of their particular interest. The latter can be compared to Western pressure groups, but lack the independence and flexibility to apply pressure at any point of the decision-making process.

The public policy formulation in Poland can be best understood by examining, first, its output side, rather than by the traditional and logical approach of analyzing inputs as the originators of the whole process. The outputs are visible, and from the outputs we will attempt to deduct the inputs. The first act classified as output is a major policy pronouncement by the First Secretary of the PUWP called the thesis. The thesis may be voiced by the First Secretary to any large public gathering, as, for example, the Trade Unions Congress, especially if the thesis is on a narrower subject of particular interest to the group in question. Most of the general and broader policy announcements are made to the Central Committee of the PUWP. In the cases of policy plans for a long period of time or of major consequences, the thesis is contained in the address by the First Secretary to the Party Congress.[5] The Central Committee passes the original thesis as its own resolution, or the Party Congress incorporates it into the new party program. From this time all party organs are formally charged with the execution of the policy. The actual implementation is in the hands of the secretariat of the Central Committee, which acts through the descending order of provincial and county first secretaries and their executive committees, down to the primary party organization and its first secretary. On all levels the party organs urge the implementation of the thesis on the corresponding government bodies—the secretariat acting on the ministries and the local executive committees on the national councils. The primary party organization explains the thesis to the public, whips up enthusiasm, and mobilizes the masses for action.

The party also presses the minor parties and the social and professional organizations, agitating for action in support of the thesis and for its smooth implementation. The minor parties bring their own programs in line with the thesis and use their organizational structures to reach the public. The same process takes place within the structure of the social and professional organizations, with the higher degree of activity evident in those organizations whose special interest is directly affected by the new policy.

On the government side the guidelines of the thesis are formulated by the Council of Ministers into a draft law. The draft law is submitted to the Parliament (*Sejm*) or to the Council of State, if the Parliament is not in session.[6] The Parliament, after a debate controlled by the PUWP, passes the thesis as an Act of the Sejm. The thesis, until now in legal terms a strictly internal matter of the party, becomes the law of the country. It is then made operational by the specific regulations of the Council of Ministers, the separate ministries involved, and the subordinate presidia of the national councils. The specific ministries are charged with the implementation. They formulate their own regulations and act through the corresponding departments of the national councils. The councils themselves implement the act by resolutions binding on the territory under their authority. The government, through the national councils, implements the law and mobilizes the population for compliance and action.

The public-policy formulation at the local level proceeds more or less in the same manner as at the national level. The ultimate source of initiation is the local first secretary of the PUWP, and the legalization of his thesis rests with the presidium of the national council, which submits it to the council for formal enactment. Two Polish professors, Sokolewicz and Zawadzki thus describe this process:

> The thought of passing a council's resolution which would regulate a specific sphere of matters originates during the deliberation of the local party organ. Participating in this party organ, members of the presi-

dium of the corresponding national council present the problem to the meeting of the presidium and consequently to the appropriate committee. The committee determines principles of solution (of the problem) and makes them known to the presidium of the national council, which—accepting these principles—instructs the department to prepare, in consultation with the committee, the proposal of the resolution. The proposal, prepared in such a way, is discussed and approved at the meeting of the presidium, and later on—as a project of the presidium—it is submitted to the council for enactment.[7]

The above description, in our opinion, assigns undue weight to the decision-making function of the committees. Our previous discussion of the committees clearly indicates their advisory character. It might be that Professors Sokolewicz and Zawadzki stress the role of the committee in the decision-making process not by design but by an unfortunate wording of their description. It may also be that their approach results from their legalistic frame of reference, rather than from observation of actual decision-making behavior. In general terms, however, their description corresponds to our own illustration of the process at the local and the national level. In the last analysis the initiative lies firmly with the party.

There is one important difference between national and local public-policy formulation. The national First Secretary is restricted only by the pressures emerging from below and by technical possibilities. The local first secretary receives his cues from Warsaw, and he looks to the thesis of the national First Secretary as inspiration for his own action. Also, his position in relation to the government is not as strong as that of the national First Secretary. The chairman of the national council receives his orders from the top through the government structure. His political survival depends on his ability to meet the demands of the government leadership, which, in turn, reaches its apex in the person of the national First Secretary of the Communist party. In a sense, both men, the local first secretary and the chairman of the local council, receive their order from the same source, the top leadership of the party, but through two different channels. The chairman, to a degree, is independent of the local first secretary since he can always refer to the orders received through his own line of command. He can also appeal the decision of the local first secretary to the higher government body.

In the Polish political system the output of public policy reaches the public from its original source, the First Secretary, through two separate channels. One is the party structure, which uses the original thesis and the resolution of the Central Committee to urge immediate action on the corresponding bodies of the national councils, the social and professional organizations and through its own primary organizations and media of communication, directly on the public. The second channel is the government, acting through the council of ministers, the Parliament, the economic administration and the unified state administration—the pyramid of councils interlocked with one another and with the ministries. The party structure is without any doubt the more important of the two, and in the last analysis it is the party and not the government which has the final say in public policy formulation and implementation.

The analysis of the inputs of the public-policy formulation is difficult in any political system. Literature on this subject in communist countries does not exist, and free inquiry is impossible since many of the most influential bodies, especially the Communist party itself, operate in secrecy. The analysis must be in the nature of an educated guess rather than a scientific inquiry based on empirical data. We begin with the assumption that the First Secretary does not formulate the policies expressed in his thesis by a personal whim. First of all he seeks the advice of his close collaborators, the presidium of the Central Committee, (the Political Bureau as it is officially called in Poland), who in their own right are important leaders of the party. They are in charge of the vital branches of party and government work. The First Secretary consults with the Political Bureau at least weekly and listens carefully to their opinions and advice. Most of them are his close supporters, at least officially, and are also handpicked by the First Secretary for their jobs.

The First Secretary relies heavily on the information and advice supplied by the secretariat of the Central Committee, especially the group of secretaries heading the main branches of the party's activities. The secretariat gathers information as to the performance of the administration and the economy and as to the attitudes of the population through the feelers of the Party organization: the first secretaries, the executive committees, and the membership grouped in the primary party organizations.

Furthermore, the First Secretary uses the government structure in the formulation of his policies. First of all he consults with his prime minister, (the use of the pronoun *his* is quite appropriate) who is also a member of the Political Bureau. The First Secretary may sit in on the meetings of the Council of Ministers if he chooses to do so. He calls individual ministers for conferences and for reports. He is supplied with a constant flow of information by the Council of Ministers and by the individual ministries. The Council and the ministries, in turn, rely on the lines of communication extending down to the presidia, departments, and councils of the national councils. The presidia and departments report on performance and obstacles and suggest modifications. The debates of the councils, even if highly controlled, serve as an indicator of public opinion and as the sounding board for new policies. Finally, the First Secretary considers the opinions and pressures of the leaders of the minor parties and the social and professional organizations, especially if he contemplates a policy directly affecting some of these organizations. Once again it has to be stressed that the communist rulers prefer persuasion and manipulated mass participation to the use of force. Their ideological orientation combined with the pragmatism of the commitment to economic development, requires of them the semblance of mass democracy.

In this entire system of the inputs of public policy, each group and each level to a degree represents a specific interest. The nature of the information sent up to the First Secretary, although often based on objective data, is colored by the subjectivity of the organ from which the information originated. The participants in the system realize the facts of its operation and consciously exercise pressure in order to obtain an output favorable to their own organizational well-being. In other words, the information and the advice which filters up from the public through the party, the unified state administration, the economic administration, the minor parties, the social and professional organizations and the media of communication is not an objective, detached evaluation of performance, attitudes, and possibilities, but is designed to produce a certain output.

The First Secretary must rely on the existing lines of communication and is himself subject to the pressures of the system. His advantage lies in his ability to use two main separate and independent lines of communication (the party and the state), as well as the several less important sources (the minor parties and the social and professional organizations). In addition the First Secretary employs yet another channel, not truly represented in our diagram because it is officially a part of the government, namely the institution of the security police (the Office of Security as it is known in Poland *Urząd Bezpieczeństwa*). The security police, through its agents, permeates the whole system and provides an additional check on the performance of subordinates and the reliability of information. Its very existence prevents all the parts of the system from using their pressure extensively. Knowledge of the secret police activities curtails freedom of exaggeration and makes the First Secretary less responsive to the particular interests of various groups and localities.

A comparison of the input and output indicates that the system relies more heavily on the Communist party for inputs and uses the government structure for physical implementation of outputs. The party plays the dominant role in connecting the top decision-makers with the public, but has a smaller role in the implementation of policy. Its function is theoretically limited to supervision, encouraging efficiency, and control of performance. In practice the party cannot avoid direct interference in actual implementation, but the unified state administration is still the physical plant of output execution.

The model can be made operational by tracing the progress of one of the theses through it. At the IX Plenum of the Central Committee of the PUWP in May 1957, the then First Secretary, Mr. Gomułka, introduced in his report the thesis for the broadening of the authority of the national councils.[8] We will concern ourselves with only one aspect of the thesis: the assignment to the county councils of all the functions of the national councils, excluding those matters explicitly reserved for the competence of councils of a lower or higher level. The thesis proposed the county councils as the *main* organ of state administration. The function of the province council was to be limited to coordination. The communes were to play only a secondary role, providing public services in their territories, stimulating agricultural production, and gathering statistical data. Up to the time of the thesis, the province had been the principle organ of state administration, the county serving as its agent rather than as an independent unit of government. Also, many of the purely administrative functions of local application were performed directly by the central government ministries—especially those in economy, transportation, and communication—and the Ministry of Internal Affairs. The thesis of the First Secretary was passed, as is customary, without any changes, by the Central Committee. The Council of Ministers, on the basis of the Central Committee resolution, introduced the draft law on the national councils to the Sejm. The Sejm passed the statute to this effect on January 25, 1958. In the meantime the party was already in full swing, hammering, at least officially, for the smooth and expeditious transfer of power to the councils and, within the councils' structure, to the counties. The Council of Ministers issued a considerable number of regulations resulting from the new law[9] and instructed its own ministries and the national councils to procede with full speed. The passing of functions from the ministries to the provinces took place without undue delay. Roughly by 1959–1960 the new law had been complied with at the central government level. The whole process was stopped by the provinces which obstructed further progress in deconcentration, claiming that the counties did not have the necessary personnel, experience, and political suavity to perform their new functions efficiently. The opposition of the provinces was highly effective despite continuous pressure by the top authorities of the PUWP and a constant stream of follow-up regulations by the Council of Ministers.

This state of affairs prompted the First Secretary to call in June 1961, the special VIII Plenum of the Central Committee, and to submit to it yet another thesis entitled: "The basic directions for further development of the activities of the national councils"[10] which became a resolution of the Central Committee.[11] It was followed by a proposal of amendment of the original 1958 statute submitted to the Sejm on June 3, 1963, jointly by the Council of Ministers and the Council of State. The Sejm amended the law on June 28, 1963, making the dominant role of the county councils in administration even more explicit. Again the Council of Ministers responded with a considerable number of regulations directing the provinces to comply with the law and setting specific timetables. This time the deconcentration began to proceed slowly, but even in 1967 there were complaints that some of the functions assigned to the counties still were performed by the provinces.

The above description of the passage of the thesis of the First Secretary shows that, contrary to the generally prevailing assumption, the First Secretary does not enjoy an absolute power of public-policy formulation and implementation. Although the structural analysis of the system singles him out as the apex of the decision-making process, and although our earlier speculation that he is the main source of formulation of the basic policies is logically correct, on the output side his power is limited by what we propose to call the *rate of absorption*. The rate is the time and degree of absorption by the system of the original thesis. In our own example the rate equals ten years in time and roughly about ninety percent in degree. The slow rate of absorption is a serious limitation on the authority of the central leadership because the time factor regulates the number of new policies which can be initiated, and it can force the First Secretary to alter his original program and perhaps even to abandon altogether some of its parts. The longer the absorption the more the policy changes from variations in degree to variations in kind. The rate of absorption is a meaningful and measurable expression of the pressure exerted by different groups within the system.

Why did it take so long to deconcentrate administration from the province to the county level? First of all, there was the human factor expressed by the province chairmen's natural opposition to transfer of part of their power. Secondly, there were technical limitations insofar as the county councils did not have sufficient staff to handle the increased volume of administration. Logically, the central authorities ordered the transfer of province personnel to the counties. This measure was opposed and slowed down by the province leaders who did not want to decrease their own staffs. There was also reluctance on the part of the province government employees to move from the large cities, the capitals of the provinces, to the smaller, less sophisticated towns, where the county seats were situated. The central government in desperation instituted special, and substantial, economic incentives for any government official moving to the counties, such as guaranteed housing in the new location, payment of the moving expenses, and permanent salary and civil service grade increases. The measure still failed to create enthusiasm among the civil servants selected for deconcentration. In addition, they were not pressed hard to move by their own provincial bosses, who were opposed to deconcentration themselves.

There was also a considerable distrust by the province leadership—government as well as party—regarding the ability of the county officials to handle efficiently the main task of administration. The province chairmen and the first secretaries of the province party organizations realized that despite the transfer of technical functions to the counties, they themselves would still be held responsible for the total performance of the provinces. They could be much surer of the results were the administration to remain in their immediate bailiwick. They preferred to control their own departments directly rather than being forced to play the ill-defined and difficult role of general coordinators.

The First Secretary and the central government were virtually helpless in the face of the combined opposition of all the provinces, short of dismissing all the province chairmen and first secretaries. The previous analysis shows that over this period all the chairmen kept their jobs, except in the province of Rzeszów, where the chairman was changed twice. Even if it contemplated such a move, which is rather doubtful, the top leadership must have realized that a wholesale purge would have been completely impractical. Firing of the chairmen alone would have produced only limited results. The new chairmen would have been under the pressure of the old province secretaries, so the purge would have had to include the secretaries as well. Such a drastic change in the leadership of the provinces would have destroyed the confidence and the image of the local administration and, what is even more important, the prestige in the eyes of the population of the whole Polish People's Republic. The province leadership was, after all, the most able and reliable from the point of view of the central leadership. Also, over a period of years it had acquired unique leadership qualities and knowledge of each region. The province leaders would have been difficult to replace, and there would have been no guarantee that the new leaders would behave any differently, though fear of another purge might have caused them to modify their predecessors' position slightly. The central leadership chose instead a different method. It barraged the province officials with a great volume of implementation regulations, culminating finally in the new thesis of the First Secretary and the amendment to the 1958 statute. At last the desired result was achieved. It took, however, ten long years.

During the whole period the province leadership fought back not only by doing very little in the line of deconcentration, but also by exerting constant pressure on the input side for slowing down the implementation. The province representation was based on technical arguments. It is typical of public debate in the communist countries that it seldom leaves the level of technical debate and that, at least on the surface, all participants accept without reservation the ideological assumptions. Of course the device of technical argumentation is often used to challenge by implication the validity of specific interpretation of ideology. In our own example, the province leadership used the party and the government lines of communication (the input side of the diagram) to convince the central leadership of the technical difficulties involved in deconcentration. It was pointed out that deconcentration without a thorough upgrading of the efficiency level of the county government would result in administrative chaos.

The First Secretary himself admitted in his second thesis the low level of the county administrative personnel. According to him, in 1959 only 7.4% of the county civil servants had university education; only 39.2% had high school education; 52.2% primary education; and 1.2% did not even finish the primary school. He also added, however, that the situation at the province level was not much better. Apparently the campaign of the province leadership had its effect and, in fact, their arguments were to a degree justified by reality. To remedy the situation the First Secretary proposed transfer of about 3,220 officials from the province to the county level.[12] The modesty of his request (in 1961 there were 22,495 employees in the province administration and 72,160 in the counties)[13] was again evidence of the effectiveness of the provinces' opposition.

The provinces also advanced the argument that the county leadership lacked political ability and warned that deconcentration might undermine the political control of the country by the center. This advice was not to be taken lightly, and the central leadership moved with considerable caution, leaving the provinces a more or less free hand as to the speed of deconcentration. Despite the opposition, effective in terms of the time span of the rate of absorption, deconcentration was constantly advocated by the center and it finally took root. What was the reason for this continuous pressure on the provinces? The whole process of deconcentration was the result of the spirit of the limited Polish revolution of 1956. To the majority of people, including the "liberal" wing of the Communist party, deconcentration meant democratization of the whole political life of Poland. It meant bringing the administration down to the level of the ordinary citizen and therefore subjecting it to direct pressure by the population. The Stalinist period of tight control was associated in many minds with the centralized bureaucracy ruling from Warsaw without any regard for the needs and conditions of the country. This centralized bureaucracy was also highly inefficient and costly in economic terms.

No doubt the First Secretary, Mr. Gomułka, was at the beginning as much committed to the general process of democratization as were other liberal sectors of the party and the general public. His personal convictions were an important motivation for the constancy of the deconcentration drive. However, the administrative and political realities ably presented by the province leadership and, perhaps also, the argumentation of his more conservative advisors who had made the comeback into the top leadership, dampened his enthusiasm for speedy deconcentration. The fact that this process was not slowed down even more and that it was not altered to the degree of impotency must be attributed to other pressure groups exercising their influence on the input side of the public-policy formulation.

The public was in favor of deconcentration and firmly against the centralized bureaucracy. Apart from the democratization aspect, deconcentration meant easier access to public officials. It was simpler to travel to county seats than to the province capital. It would have been still simpler to deal with the commune administration. The public attitude was known to the top leadership through the reports of the councils' sessions, meetings of councilmen with the public, letters to the editors of the local newspapers, and the reporting by local and national journalists.

More important, however, was the pressure brought about by the minor parties and the social and professional organizations (circles

4 and 5 on the diagram). The parties hoped to obtain more impact on the administration by pushing it down to a level under less direct control of the PUWP, since in county councils the communists have a smaller majority and must cooperate more meaningfully with the minor parties. The social and professional organizations pressed for reforms for a variety of reasons. Some desired to take over certain administrative functions, such as licensing, and felt themselves to have a better chance for this by dealing with the counties; some represented genuine public opinion; some, such as women's organizations, were concerned with more efficient distribution of consumers' goods. The economists pressed for deconcentration in a belief that it would improve the management of the economy and would lead to a better utilization of resources. All of them, including the managers of the economy, thought the relatively weak counties to be more easily managed in favor of their own particular interests.

Many of these pressures were brought about not only through the official lines of communications—the debates and private discussions in and around the national parliament, the meetings of the Central Committee and the supreme committees of the minor parties, and the gatherings of the central councils of various social and professional organizations—but also by informal consultations by leaders of all these bodies with the members of the Council of Ministers, the members of the politburo of the PUWP, and the First Secretary himself. The supporters of deconcentration finally won, perhaps only because the First Secretary and most of the top leaders themselves believed in the advantages of this policy. The effectiveness of the province opposition, isolated to the province officials and the province first secretaries, must be measured by the slowness of the rate of absorption.

The analysis of the public policy formulation and the role played in it by the national councils, as illustrated by our example of the thesis of deconcentration, suggests that the system, although not representative is responsive to a number of pressures which influence the input of public-policy formulation. The policy outputs depend on the rate of absorption, and here the role of the national councils as the unified state administration is fully evident, with the councils subject only to the control and active direction of the party. The party, however, is divided into the top leadership, the local first secretaries, and the membership at large. The impact of the leadership on the rate of absorption depends on its ability to spur the first secretaries to action. In our example the province secretaries were united with the province chairmen, and the leadership pressure was not any more effective through the party channels than it was through the unified state administration. In the last analysis the First Secretary must rule through his subordinates and through the structure of the Polish system. He is as much a prisoner of the system as the system is under his command.

POPULAR MOBILIZATION

The best method of effecting willing cooperation with the government is the involvement of ordinary citizens in the political process. It creates in them the impression of participating in the decision-making and, to some degree, also gives them a feeling of responsibility for all the activities of the state. The structure of the councils brings into the political process hundreds of thousands of people. The matters they deal with may be regarded as of only secondary importance, but nevertheless their participation in local government activities to some extent unifies them and identifies them with the existing regime in their own minds as well as in the eyes of the rest of the population. An individual may agree to election to the local council because he wishes to work for the improvement of his own small community, but by this act he assumes at once the position of an official and is considered to be part of the ruling elite, even if his own personal ideology is contrary to the communist dogma. Soon he finds himself not only propagating the policies of the communist leadership, but also defending its failings, since the policies are part of his own activity and the shortcomings are often his own deficiencies. The local deputy "is supposed to be a priest and ward heeler rolled into one,"[14] and he is bound to identify himself more and more with the communist state. Multiplying one citizen by thousands we obtain a vast army of government supporters, who, although greatly varied in their enthusiasm for communism, perform the vital role of perpetuating and strengthening the communist rule.

With these thousands of servants of the communist state, the leadership can practically relinquish the use of force for political reasons, employing it only in the most drastic cases of overt opposition and as a reminder of the central authority's unlimited power, because "the political principles of the functioning of the apparatus of power in the socialist state dictates the duty of persuading the citizens, while force remains only as the final method when other methods fail."[15] The councils engage in mass mobilization through their so-called work of "mass-organization,"[16] in which the councils explain the goals and directives of the communist leadership, popularize policies of the councils, and attempt to draw the population into active participation in the execution of these policies.

The councils also provide organizational help for the formation of the social and professional groups designed to contribute to the political indoctrination of their members and, in some cases, to the development of higher economic production. The "mass-organizational" work should actively involve all the councilmen, as well as the members of the presidia and even the heads of the departments. Ideally, at least from the point of view of the mobilization function, all these people should be in constant motion. They should attend the village and urban block meetings, the meetings of social organizations and cooperative societies, and the meetings of the voters with their representatives. They should argue, persuade, explain, and take in suggestions and complaints. The previous discussion of the functions of the presidium members and the department heads already suggests that a considerable amount of their time is spent in this type of endeavor, in many ways to the detriment of their primary function as administrators.

Of course, by virtue of their political nature the councilmen should be the main vehicle of mass mobilization. In theory, they are the link between the administration and the population. They should, on one hand, identify closely with the people whom they represent and on the other hand bring the government policies to the level of their localities and explain their significance in terms of national or regional well-being. They have an obvious advantage over the administrators in their mass-organizational work. They are not directly identified with the government and are expected to be free of partisan interest in promoting the party and the administration policies. The ordinary people should be more susceptible to their arguments than to the mobilization effort of the administrators. They are, to a certain degree free of the mistrust characteristically felt by the ruled toward their rulers, an attitude especially evident in countries like Poland, where the officials are traditionally viewed as serving the central power rather than the public. Their roles as "priests" and "ward heelers" are of prime importance if the masses are to be mobilized effectively for the support of the national and local policies.

In terms of pure numbers the councilmen should have effectively mobilized the population. In 1971 there were, in round figures, 165,000 potential mobilizers.[17] Since the total population of Poland was (1970) around thirty-two million,[18] there was roughly one councilman for every one hundred and ninety people. It would have been quite possible, say in the course of a year, for a councilman to contact personally each member of his constituency.[19] Their effectiveness in popular mobilization was much less than their numerical strength suggests. The following excerpt is a highly typical comment of the Polish press on the political involvement of the councilmen:

> Voters generally know very little about the work of the councilmen. They don't know—because from where—what the councilmen discuss at the sessions, if they are capable of defending their interest, if they know at all what is happening in their electoral districts? The councilman—especially in larger cities—is for the electors an anonymous person.[20]

Crucial for the mobilization process is, of course, the enthusiastic political involvement of the councilmen at the commune, settlement, urban ward, or small city level. Here, not only in Marxist theory but in practice, the councilman comes in most direct contact with the population. At this level of government it is only natural for the local representative to be in a close relationship with his electors. The whole success of mobilization depends on the government's ability to politicize the local representative and to infuse him with the values of the national and local leadership. Our own observation as recorded in the previous discussion, the Polish press criticism, and the communist leadership's concern over the political apathy of the councilmen indicate their lack of effectiveness in the process of popular mobilization. Despite the constant barrage of propaganda and despite the theoretical assumptions, the councilman in his own role perception does not think of himself as a mobilizer for the popular support of "our" policies. He is well aware that the policies which he is to promote are in most cases formulated without his active participation, and hence he does not regard them as his own. The apathy of the councilman results from the schizophrenic dichotomy of communist political theory which advocates at the same time popular participation and tight controls from above founded on the dogmas of the absolutist ideology. The end result must be the councilman's withdrawal from his role of mobilizer. Generalizing from the Polish communist experience, we cannot expect enthusiastic participation in the popular mobilization process without at least some degree, however small and regionalized, of meaningful involvement in the public-policy formulation.

The party in Poland is aware of the problem and is aggressively attempting to politicize the councilmen. It stops short, however, of curtailing its own monopoly in the policy-making process. The party pressure on the councils resulted in the introduction of the practice of having the councilmen's work evaluated by their own councils or rather by their mandate committees, and in some councils by the political clubs.[21] The evaluation may get some of the councilmen into the field, but it is bound to fail in increasing their enthusiasm for the policies which they are required to support. Administrative control cannot substitute for the genuine personal commitment which results only from active participation in the policy formulation.

The second important factor in the mobilization process is the activity of the standing committees. Potentially their membership could be double that of the council. The actual number falls short of the maximum, but involves thousands of people co-opted from outside the councils' membership. They could become effective mobilizers, but in view of their minimal impact on the public-policy formulation, their role is in general terms highly limited. The committees' members are active in narrow, technical fields, where their participation bears fruit not in the general output of the councils, but in the technicalities of separate bills and in the administration by departments and other government agencies. For example, the committee on public law and order, which includes in its membership police officers as well as lawyers, has little impact on the formulation of laws, but exercises through its membership some influence on the application of the existing regulations.

In no way can the committees substitute for the councilmen in the role of general mobilizers, especially since their freedom of operation is greater, the more technical, and less political their activity. Their members can and do become enthusiastically involved in the application of specific government policies, but it is unrealistic to expect that they would mobilize the population for the general and broad issues. Their service to the communist leadership lies in the aggregate effect of the activities of all the committees, and primarily in the spheres of social change and technical modernization. The committees draw a substantial number of citizens into the ranks of the modernizing elite, and they could be used as an effective device by any developing political system. The committees can also provide a voluntary corps of administrators, thereby reducing the state bureaucracy, providing that the bureaucracy is willing to transfer some of its functions to the committees. This is not the case in Poland, and the committees' role as social and political mobilizers is even more restricted than that of the councilmen. The practice of staffing their membership with public officials reduces their potential for drawing independent citizens into the group of mobilization activists. And, finally, most of the committees suffer from the serious malady of dormancy.

Theoretically, the councils should employ social and professional organizations as vehicles of mobilization. The councils should "utilize initiative and participation of social organizations,"[22] through them connecting the state with the population:

> The cooperation results from the membership of councilmen in the social organizations, from the combined local conferences, from the coordination of tasks within larger political actions, from utilization of the plans of work of the organizations and participation of their members in the realization of the tasks of the councils, as well as from the duty of the councils to capture and popularize the initiative of the organizations.[23]

In practice, the effectiveness of utilizing social and professional organizations for mobilization purposes depends on the character of their specialized interests. They are, in a way, similar to the committees and can be utilized in a narrow sense—not for the broad overall mobilization. Their number, diversity, and large membership[24] would produce a broad spectrum of mobilization if they could be employed for this purpose, but their diversity renders the task difficult and limits the import of their utilization by the councils. The councils do employ the leaders of the social organizations as mobilization agents, but the ordinary membership is beyond the councils' reach since it is even more politically apathetic than the councilmen. The interest of the members of the social and professional organizations is directed toward obtaining benefits for themselves—either materially or through association with other members of the profession—and not toward promotion of somebody else's policies. There are, of course, important exceptions in the case of organizations which have a purpose of social welfare, as for example the Polish Red Cross. But even they can only be utilized as mobilizers in the field of their own narrow and specialized interest. Furthermore, the party uses the social and professional organizations to promote its goals directly omitting the local government channels.

In the last analysis it is the PUWP and not the councils which plays the major role in the mobilization process. The party is, however, clearly identified in the mind of the population with its doctrinaire ideology and its totalitarian dominance. The effect of the party mobilization effort depends on the acceptance or rejection by the individual of the party's *Weltanschauung*. The rejection by the people of local programs may have nothing to do with their value to a particular locality, but is often based on a rejection of the PUWP's domination. The party would be well-advised to use the councils more effectively in the mobilization process, but this move would entail delegation of the decision-making process to the councils and would erode the power hegemony of the party. For ideological reasons, the party believing in its own mission is not prepared at this stage to share power with anybody, not even with the local councils, which the party can control internally.

The Party realizes that its program of "making Poland a modern country with a high level of economic development, culture and prosperity of its people"[25] depends on its ability to mobilize the whole society for the task of this "socialist construction." The First Secretary, Edward Gierek, closing the deliberation of the VI Party Congress in December, 1971, stated: "The tasks which face us are difficult. They demand maximum mobilization of efforts, universal action and initiative. It is a matter for the whole nation; for all of its patriotic and creative forces."[26] The First Secretary admitted the national potential to be far from full utilization. Mass mobilization was necessary for the ambitious task of continuous modernization and industrialization which would, hopefully, lead to a high standard of economic well-being. But at the same time the Congress reaffirmed and strengthened the party's determination to remain in the exclusive political and social leadership. The party was not in 1971 and is still today not ready to abdicate the principle of its own dictatorship.

Realizing the necessity for popular mobilization and admitting that the society is far from being mobilized the party accepts mobilization only on its own terms—mobilization by the party and for the party. The local councils' role is restricted to the support function; the councils become an extension of the party and are not able to assume any independent political significance. The politicization of the councilmen cannot be achieved if it must be paid for with their meaningful participation in public-policy formulation—by definition an exclusive right of the PUWP. The party mobilization drive is to be carried by its own cadre, because the party fully recognizes that a mass following organized by an outside body, say the national councils, can lead to the eventual destruction of the party hegemony and of authoritarian communism in Poland.

POPULAR CONTROL

In all modern industrial states the burgeoning bureaucracy which results from the increasing involvement of the government in the socio-economic matters is of prime concern to the political leaders—the lawgivers. It is also the whipping boy of the general public. Communists are especially sensitive to the problem of a large public administration growing out of reach of the political control. Just such an independent bureaucracy played an important role in the criticism by Marx and Engels of Western liberal democracy.[27] If it were to be proven that the bureaucracy of the socialist state, the new type of political system, is as independent and uncontrollable as that of the bourgeois state, then the socialist state would be basically no different from its predecessor criticized by Marx and Engels. It would have no right to the communist claim of superiority and uniqueness. The criticism Marx and Engels leveled against the liberal democracy would apply at least partially to the socialist state. It is ideologically vital for the communists to develop methods of public control of bureaucracy, because

> The influence of the sovereign people on the activity of the state apparatus should not limit itself to the selection, control and recall of the representatives to the organs of the state power, but should embrace the whole state apparatus in its concrete, everyday activity. The cooperation of society with the state apparatus, control over it, and also initiative in relationship to its activity, is the guarantee of its correct functioning and the phenomenon of democratization of public life.[28]

The size of the bureaucracy, or rather the number of specialized bureaucracies, in the communist states is much larger than in the liberal democracies, not only because of the Communist party and the extensive state control of the social and political expressions of human behavior, but also because of the centralized ownership, planning, and administration of the economy. The very number of agencies, with their enormous staffs, all juggling and competing for power and influence, must be a nightmare to the top decision-makers. Whether the First Secretary and the top leaders of the presidium are the actual rulers of the communist state and not the victims of a bureaucratic monster is a highly relevant question, as suggested by our own case study of local government deconcentration.[29]

The top leadership has at its disposal a number of control channels over the administration—none of them completely reliable and efficient. The party burdened with its many tasks serves as watchdog over the activities of administration by duplicating the state administrative organs in the departments of the secretariat of the Central Committee and in the executive committees of the provinces and counties. The party also controls the administration by permeating it with party members, for whom the top executive offices are reserved.

The control of the legality of the administrative acts, or rather, of their correspondence to the party will as expressed by the legal norms, is performed by the Office of the Procurator, which scrutinizes all action of the state organs. The normal for all states financial supervision lies in the hands of the Supreme Control Board. The Security Police watch over not only the political orthodoxy and purity, but also the efficiency, corruption, and performance of the administration. Finally, the administration controls itself through the Council of Ministries, individual ministries, and the departments of the local councils. These five channels of control should be more than ample to insure the swift passage of commands issued by the top decision-makers and should prevent the possibility of any bureaucracy's acting in its own interest to the detriment of the efficient execution of public policies. The problem is, however, that the five agents of control are bureaucracies themselves. They are not free of their own vested interests, which may or may not be interlocked with the vested interests of the agencies under their control, but which in any case diminish their control usefulness to the top leadership.

The communist state is no less free from the necessity for an independent, nonadministrative control factor than any other modern political system. In liberal democracies this is provided by the political parties in their competition for power, and especially by the institution of the "loyal opposition." In the communist states the institution of the local councils is viewed as the independent agent of public control of the bureacracy, ultimately in the interest of the top leadership of the Communist party.

Within the structure of the national councils the most important channels of control are, to my mind, the committees. Even if their participation in the public policy formulation is much less effective than intended by law, the very fact that they keep under constant observation the departments of the council and the other government agencies under the supervision of the council forces the bureaucrats to exercise more caution and vigilance in the execution of their duties. Although the committees are far from being able to get at the "secrets" of the departments, the high technical qualifications of many of the committee members permit them to see beyond the official reports and, by this very fact, to upgrade the general technical performance of the administration.

The reason for the lack of truly effective control by the committees does not lie in their inability to discover faults in the administrative performance, since many of them, depending on the qualifications and the zeal of their members, are perfectly capable of doing so. It lies in the deficiencies in the lines of communication between the committees and those higher authorities capable of putting pressure on the departments. The committees' advisory character prevents them from expressing their findings as direct orders to the department heads. They have to act either through the whole session of the council or through the presidium. The council meeting in sessions of one day's duration a few times a year hardly has time to consider reports of its committees. Most of the councils do not plan the committees' work and do not charge them with any specific control-investigations. The presidium, under pressure from the party, the higher presidium, and the higher departments, seldom welcomes the committees' inquiries. As far as the presidium is concerned, the committees might produce a few embarrassing skeletons. The presidium invites committee chairmen to its meeting if it must, but they function strictly as advisors.

The presidium prefers to control its departments through its own members, each of whom is formally in charge of a bloc of administrative business. In this way any irregularities are kept within the close "family" of the presidium and are not handled by a group of outsiders, the committee members, who by virtue of their professional or political occupations might give embarrassing information to some higher authority, to the newspapers, or to the general public. It is once again the old story of the organization guarding its own secrets, defending its own cohesiveness, and presenting a unified front against outsiders. A few of the committees have greater control ability than is generally true of the majority. They have greater penetration of the administration, and their channels of communication are more open due to the inclusion in their membership of individuals who can command substantial authority stemming from their party or presidium connections. Such committees are rather an exception, and the central leadership realizing the value of the committees' control function and their inability to perform it efficiently, presses for their greater involvement in the actual administrative processes of the department.

The 1963 amendment to the 1958 statute increased considerably the committees' authority and obliged them to take more interest in the work of the departments under their supervision. The post-amendment reports of the newspapers and the evaluation of the committees' performance by Polish scholars do not indicate any considerable increase in their aggressiveness.[30]

Polish professional literature and the pronouncements of the party and government leadership constantly stress the control function of the councilmen as the expression of popular socialist democracy. In reality, however, the councilman is not in a position to exercise constant control of the administration. First of all, his professional occupation permits him only a limited time for political and social work. Secondly, his authority as the representative of the people is undermined by the well-known fact that his role in public-policy formulation and in personnel-appointment policy is virtually nil. Thirdly, his investigation of the administration is resented by the departments as well as by the presidium. The latter affords him no encouragement in his control function for the same reason as its resistance against the committees. He is even more of an outsider than the committee members, and he lacks their organizational and group-power capacity. Finally his own role perception of himself as the nominee of the party renders unthinkable the possibility of his challenging the all-powerful state as represented by its officials. He may sporadically intervene with the administration on behalf of one of his constituents, especially if the matter is an obvious bureaucratic oversight, involves a minor official, or is exclusively technical. He will shun any question which even slightly smells of politics.

Another important feature of the council's system which plays a significant role in the control function is the institution of public complaints and suggestions: "Complaints and suggestions institute the patterns, specific to the socialist state, of social control over the activity of state organs and institutions and also the pattern of influence by citizens, social organization and press on their work."[31] The institution of complaints and suggestions is given a constitutional foundation. Article 73 of the Constitution requires all state organs to deal with complaints "keenly" and "speedily" and also to punish civil servants, who disregard them. The specific legal bases go back to the years 1950 and 1951.[32]

Complaints can be made concerning neglect by the state institutions and their employees of their duties and the valid interests of the citizens, violations of legality, bureaucratism and undue slowness in dealing with the citizens' business. The suggestions should concern themselves with improvement of the organization and work of the administration, enforcement of legality, protection of public property and prevention of corruption. The suggestions can also deal with the efficient supplying of the population's needs. The citizen cannot be put in any jeopardy as a result of his complaint or suggestion, providing that he acts within the limits sanctioned by law.[33] All administrative organs must counteract any attempts to prevent public criticism or to intimidate individuals lodging complaints or suggestions.

Complaints and suggestions are not constrained by any formal requirements, as for example time limitation. They can be directed to any state institution and can be submitted not only by the individuals personally interested and involved in the matter, but also by other citizens, social or professional organizations, press, radio, or television. The authority to review complaints and suggestions regarding the national council, the presidium, or the department lies with the same institution in kind one step higher; e.g. for the county national council, the province council; for the county presidium, the province presidium; and for the county department, the province department. In case of local enterprise under the supervision of the council, the same level in the presidium or the department has the review authority.

The subject matter of a complaint or suggestion must be deliberated upon within two months, counting from the date of its receipt by the appropriate organ. The institution which receives a complaint or suggestion, but which has no authority to deal with it, must within seven days transmit it to the proper office. Every petitioner should be notified of the transfer and of the final decision in his case. All offices of the council must daily, in the specified hours, receive citizens with complaints and suggestions. The presidium can also instruct the heads of its departments to see visitors on some days after normal working hours. Each institution of socialized trade, such as shops and restaurants, has a book of complaints and suggestions, and it must be displayed so that the customers can make entries. The book should be inspected by the supervisory department of the council every three days, and the matters must be treated in the same way as the formal complaints or suggestions logged with the national councils. In the presidium the chairman himself or a designated permanent member of the presidium receives citizens in the announced time and, at least once a week, also at night.

All complaints and suggestions are collected, grouped statistically, and reviewed every six months by the presidium in consultation with the appropriate committees and the departments. The complaints and suggestions are one of the criteria on which the efficiency of the administration is judged. The province presidium periodically evaluates the activity of those state institutions within the province which are not under the direct management of the councils regarding their treatment of complaints and suggestions and communicates its findings and recommendations to the higher authorities. All institutions required by law to receive complaints and suggestions must use the materials so obtained for the protection of the social interest and of the justified interest of the individual, as well as for the improvement of their own administrative efficiency.[34]

The line of communication created by the institution of complaints and suggestions is without any doubt the most independent control function within the whole communist political system. Its magnitude testifies to its importance as an open channel of communication between the citizens and the state. In the course of one year the councils received millions of complaints and suggestions.[35] The analysis of one city indicates that most of this communication is of a personal nature. In 1961 in the city of Grudziądz, the inhabitants, during their preelection meetings and other meetings with the councilmen, formulated a total of 806 suggestions and demands.[36] An overwhelming number (87%) was in the form of claims of small groups or individuals. By far the largest category was the improvement of housing and communal economy (see table 14),[37] followed by the categories of trade and services, and allocation of housing. The fourth relatively large group of suggestions was in the field of health and sanitation. Together these four accounted for 71.6% of the total number of suggestions and demands, but these matters received low priority

Table 14

Suggestions and Demands Submitted by the Citizens of Grudziądz

	Suggestions	% of Total	All Decisions	Favorable Decisions	% of Favorable Decisions
Housing/Communal Economy	352	43.7	272	166	61.0
Trade/Services	89	11.0	84	29	34.5
Allocation of Housing	71	8.8	. . .	. . .	. . .
Health/Sanitation	65	8.1	62	26	41.9
Public Order	45	5.6	45	. . .	. . .
Education/Culture	38	4.7	38	. . .	. . .
Building Construction/ Renovation	36	4.5	36	14	38.9
Transportation/Safety	24	3.0	. . .	. . .	. . .
Industry/Trade	7	.8	. . .	. . .	. . .
Referred to Province or Central Government	30	3.7	. . .	. . .	. . .
Other	49	6.1	49	. . .	. . .
Total	806	100.0			

in the councils' activities as expressed by the presidia resolutions.[38]

It is interesting to note that where the data was available, there was a relatively high percentage of decision in favor of the petitioners. This was especially true regarding the suggestions for improvement of housing and communal economy (61.0%). It could be that the city fathers of Grudziądz were exceptionally civic minded, and indeed this author found a number of dedicated officials in that city's administration. On the other hand, it seems that it pays off to petition the local council. Complaints or demands cannot worsen the matter, and in many cases they force the departments to take action and to render more favorable decisions. The whole institution of suggestions and complaints is used by the population as a last resort for applying pressure on the administration.

Yet another example draws our interest. During the preelection period of 1965, Janusz Zarzycki, the Chairman of the City Council of Warsaw, instituted a new, and in many ways challenging, method of accepting complaints and suggestions by telephone. Mr. Zarzycki personally listened to citizens' problems and often offered solutions or promised further action. Here is one example of a conversation:

> CITIZEN—Sir, I have lived for the last six years in Marszałkowska street as a "wild" tenant.
> ZARZYCKI—It is not a very nice word "wild." Judging by your voice, my dear lady, you are not "wild." . . . Perhaps, let's say "illegal."
> CITIZEN—Really "wild." And I had very serious problems because of it: I couldn't vote, because I was not on the roll; I couldn't enter my child into a school, because he was not registered anywhere.
> ZARZYCKI—Well! All right! But why were you not registered anywhere?
> CITIZEN—They didn't want to register me. Some time ago I moved illegally to this apartment. The Province Housing Committee allocated to me a substitution apartment, and I have been waiting six years for it. In the housing office (of the city council) they didn't want to talk to me because I was not registered. I only want registration, because I have the apartment.
> ZARZYCKI—Where is your husband employed?
> CITIZEN—In the Housing Administration.
> ZARZYCKI—What? In the H.A.?! And during six years you were not able to settle this registration business? Write the whole story and send it to me please. We will try somehow to solve the problem, because it is indeed an unusual and even slightly humorous business.[39]

We admit that the selection of this conversation was made for its theatrical and tragicomical quality, but most of the other problems were also in the nature of personal grievances. Chairman Zarzycki's exercise in "direct democracy" is highly unusual,[40] but in the preelection period there is a considerable increase in the complaints and suggestions submitted through the normal channels.

Both the examples of complaints and suggestions and the impressions obtained by this author in his talks with the officials and councilmen indicate that most matters brought to the attention of the higher levels in the council structure are of this personal nature. What is even more, the complaints generally do not challenge the bureaucracy on the grounds of legality or propriety, although many are directed against its slowness in reaching a decision. They are, in the majority, pleas for reversal of administrative actions arrived at on the basis of existing laws and regulations. They are generally hardship cases which result from the a priori allocation of resources, and as such, their control value is minimal. At best they can bring to the attention of the higher authority the lower officials' lack of aggressiveness in utilizing their own resources to solve such particularly pressing shortages as housing, supplies for population, and public health services.

Of much more general value in uncovering real abuses of power, bureaucratic negligence, or waste of public property and human resources are the articles of local newspapers centered on the activities of the councils proper, the presidia and the departments. The reader no doubt has already noticed that much of the data used in this study was provided by often the frank and biting Polish press (represented in our input-output diagram by circle 6). The newspapers, employing their own investigators and utilizing the letters to the editor and the complaints and suggestions lodged with the national councils provide an important, and perhaps the most effective, control function independent of the council structure. The bureaucracy is kept in tow by the knowledge that the press is encouraged by the central leadership and by the general policy of the party to attack it without mercy. This is not to say that the press is free. It is used and manipulated as the watchdog of the party, especially for the lower levels of administration. Many articles are followed by administrative action rectifying the wrong done. Many are answered by letters to the press from top local officials defending the positions taken by themselves or their subordinates. But by far the largest number of complaints and suggestions is sent not to the national councils or the newspapers but to the local party headquarters. The citizens recognize the real power to be with the party, and they rightly assume that there will be faster action on their grievances if their petitions are lodged with the supreme center of the decision-making process. They know the party to be capable of chastising the government officials, of reversing their decisions, and, on some occasions, even of violating the law or local regulations. The party is the last resort of arbitration between the population and the bureaucracy and is the most trusted control agency of the central leadership.

Some device for effective control of the bureaucracy by the top leadership is essential to the maintenance by the leadership of its monopoly of power. Our study of public-policy formulation shows that this monopoly is not as absolute as is generally assumed. Although the several bureaucracies, considered as interest groups, cannot reverse the decisions of the central authority, they can slow down their implementation and render them ineffective in time.

There are many formalized channels of control designed to prevent these occurrences. They are, however, also bureaucracies—and therefore interest groups—which may, and often do, ally themselves with the institutions under their control.

Even the party is bureaucratized, and it forms a specific interest group, as our example of the coalition of the province chairmen and the province first secretaries has shown. In this context it becomes imperative for the top leadership to operate unstructured and independent control channels. Despite repeated efforts to achieve more effective control, however, these independent channels cannot perform a meaningful service. The council committees lack the necessary lines of communication; the councilmen have minute roles in public-policy formulation and are only too aware of the appointive character of their jobs. They are not in a position to challenge the all-powerful state officials, who are at the same time important party leaders. The complaints and suggestions of the public seldom deal with questions specified by law—questions which would provide an effective control function. They are mostly personal pleas, designed not to criticize the administration but to extract from it certain favors. The newspapers and other media of communication remain the only truly independent channel exempt from pressure by the administration and therefore capable of fruitful criticism. For this reason they are allowed by the party more freedom of expression than any other interest group or than the society in general. They are also, however, more carefully watched and censored as to their ideological and political purity.

In conclusion, the control function of the system of national councils does not work effectively because it demands, on one hand, free expression and criticism of the administration and, on the other hand, ideological and political orthodoxy and unquestionable submission to the communist monopoly of power. How is the public to know which decisions originate at the top and are therefore, by definition, outside the realm of public criticism and which are the product of local officials and hence free game for all? The local officials are also the dispensers of state power and the distributers of the scarce resources. On both counts it is safer not to annoy them. An effective control function requires a source of power independent of the institution it controls. With the possible exception of the media of communication, nobody in Poland at the local level can claim such a detachment.

COMMUNICATION AND THE SAFETY VALVE OF PRESSURE

The criticism of local officials by the councils, by the media of communication, and by the population in general is useful to the leadership for yet another reason: it provides the leadership with a shield, guarding it against the sword of public discontent. Although most of the policies originate at the top, the local officials are in the first line of attack for criticism because they themselves have to implement and enforce the decisions of the top leaders. The public is thereby prevented from placing direct blame on the central authority or on the tenets of communism. The local officials, who are part of the council structure, serve as a scapegoat for some of the misjudgment of the top communist bosses, and they can be conveniently removed from their posts in order to pacify the public wrath. This is also an effective device for the reversal of top policies when the leadership does not wish to admit that it was mistaken. And the semidemocratic elections of deputies to the councils and the internal elections of the executive committees, in which the electors have some, even if very limited, choice by selection from a communist-sponsored list, offer a useful method of eliminating candidates who are most disagreeable to the population. Furthermore, the elections again give the public a feeling of participation and of identification with the council and with the official who "represent" the region. The people "elect" their own local parliament and their own local government.

Public criticism provides some valuable information on the attitudes and grievances of the population. On the basis of the public's involvement in the "direct democracy" of the national councils, the leadership at the local and the national level can adjust its manipulation instruments by shifting its policies, alternating the carrot and the stick. At the same time it does not have to compromise its ideological determination nor relinquish its monopoly of power. Because the party controls the councils as well as the economy and the social and professional organizations, the communist society of today is not terrorized, but skillfully and "gently" manipulated into acquiescence. But "direct democracy" is not without its dangers to the communist rulers. It sometimes forces the local leaders to perform a tightrope balancing act between pressures from the top and demands from below. It often results in the heresy of "localism," in which local officials try to obtain a bigger slice of the national cake than that allocated to them by the central authority, especially by retaining local production exclusively for local use. They may also attempt to circumvent directives of the national government in the interest of their region.

Finally, popular criticism, once permitted and encouraged to a degree, may grow unpredictably out of control and exert pressure on the central leadership itself, flooding it with the unmanageable turbulence of public dissatisfaction (the revolutions in Poland and Hungary in 1956, the 1968 events in Czechoslovakia and the 1970 workers' "uprising" in Poland). In general, however, the skillful use of controlled popular participation and criticism within the framework of the councils provides the leadership with valuable channels of information and indoctrination. The criticism provides a safety valve for pressure, which can be loosened up or tightened according to the leadership's evaluation of the situation. Its psychological effect is to prevent desperate resorts to illegal conspiracy, since most people are not likely to risk physical repression if they can vent their dissatisfaction by verbal expression of criticism. For all these reasons the shield of the councils serves well, guarding the Olympic heights of the communist gods and their dogmas.

PUBLIC INVOLVEMENT

The final measure of the effectiveness of mobilization and, directly related to it, the control function of the national councils must be, in the last analysis, the degree of public involvement and interest in the activities of the councils. We know from the Polish statistics that hundreds of thousands of citizens participate in the council system as councilmen and committeemen. The bare numbers do not, however, give us any indication as to the degree of involvement and interest by the public in general. The sure answer could be given only on the basis of an attitudes survey. However, the Communist leaders shun away investigation of public opinion which may reflect, even if indirectly, the political composition of the public. They show by this a lack of faith in the potentials of their own ideology and in their own methods of public mobilization. In short there is in Poland no survey of public involvement and interest in the activities of the councils. Again we are forced to utilize our own imperfect attempt at sampling, bearing fully in mind the smallness of the group investigated and the crudeness of our techniques. The results may at best be treated as an indication of general trends and in no way should they be evaluated by our reader as final, definite answers.

To measure their involvement and interest, the subjects were asked to answer affirmatively *only* one of the five questions (see table 3, appendix 5). An affirmative answer to question 1 indicated gladiatorial activity and, hence, the highest degree of involvement and interest.[41] Subjects choosing questions 2 and 3 were classified as spectators—2 signifying participant spectator, 3, passive spectator. Answers 4 and 5 were regarded as given by apathetics—4 suggesting a "couldn't care less" attitude, 5 an act of withdrawal as an expression of opposition. Of our sample of 80 people, 73 answered the question. A relatively large number were gladiators (19.1%). Similar studies in the United States show that only about 5–6% of Americans engage in gladiatorial activities.[42] Accounting for nearly the same percentage as the gladiators were the apathetics 2 (17.8%), whom we have classified as being in opposition to the system or as considering themselves not a part of the system. These individuals belong to the political field, but not to the political system.[43] The number of people who qualified as gladiators within the system was approximately equal to the number of those who were negative gladiators, apathetics 2, outside the system. Combining the apathetics 2 and 1, we find 26.1% of our sample not interested in the councils' activities. This is slightly lower than the number of apathetics to be found in American politics.[44] The largest group was that of spectators (54.8%), and it was divided equally between spectators 1 and 2. Again this is similar to the American scene, where 60% "play largely spectator roles; they watch, they cheer, they vote, but they do not battle."[45] Of course the method of battle in Polish politics is of a different character. The struggle takes place not in the elections, but in the manipulations which precede and follow them.

The division of attitudes displayed in our Polish sample is what one would generally expect, and it is verified by studies of American political process. Most people aggregate in the middle of the participation scale, neither radically supporting nor opposing. Generally speaking, the mobilization effort in Poland is not any more successful than the mobilization effort in the United States. The larger percentage of gladiators was matched by the number of apathetics 2, and they therefore canceled one another. The mass in the middle expressed "normal" mild interest and involvement.

Divided into statistical groupings, our study showed a high level of participation to be most likely among middle-aged males with university education in managerial or professional occupations, of peasant origin, high economic status, PUWP or UPP affiliation, and urban and industrial region domicile. A high propensity to nonparticipation was observed among either the very young or the very old, women, those with primary or high school education, independent farmers, housewives, and persons of intelligentsia origin, low economic status, no party affiliation, inhabiting villages and agricultural regions. Both groups correlated perfectly with the typical high and low participation observed in other societies, including western Europe and the United States.[46] The study shows a lack of effective mobilization results as measured by the scale of participation. The Polish local councils, with an intensive mobilization effort backed by the professional and social organizations and by the minor parties and with an even more intensive effort by the high-geared propaganda machinery of the PUWP, did not achieve higher results in terms of participation than the lower intensity mobilization of the political processes of noncommunist systems.

APPROVAL—DISAPPROVAL

Another measurement of mobilization results, especially in a one-party system, is the degreee of approval or disapproval expressed by the people of the government's performance. For this purpose the responders were asked the following question: "How do you evaluate the work of your council?" They had only two choices of answer—positive or negative. Altogether, 75 persons responded. Thirty-nine (52.0%) felt their council to be doing a decent job, 36 (48.0%) answered negatively (see table 4, appendix 7). In general the sample divided nearly equally between the two answers. A propensity toward positive evaluation was observed among the younger established group, men with trade school or university education, in clerical or managerial positions, and of peasant origin, high economic status, and PUWP or UPP political affiliation. The individuals who tended toward the negative stand were found among the very young, middle-aged, or old; women; those with primary or higher technical education; independent farmers and housewives; those of worker or intelligentsia origin; and those with low income status and no party affiliation.

The overall evaluation of the responses to the two sets of questions indicated high mobilization (measured by participating supporters) among the 36–45 age group, men, people with university education, managers, and individuals of peasant origin (the lowest class origin), high economic status, and the PUWP–UPP affiliation. Low mobilization (nonparticipating opponents) appeared among the very young or very old, women, those with primary education, independent farmers, housewives, and those of intelligentsia origin (the highest class origin), low economic status, and no party affiliation. The high mobilization group were the obvious beneficiaries of the system; the low mobilization individuals represented the losers. Only two groups on the negative side vary from the normal pattern of mobilization propensity observed in other systems.[47] Women, although generally participating less than men, support the government of the day to a similar degree as men. Their decisive negative stand in Poland is atypical and must be blamed on the communist system. Individuals of intelligentsia origin (the highest class origin) show more propensity to mobilization in the stable systems. Their slightly negative attitude in Poland is the result of the social upheaval brought about not only by the communist "revolution," but also by the rapid industrialization and modernization. Their relative negation of the system does not mean a lack of desire for cooperation with the communist government, but rather signals their frustration with their class's loss of elite status to a growing number of upstarts from the lower classes. Their negative evaluation of the local government work may be based not on a rational examination of its possibilities, failures, and achievements, but on a snobbish attitude towards the expeasants running local government affairs.

On the whole the interviews do not indicate any special ability to mobilize the masses by the system of national councils. The findings of the sample are supported by the impressions gathered by this author as well as by the relevant articles appearing in the Polish press. The local government bodies fail in their function as general mobilizer. Their ability to mobilize does not extend beyond the groups who are customarily participants and supporters in any other political systems. On the other hand if we assume that the communist system operates (in terms of mobilization) under a disadvantage because of its limited representation and the dogmas of an all-exclusive ideology, then the mobilization achievement of the national councils must be evaluated positively. Their success lies in their ability to uplift the society politically to the level of Western liberal democracies. In our opinion, however, the more realistic explanation for the similarity of participation and support levels in Western and Polish societies lies in the relative economic and social attractiveness of the Polish system for certain groups of individuals. The groups are the same as in the West, but their motivation may be not so much an acceptance of the system for its own virtues, but an adaptation to an existing pattern which they must consider as given and as fundamentally unchangeable. In that case, the communist victory in mobilization is due not to the national councils' activity and not even to the high geared propaganda barrage, but to the government's capacity for economic and social manipulation in a rapidly industrializing and modernizing society in which the career patterns offer an attractive incentive for cooperation.

THE POLITICAL FUNCTIONS

The national councils in the communist political system perform three basic functions. First, they are the implementors of public policies as a part of the unified state administration. Second, they are a channel of information, along with the Communist party, the minor parties, the state control boards, the procuracy, the political police, and the social and professional organizations. Third, they are mobilizers of the public for the support of the system and of the specific policies.

For administrative activity the central government must rely on the local government bodies, as there exists no other direct channel of implementation. The fusion of the central and local governments permits adjustment of central policies to local conditions. This is vital for a system in which there is a strong centripetal force due to ideological rigidity and nearly complete government monopoly of economic management. Overcentralization in a complex modern society is administratively and economically wasteful and produces latent political opposition dangerous to the system's future stability. The unified state administration provides the necessary local participation and deconcentration, while at the same time maintaining a high degree of centralized control and preventing the development of politically independent local centers.

Our model of the communist public policy formulation and implementation mechanism indicates that the local government structure's role as exclusive general administrator is of some danger to the central leadership. Its monopoly of general administration permits the local bodies to manipulate the rate of absorption, thereby affecting policy formulation by exercising pressure on the top leadership. The slowing down of the rate of absorption cannot halt the implementation process, but it can limit the number and the magnitude of policies which the system can digest. The top leadership can in fact be forced to alter, to postpone, or even to abandon parts of its program. Its political success, as measured by administrative efficiency and by the constant economic growth, depends on the rate of absorption. The First Secretary may receive severe criticism from his lieutenants, and party bosses, the party in general, and the population, if he cannot make the system work. However bright his ideas his success depends on their implementation. For that he needs the active cooperation of the local councils or, at least, of their leadership. The nature of the industrial society prevents him from using strictly administrative measures. He must rely on persuasion. Hence, he is subject to manipulation by his subordinates.

The management of policies, men and resources requires a constant flow of information from below to the top leadership.

The national councils share this function with other state, police, and social organizations. The information flow plays a dual role. It supplies data on the efficiency of the administration as well as on the public opinion. In both cases the usefulness of the national councils is limited. The system is not able to develop sources of control and information independent enough to be effective. The councilmen, in theory the controllers and the informers, are nominated for their jobs by the party and by the administrators. They are in no way in an independent position to challenge the bureaucracy representing the all-powerful state. The committees have exactly the same impediment. In addition, the inclusion in their membership of large numbers of public officials emasculates their control faculties. The public, theoretically plugged into the control and information channel by the institution of complaints and suggestions, realizes its politically subordinate status and uses this vehicle for the promotion of individual interest. It does not criticize nor check the bureaucracy, but it begs for personal favors. Whatever the control and information mechanism, it cannot substitute for free elections and for democratic opposition. Only elections and opposition can effect valid criticism of the administration and create the true picture of public opinion.

The use of local councils as mobilizers is, on the surface, not any more successful than mobilization methods employed in other political systems. The supporters and the activists are recruited in Poland from the same groups as in the West. They are generally individuals who are close to the core of the system. Attempts to involve the fringes of the public have proven fruitless, and those who have been successfully mobilized would have been participating under any other institutional structure. On the other hand, were we to assume the communist government to be working at a mobilization disadvantage because of its ideological rigidity, then the national councils' mobilization achievement must be measured by their success in bringing the public to a participation and acceptance level similar to that of Western democracies. Our own contention is that the relatively high level of mobilization in the communist systems is due not so much to the employment of this or that mobilization technique, but to the ability of the modernizing systems to manipulate participation by means of economic and career rewards. The main role of the national councils does not lie in mobilization or in gathering information on public opinion, but in their adjustment of central policies to local needs and capacities. In Poland this is strikingly evident in the council's participation in the administration of economy, the subject of our next chapter.

NOTES TO CHAPTER IV

[1] In our studies of the communist revolutions we concentrate on the tactics of the use of force and on the organizational aspects of the Communist party. The communist underground state, based on the conspiratorial councils—so vital to the success of the communist revolution—awaits extensive research and evaluation.

[2] On this subject see: Mieczysław Janikowski, *Próba Tamtych Dni* (Warszawa, 1964); Wacław Czyżewski, *Więc Zarepetuj Broń* (Warszawa, 1964); Józef Sobiesiak, *Brygada Grunwald* (Warszawa, 1964); and more specifically on the underground national councils see: A. Weber, *Podziemne Rady Narodowe w walce o Polskę Ludową* (Warszawa, 1954).

[3] The Provisional Government originated from the group of Polish communists who, during World War II, organized themselves in Moscow under Soviet auspices into the Committee of Polish Patriots. The Committee followed the Soviet troops into Poland, declaring itself the Provisional Government, and was unilaterally recognized by the Soviet Union in January, 1945. After the inclusion in the government of the Prime Minister of the Polish Government-In-Exile from London, Stanisław Mikołajczyk, and three other "London Poles," the Provisional Government was recognized by the Western powers in July, 1945.

[4] F. Petrenko, "People's Power," *Izvestia*, December 5, 1964, in *The Current Digest of the Soviet Press* 16, no. 49 (December 30, 1964): 15.

[5] The Central Committee meets about twice a year and the Party Congress once in four or five years.

[6] The Council of State is the collective head of the Polish People's Republic, a sort of collective president, with the important authority to pass, when the parliament is not in session, legally binding acts with immediate validity, subject to the parliament's confirmation. During the whole history of the People's Poland, there has not been even one instance of the parliament's not confirming the act of the council.

[7] Wojciech Sokolewicz and Sylwester Zawadzki, "Wyniki Badania Uchwał Rad Narodowych i Ich Prezydiów," *Problemy Rad Narodowych, Studia i Materiały*, no. 3, p. 167. The same process was observed by Dr. Winicjusz Narojek in his study of a city, *System Władzy w Mieście*, pp. 130–35. Yet another pair of Polish writers thus describe the process at the county level: "The local political system should be viewed as the pattern of interaction between the Council, the political parties, and the social and economic institutions located on the territory of the poviat." Ostrowski and Przeworski, "Local Leadership in Poland," p. 55.

[8] *Nowe Drogi* 11, no. 6 (August 1957): 5.

9 Among the most important were: "The Resolution of the Council of Ministers No. 469, December 4, 1959, regarding the enlargement of the competence of the national councils," *Monitor Polski*, no. 8 (Warszawa, 1960), entry 36; and "The Regulation of the Council of Ministers of October 4, 1958, regarding the duty of coordination by the state organs, institutions, and economic units of their activities with the activities of the national councils," *Dziennik Ustaw*, no. 59 (Warszawa, 1958), entry 296.

10 "O podstawowych kierunkach dalszego rozwoju działalności rad narodowych," *VIII Plenum KC PZPR* (Warszawa, 1961), pp. 7–39.

11 Ibid., pp. 43–85. Our study of the debates of the county national councils in the Wrocław province (see table 7, p. 125, shows the councils not to be especially preoccupied with the resolution of the VIII Plenum. In 1961 only twelve councils out of the total of thirty-one debated the issue, and in 1962, only two.

12 Ibid., p. 12.

13 Ibid., p. 10.

14 Howard R. Swearer, "Popular Participation: Myths and Realities," *Problems of Communism* 9, no. 5 (September–October 1960): 48.

15 Rybicki, *Działalność i Organizacja*, p. 332.

16 The Statute of 1958, Art. 68, par. 3.

17 *Rocznik Statystyczny* (1971), table 4, p. 58.

18 The figure for 1970 was 32,605,000 (ibid., table 2, p. 68).

19 At the same time the membership of the PUWP stood at 2.3 million, making it in simple mathematical terms a much more effective vehicle of mobilization (ibid., table 7, p. 60).

20 Jadwiga Mikołajczyk, "Radny—Anonim?," *Trybuna Ludu*, April 13, 1964.

21 Ibid.

22 Gebert, *Komentarz do Ustawy O Radach Narodowych*, p. 102.

23 Ibid.

24 In 1970 there were in Poland 62,000 social organizations (400 national in scope) with a total membership of over 18 million (*Rocznik Polityczny* [1970], pp. 244–45).

25 Ibid. (1964), p. 130.

26 *VI Zjazd Polskiej*, p. 306.

27 See chapter 1, p. 14.

28 A. Burda, *Polskie Prawo Państwowe*, as quoted by Z. Izdebski, "Zespoły Obywatelskie w Administracji Jako Wyraz Realizacji Konstytucyjnej Zasady Udziału Mas w Rządzeniu Państwem," in *Problemy Rad Narodowych, Studia i Materiały*, no. 1 (Warszawa, 1964), p. 56.

29 See this chapter, pp. 179–185.

30 See chapter 3, pp. 150–152. And also, for example, see Surmaczyński, "Aktywność Radnych," p. 15.

31 Tadeusz Bocheński and Stanisław Gebert, *Zadania i Organizacja Pracy Rad Narodowych* (Warszawa, 1966), p. 441.

32 The Statute of the Council of State and the Council of Ministers of December, 1950 and the Executive Regulations of the Council of Ministers of December 10, 1951, in *Monitor Polski* (1951), no. A–1, entry 1, and no. A–2, entry 16; and the Statute of the Council of Ministers, no. 151 (July 1971), in *Monitor Polski*, no. 41, entry 260.

33 The Code of the Administrative Procedure, Art. 155.

34 The Statute of the Council of Ministers of October 13, 1960, on the

organization for acceptance and examination of complaints and suggestions *Monitor Polski* (1960), no. 80, entry 367, and Bocheński and Gebert, *Zadania i Organizacja*, pp. 442–43.

[35] In 1955, one and half million of complaints and suggestions were lodged (Gebert, *Komentarz do Ustawy o Radach Narodowych*, p. 73, note 35). The author was unable to obtain a more recent figure for the whole country. The number today, with the relaxation of police terror and with the general deconcentration of administration, is no doubt much larger than in 1955. For example, during the 1965 election campaign alone 140,000 suggestions were transmitted (Wendel and Zell, *Rady Narodowe W PRL*, p. 26), and in the 1969 elections 104,000 (Bocheński, et al., *Rady Narodowe*, p. 194).

[36] Prezydium Miejskiej Rady Narodowej w Grudziądzu, *Materiały Informacyjne*, no. 1/62 (Grudziądz, 1962), p. 3.

[37] Compiled from ibid., pp. 3–6. Grudziądz is a city of about 71,000 situated in North-Central Poland.

[38] See chapter 3, pp. 133–142. Another study thus groups the priorities of the suggestions: communal economy, housing, water supply, education and culture, trade and services, communication, health and agriculture (Bigo, et al., *Pozycja Ustrojowa*, p. 94).

[39] "Poselska 'audiencja przez telefon'—Warszawa—miasto i ludzie—Janusz Zarzycki odpowiada na pytania wyborców," *Życie Warszawy*, May 31, 1965.

[40] The author never heard of anybody using the same method. Mr. Zarzycki should be commended for his obvious concern and also for his political flair and style. By the way, he lost his job in 1968.

[41] The author is using a slightly modified scale of Lester W. Milbrath, *Political Participation* (Chicago, 1965), p. 18.

[42] Ibid., p. 19.

[43] The political field is a broader concept than the political system, and it includes not only those individuals who accept the system and are prepared to compete for power within the framework of the system, but also those persons or groups who reject the system and either withdraw from it or attempt to destroy it. The best example of field members who are not system members is presented by many American Blacks. I am grateful for this concept to professor Wayne Penn.

[44] Milbrath claims that one-third of the American adult population can be characterized as politically apathetic or passive (ibid., p. 21).

[45] Ibid.

[46] For comparison see Milbrath. My own findings are collaborated to a degree by a Polish study of the presidium membership (Szymczak, "System Powoływania"). Also according to yet another study, young people (63.6% of the age groups up to 25), find the work as councilmen the most difficult (Surmaczyński, "Aktywność Radnych," p. 29).

[47] Milbrath, *Political Participation*, and Gabriel Almond and Sidney Verba, *The Civil Culture* (Princeton, 1963). The same variation was observed in Czechoslovakia (see my *Public Opinion Polling in Czechoslovakia*).

5

THE ROLE IN THE ECONOMIC STRUCTURE

In the early stages of industrialization of an underdeveloped country, one of the main limitations to economic growth is the relative scarcity of capital. Labor, with the exception in some cases of skilled personnel, is plentiful, and there are usually ample potentialities for a fuller utilization of land.[1] The planners have many possibilities of choice among different combinations of factors of production, any of which will result in comparatively spectacular growth. As the economy matures and approaches full employment of resources, the planners become more and more constrained in their choice of alternatives. More plentiful capital would then produce desirable growth only if it were combined in certain proportions with land and labor. The economy becomes more complex, and a scarcity of factors of production occurring at different levels of the economic structure produces bottlenecks which hamper further growth. Increased growth can no longer be achieved by taking advantage of a slack in the economy. Furthermore, replacements and repairs of stock and investments in services which are of lesser significance in the early stages of industrialization cannot be postponed any longer. Buildings and machinery must be either repaired or completely replaced with newer and more modern units. The pattern of roads and railroads must be expanded, new means of rapid communication constructed, and services enlarged and improved. The approaching scarcity of labor, expressed first of all in the shortage of skilled personnel, necessitates the employment of more sophisticated economic incentives and leads to competition for labor between different units of production. This development increases the general level of personal incomes and, in turn, forces the planners to divert their attention and economic resources to the production of consumer goods. The natural increase in population, combined with the growth of affluence in society, demands increased production of food. Also, the growing industry requires larger outputs of industrial crops. Agriculture must be allocated more resources to keep pace with this growing demand.[2]

The development of the economy makes planning more com plex. It increases enormously the number of decisions which must be made by the central planning authority. The possibility of erroneous decisions multiplies with each step of economic growth. The importance of error, measured by its far-reaching impact on the entire system, makes the direction of the economy even more hazardous. The scarcity of resources requires deep fishing with a fine net in all parts of the country for untapped reserves. All the above considerations compel the central government to deconcentrate planning and the direction of the economy. Similar problems face a number of East European countries in the process of industrialization. In Poland the need for deconcentration increased the importance of the national councils: "In their search for new sources of efficiency, the authorities were certain to discover the advantages of delegating administrative responsibility and developing local initiative."[3]

The difficulties of coordination in the Polish economy are magnified by the existence, side by side, of three distinct sectors, namely:

1. The state sector, which embraces trade, distribution and services, and most of industry.
2. The cooperative sector, which is composed of business, service, industrial and agricultural ventures.
3. The private sector, which includes most of the agriculture, many crafts, some trade, and even small scale manufacturing.

The state sector dominates the economy. In 1970 it produced 73.3% of the national income, while the cooperative sector produced only 8.6% and the private sector 17.9%. Most of the manufacturing is state or cooperative owned (socialist sector). Together they produced 51.8% of the 1970 national income (96.5% of the total value produced by manufacturing). Private manufacturing accounted only for 1.9% (3.5% of the total value). Building and trade are also firmly in the hands of the state or cooperatives. In building, the socialist sector produced 8.1% of the N.I. (84.3% of the total value) and the private sector only 1.5% (15.7% of the total value.) In the retail trade, state-owned shops sold 47.8% of the total value of sales, cooperatives 50.9% and private shops

1.2%. Here the cooperatives played a slightly dominant role, mostly for their near monopoly of the rural trade. In service, the trade owned enterprises produced 54.6% of the total value, co-operatives 10.0% and the private sector 22.4%. Only in agriculture can the role of the private sector go undisputed. In 1970 it produced 13.1% of the national income (89.7% of the total value produced) to 1.5% of the state and cooperative forms and agricultural circles (10.3% of the total value).[4]

It would be impossible to coordinate the three sectors effectively from one central seat of power. Agriculture presents an especially difficult case for coordination. A private farmer can only be coaxed into the desired type and scope of production by direct persuasion and supervision. The central government is too far removed for the village to be able to perform this delicate task, and so the national councils bear the main burden of directing agricultural production. They also coordinate the activities of the three sectors in accordance with the uniform economic plan. They coordinate all economic activities in their territory by a combination of measures: they direct the administration of local industries, transportation, and trade; supervise local economy, especially agriculture; enforce the centrally and locally determined prices; and cooperate with the centrally administered enterprises (key industries). In addition they enact local economic plans and local budgets.

LOCAL INDUSTRIES

The national councils administer their own local industries and coordinate the activities of cooperative and private industries and crafts. The Polish industries are divided into two types, according to their organization: key industries, which include most of the producer goods industries and are administered centrally; and local industries, which are composed of enterprises producing consumer goods and are administered by the national councils or cooperative societies. The large consumer goods factories are also administered directly by the central government, although theoretically they do not belong to the key industries. Because of their large size, they supply the whole country and they therefore are considered to be of national importance. The local industries include those involved with production of household goods, furniture, wearing apparel, and processing of food, as well as tanneries, quarries, and light chemical industries, and those producing fertilizers, and building materials. They are primarily based on the local supply of raw materials and labor, and they supplement the production of key industries.

The share of local production, already quite impressive, is constantly growing, thereby enlarging the role of the national councils in the economic structure of the country.[5] The county councils operate on their own account enterprises producing approximately three-fifths of the total production of the local state industries, and they employ three-fifths of the total labor force of these industries.[6] The bulk of the rest of the local state industries are included in the budget of the province council. A very small number are connected with the commune councils, mostly flour mills and other small food-processing plants, quarries, and sawmills. All the local state industries are united in the province associations. An association groups together all enterprises in the province which produce the same commodity, such as the Association of Shoe Factories. It coordinates and directs the activities of its enterprises in accordance with the national and provincial plan and represents the common interests of its member enterprises. An association is formed by action of the presidium of the province national council. Through the associations the presidium controls the activities of the state local industry in the province. In practice the associations actually supervise strictly even those enterprises which are financially connected with the county or commune councils. The associations are not organs of state administration, but they possess a legal personality as independent business ventures.[7]

Theoretically, the national councils coordinate the production of the industries owned by the cooperatives and include this production in the province economic plan. In practice the cooperatives disregard the directives of the national councils. During the period of a plan the agreed-upon plans are changed by the Central Board of Cooperatives (provincial or national). The boards determine production and investment even without prior consultation with the councils. Cooperatives do not pay any attention to the local plan of development, but are motivated strictly by the profit and loss account. Their industries are often concentrated in highly industrialized regions with a scarcity of labor and resources.[8] Many cooperatives act in the manner of private businesses and successfully escape the bureaucratic control of the state.[9]

AGRICULTURE

Agricultural production is included in the local economic plan. The province national council directs the total development of agriculture in the province by coordinating the work of the county national councils and by administering the state farms, machine stations and drainage enterprises. The county council acts as the transmitter of the province agricultural policies, and the commune performs the function of executor. Implementation of the policies is insured by a careful balance between administrative pressure and economic incentives offered to the farmer.

The fulfillment of the plan is secured first of all by a constant agricultural education drive designed to improve and modernize the methods of agricultural production. The county and commune councils employ agricultural advisers, many of whom are attached to the agricultural circles or the producers' cooperatives. Secondly, especially desired production, such as meat, and industrial crops, is stimulated by favorable prices and long-term investment loans and by priority in the allocation of raw materials and of the services of machine stations. Finally, the full blast of propaganda descends on the farmers, urging them to serve by their work the interests of People's Poland. Because of the private ownership of Polish agriculture, remunerative power is the most effective tool which could be employed to increase production. The importance of that production to the Polish economy is expressed by the constant pressure applied by the central government and the province councils on the county and commune councils. The official life of the county or commune chairman often depends on his ability to fulfill in a reasonable manner the demands of the plan of agricultural production.

SUPPLIES FOR THE POPULATION

The national councils ensure supplies for the population and direct local trade, services, and distribution. The local production is basically designed to satisfy local demands, utilizing local supplies of raw materials, labor, and capital. Some of the local industries surpass the narrow limits of this objective and deliver their wares to other provinces and even to foreign countries.[10] The national councils supervise in their territory all the activities of retail trade, services, and craft shops. They also direct the purchases of agricultural commodities and coordinate and are responsible for the distribution of food and other consumer goods. The presidium of the province national council scrutinizes systematically the province's balance of incomes and expenditure for the entire population of the territory, prepared by a local unit of the Polish National Bank, in order to determine the size of effective demand and to adjust to it the supply of goods and services as to quantity and distribution. The Province Planning Commission composes balances of supply and demand of basic articles. The national councils should take action to avert local shortages of supplies by organizing local production to fill the needs, and they should ensure that the local industries produce their commodities in the desired quality and that the commodities produced by the key industries are distributed in accordance with local demands in cities, towns, and villages. The councils should organize the distribution of supply in such a manner that long hauls and crisscross transportation are eliminated. One of the basic functions of the national councils is to see that the service enterprises improve their performance in accordance with the plan.[11] The enterprises of the key industries are encouraged by the councils to organize "sideline productions" of articles in short supply in the regions where they are located. All profits from such production are accumulated in the Enterprise Fund.[12]

Despite the soundness of the theory that the supplies for the population are directed more effectively by local government than by central ministries, the Polish consumer is constantly frustrated in his demand for consumer goods. The production in this sector of the economy is still grossly insufficient in quantity and in variety of commodities. The consumer goods industry has always been, in People's Poland, the stepchild of the planners, who devote large investments to the development of heavy industry.[13] The practice of burdening the national councils with the responsibilities for supplying the population was designed precisely to allow the central planners to continue their preference for the development of heavy industry.

However, supplies for the population have improved with the deconcentration of decision-making. This deconcentration has allowed the planners to tap unused local resources and energies. Also the system of distribution has lost some of its central bureaucratic grossness and slowness. The general supply of locally grown food is fully sufficient, although shortages of single commodities do occur periodically. Imported foodstuffs appear and disappear as if by magic. To a large degree the serious shortages of basic articles result from the still extremely chaotic system of distribution. It seems that the bureaucrats of the national councils have been able to cope with this problem only a little better than their colleagues in Warsaw. We never did discover why, on some occasions Warsaw was without coffee, while Lublin, one hundred miles to the east, had a plentiful supply. At other times the opposite was true. Crisscross transportation has not been eliminated, and bricks from Lublin were transported to Opole, while bricks from Opole were hauled to Lublin.[14]

COMMUNAL ECONOMY

Communal economy and administration of state housing are in the hands of the national councils. The supply of public utilities and housing is a trouble spot in the fast-growing Polish economy. This branch of the national economy suffered long neglect and was starved for investment, first by the Germans during their wartime occupation, and most recently by the communist leadership, which devoted most of its attention to the growth of industry. Twentieth-century factories operate in cities with nineteenth-century facilities. Only an extremely heavy capital outlay would bring the communal economy in step with the modern, growing industrial sector. Table 15 clearly indicates that many towns still lack complete urban facilities. In others, including the capital, Warsaw, the machinery and equipment is old, inadequate, and in serious need of repairs and replacement. In many cities and towns the existing plants were constructed from thirty to a hundred years ago, and the demand for their services has outgrown their capacity in the rapidly expanding communities. The

Table 15

Urban Services in Polish Cities (1950–1970)

Year	Total Cities	Water Supply	Sewer System	Gas Supply	Elec- tricity Supply	Urban Transporta- tion	Hotel	Public Bath	Public Laundry
1950	706	367	324	237	669	75	...	...	...
1955	815	513	498	248	806	93	326	306	327
1960	893	595	561	282	893	149	353	332	350
1963	891	653	620	300	891	161	351	356	498
1964	890	661	630	303	890	164	348	355	566
1965	891	669	640	306	891	161	346	347	628
1966	891	680	658	307	891	166	340	341	660
1967	891	690	665	309	891	166	342	...	706
1969	889	702	673	320	889	180	343	...	728
1970	889	714	677	327	889	181	338	...	742

SOURCE: *Rocznik Statystyczny* (1965), p. 372; *Rocznik Statystyczny* (1968), p. 402; and *Rocznik Statystyczny* (1971), p. 444.

pressure of gas and water is so low that during the day one can hardly cook or take a bath. Public transportation is extremely overcrowded during rush hours (we suppose it is no worse than that of New York at 5:00 p.m.).[15] All services are very inadequate and repairs take a long time. It is not unusual for a city or a city district to be without water, gas, or electricity for twenty-four hours. Many new and some old districts in cities lack utilities be- cause of the limited, outdated capacities of the plants. The city of Lublin, with a population of 236,000 is supplied by the same gas works which served it in 1931, when the population was only 112,000.[16]

The urban national councils spend a large part of their funds for repairs of existing facilities of communal economy, often at the expense of other objectives such as housing. This is a result of the low total investment by the state in communal economy in general. In 1967, for the upkeep of the existing plants, the coun- cils used 57.2% of the total communal investment funds.[17]

One of the most annoying hardships to which the Polish popu- lation is subjected is the persistent shortage of housing. It is still not unusual to find two different families sharing one apartment. This is an indirect cause of many social problems, such as alcohol- ism, a relatively high divorce rate, juvenile delinquency, crime, and mental disorders. It influences adversely the productivity of labor, especially for those engaged in mental work, many of whom have to work in their homes, and it contributes to the high degree of nervousness so very noticeable in the Polish people. A comparison with other European countries clearly illustrates Poland's housing shortage (see table 16), although it is of a similar magnitude as in other East-Central European communist countries. The Polish neglect of this most serious problem is not unique, but is, indeed, characteristic of all the communist systems.

Table 16

Average Number of People per Room in European Countries

Country	Year	Amount
Austria	1961	.9
Bulgaria	1965	1.7
Czechoslovakia	1961	1.3
Denmark	1965	.7
England & Wales	1966	.6
Finland	1960	1.3
France	1968	.9
German Democratic Republic	1965	1.1
German Federal Republic	1963	.9
Greece	1961	1.5
Holland	1960	.8
Hungary	1960	1.4
Italy	1961	1.1
Norway	1960	.8
Poland	1960	1.7
	1970	1.4
Rumania	1966	1.4
Spain	1960	.9
Sweden	1965	.8
Switzerland	1960	.7
Yugoslavia	1961	1.6

SOURCE: *Rocznik Statystyczny* (1971), table 34, p. 723.
NOTE: Total rooms include kitchen, except in Bulgaria. In France, kitchen below 12 m² not included.

Poland rates far below other industrial countries of Europe in housing construction, and it has not really made much progress since 1931, when the average in urban areas was two persons per room.[18] Some of the postwar gain was achieved by the transfer of population from the eastern provinces lost to the Soviet Union, which had suffered a great housing shortage, to the western provinces gained from Germany, which had comparatively sufficient housing. There are three reasons for the persistent housing shortage:

1. Lack of investment and the apalling destruction of property during World War II (in some cities such as Warsaw, Gdánsk, and Wrocław, 80–95% of all buildings were destroyed).
2. The fast growth of population after the war, and the large emigration of the rural population to the cities (see pp. 6–7 and table 17).
3. The comparatively low investment and rate of construction after the war (see table 18).

Thus Poland led other countries in the increase in population and over the years trailed them in the rate of construction. The serious shortage of housing was bound to persist, although there was a considerable improvement between 1954 and 1970. The relative

Table 17

Population Increase of Poland Compared to Other Selected Countries
(Average net increase per 1,000)

	1950–1960	1961–1970
Czechoslovakia	8.9	5.0
France	7.0	6.0
Great Britain	6.3	5.8
Hungary	7.3	3.1
Poland	17.8	8.9

SOURCES: *Rocznik Statystyczny* (1961), p. 461; and *Rocznik Statystyczny* (1971), p. 653. The Averages calculated by the author.

Table 18

Apartment Construction in Poland Compared to Other Selected Countries
(per 1,000 of population)

	1954	1960	1966	1970	Average
Czechoslovakia	2.9	5.6	5.3	7.4	5.3
France	3.8	6.9	8.4	8.9	7.0
Great Britain	7.0	5.9	7.3	6.5	6.7
Hungary	2.8	4.2	5.5	7.7	5.1
Poland	2.7	4.8	5.6	5.9	4.8

SOURCES: *Rocznik Statystyczny* (1961), p. 515; *Rocznik Statystyczny* (1968), p. 695; *Rocznik Statystyczny* (1971), p. 724.

share of investment increased from 2.6% in 1955 to 3.2% in 1960 and further to 4.5% by 1967. It remained the same by 1970.[19] It was still low in view of the housing crisis.

The national councils are responsible for coordination of all construction. They were direct investors in a considerable share of the total state apartment building.[20] The Fifth Congress admitted that the further solution of housing shortage must lie not in state, but in private construction for villages and small towns and in cooperative building for the cities. They administer most of the existing property and are in charge of allocation. The population often blames the national councils for the shortage of housing because local authorities have such large responsibilities in this sphere. Local officials are accused of not building enough, of misappropriating funds, and of allocating apartments to their friends or to people who can afford a bribe. Although this was true in many instances, the shortage of housing resulted from the conscious policy of the central leadership, in whose favor the development of housing occupied only a minor place. A drastic change in the housing policy took place in 1966, when the main emphasis was put on construction of cooperative apartment buildings, diminishing thereby the role of state construction in general, and construction by the National Councils in particular (see table, note 20). By 1967 the cooperatives built about 25% more apartments than the state; by 1968 50% more, and by 1969, twice as much. This proportion continued throughout 1970. Since individuals buy apartments in cooperative housing this meant abdication by the socialist state of direct involvement in housing allocation, leaving the distribution to market forces. Cooperative apartments are expensive by Polish standards and naturally only those better situated can afford them. The upper classes can buy luxurious housing. Opening of the housing market created incentives for savings and dampened consumption. (With the shortages of various consumer goods lack of saving incentives is a constant nightmare to the communist planners.) The state retained control of the building trade in general by direct management of production of building materials and their distribution. The new administration under Gierek noted the dire Polish housing situation, stepped up production of building materials and building construction, and promised to build "one more Poland" by 1980.[21]

"Social deeds" play an important role in construction connected with communal economy, especially on the commune level. They utilize local sources of labor and capital not included in the state plan, and they are from the point of view of the central planners, a clear savings, with the exception of state grants which generally account for about 1/5 of the total outlay. Their total capital outlay grows constantly, as illustrated by table 19:

Table 19

Total Capital Outlay for Social Deeds (1956–1970)
(*in Million Zlotys*)

Year	Amount	Year	Amount
1956	863	1964	4,871
1957	947	1965	4,629
1958	1,098	1966	5,087
1959	1,411	1967	5,012
1960	1,425	1968	5,803
1961	1,742	1969	6,375
1962	2,538	1970	6,572
1963	3,020		

SOURCES: *Rocznik Statystyczny* (1971), table 17, p. 159 and for the calculation of the general prices increase, table 6, p. 401.
NOTE: General price increase between 1956–1970 was about 29%. Accounting for this increase, the value of social deeds in 1970 (in 1956 prices) was about 4,666 million zlotys. At constant prices then, the increase in the value of social deeds between 1956–1970 was roughly five times.

PRICES

The important weapon by which planners direct, control, and stimulate the economy is the manipulation of prices. Most of the prices are set by the state at different levels of its structure, depending on the importance of a commodity. The prices of the significant raw materials are decided upon by the Council of Ministers, and those of the great majority of other commodities by the State Commission on Prices of the province national councils (about 30% of the total amount of the state controlled prices). In agriculture, in addition to the centrally established prices there exist prices for articles which the state allows to be sold on the free market—vegetables, fruit, poultry and eggs. These prices are determined solely by supply and demand, and the state influences them only in a roundabout way by fluctuating the prices of the same commodities sold in the state shops. The role of the national councils in the formulation of price policy is insignificant, as most of the prices are centrally controlled. It is limited in most cases to the enforcement of the regulations of the central government.

COOPERATION WITH CENTRALLY ADMINISTERED ENTERPRISES

The province councils are legally in charge of coordinating all of the economy of the province. Specifically, they supervise the fulfillment of the national and territorial economic plans. For the centrally administered enterprises, the province councils advise the appropriate ministries and national associations of the performance of the economic units under their administration. The centrally administered enterprises must file periodic reports with the province council. The province councils participate in the preparation and reevaluation of the major investments undertaken on their territory. They also must be consulted or, in some cases must decide on the localization of industries. Furthermore, they participate in an advisory capacity in decisions to establish new enterprises and to recognize or liquidate existing firms. Finally, they initiate combined investments and other cooperation between locally and centrally administered enterprises.

It is obvious that the position of the province council in relation to the national economic administration is strictly advisory. The 1963 amendment to the 1958 statute did not allocate any decision-making powers to the councils (with the possible exception of localization), although it enlarged the provisions of the original law for further involvement of the councils in advisory-coordination functions.[22] The amendment also retained the right of the Council of Ministers to determine the specific principles and methods to be used by the province councils in the coordination and supervision of centrally administered enterprises. The 1960 decree of the Council of Ministers, which as far as we know has never been superseded, diluted the spirit of the 1958 statute (and its amendment) in two ways.[23] First, the consultation clause obliged the enterprise only to ask the presidium of the province national council for an opinion. And second, the Council of Ministers was no longer required to consult with the presidium of the province national council before establishing certain key industries. This formulation left the presidium of the province council with very little legal means for coordinating activities of the key industries operating in the province.

In practice, the cooperation depends to a large degree on the willingness of the specific ministry and of the directors of the association or the individual enterprise to make use of consultation.[24] In many instances the people in charge of key industries find it to their advantage to cooperate with the local government, and such cooperation often proves mutually beneficial. By cooperating with the councils, the directors of key industries are assured of their supply of energy, raw materials, and labor. The national councils, in turn, can more effectively plan their development. Our own experience indicates that such a cordial and fruitful relationship is rather rare.[25] Usually the national councils and the directors of the key industries are at loggerheads. The councils try to preserve the resources for local use, while the directors change their plans of production and budgets without informing the presidium of the province council. This, of course, plays havoc with the local plan, often causing it to be continually revised.

The key enterprises are allowed to conclude agreements with producers' cooperatives or independent artisans for various services, and they can make purchases from cooperatives, nonsocialized firms, and private individuals. The directors must fulfill the plan or perish, and in order to secure vital supplies or services, they resort to paying higher, "illegal" prices above the official state margins. Thus they compete effectively for these services and materials with the local government, which operates on a limited budget. Local craftsmen are inclined to refuse their services to private individuals and to concentrate on work for the industries, where their high bills are settled without question. The local plan is also jeopardized by the curious method by which all enterprises in Poland operate. In the first quarter they fulfill only about 5–10% of the yearly plan; at the end of the third quarter, they have produced only 50–60% of the plan; and in the last quarter they rush to reach 100% or even to over-fulfill the plan. In the case of a large plant of a key industry, this erratic performance produces depressions and sudden booms in the local economy.[26]

Each enterprise must participate in the cost of investments for the communal economy, provided that the new investments are necessitated by an increased or new demand for services by the enterprise and that this demand cannot be satisfied by the existing facilities.[27] The definition of this participation by the key industries in local investment is ambiguous and leads to constant disputes between the directors of the enterprises and the presidia of the councils on what is and what is not an additional demand for communal services. The dispute is aggravated by the fact that the law does not specify what percentage of the total investment must be supplied by the key industries. The argument is usually finally settled by the minister in charge of the key industry in question. Generally speaking, the financial participation of key industries in local investment covers only a small part of the total investment. For example, in the city of Lublin the total investment between 1959 and 1961 was 559 million zlotys. The key enterprises actually provided only 8 million and owed the city 175 million.[28] Often the additional demand for services by a factory places a heavy burden on the local budget.

Even after the enterprise has agreed on the size of its contribution, the council has no legal sanction in case of refusal or postponement of actual payment of the obligation. The enterprises interpret the regulations narrowly. For example, an enterprise may agree to contribute toward the establishment of new bus or streetcar routes. The size of the contribution is determined by the number of employees, but the enterprise often refuses to pay for routes which are some distance from its location, even though the routes run directly to its location and carry its employees to work.[29] It seems clear that the enterprises wish to contribute as little as possible, and that the councils have no real power to force the key industries to participate in the development of the communal economy.

LOCAL ECONOMIC PLAN

The councils enact long-term and yearly economic plans. These plans should be consistent with the directives and tasks established for the national economy in the National Economic Plans. They should include the most important tasks of the centrally directed enterprises which affect the territory of the councils. The yearly plans together with the budgets, should be enacted by the province and county councils before the end of January of the year of the plan, and by the commune councils before November 15 of the year preceding that of the plan.[30] The plans are enacted in an upward progression: first by the rural and urban communes; then by the counties, which incorporate in their plans the plans of the lower bodies; and finally by the provinces. The plans of a province include the plans of all the counties and therefore, indirectly, the plans of all the communes of the province. At the top these plans are combined in the National Economic Plan, which is enacted by the Sejm. The plans of the councils are prepared on the basis of directives issued to them by the Council of Ministers which originate from the planning proposals prepared for parliament. During this process of enactment progressing gradually from the lower levels of local government to parliament, it may be necessary to change the plans of the lower councils in order to achieve consistency with the higher plan. The changes are simply executed by the presidium, which then informs the council of this step at the earliest session.[31] The Council formalizes it by resolution.

In this procedure for the formulation of the economic plan, we detect the same principle of democratic centralism on which the political and administrative structures of a communist state are based and which supposedly bind together "in complete unity the necessary amount of centralism with true democracy."[32] In economic planning the lower councils have more independence than in political or even administrative matters, because planning, as it progresses upward, becomes more general. This is a result of the complexity of the economy. The central planners, even if they would wish to, are not capable of including in their considerations every minute detail because of the sheer limitation of the human mind's ability to understand the interplay of too many variables. This limitation is God's gift to people living in communist states.[33] Because of it the lower bodies have some freedom in decision-making inside the general economic framework.

Planning for the following year starts in the spring. Each presidium decides on the main targets on the basis of general directives received from above, previous debates in the council, and the suggestions and pressures of the Communist party, the standing committees, individual councilmen, the local newspapers, and, finally, the general public. The main targets may be building a school, constructing a new road or street, opening a new shop, starting a new bus line, or increasing the supply of shoes. These targets are handed to the planning commission of the national council, which in turn calculates the necessary supply of resources for their fulfillment. At the same time the commission receives the proposed production plans from the economic units directed by the council (state, cooperative, and private). The commission tries to balance the demands for materials created by the targets with the outputs as indicated in the proposed plans of the economic units. Of course it can use only the net output, which is obtained by the following calculation: total output minus output used in production equals net output. Total output is the total output of a given territory. The output used in production is supplemented by the commodities produced by the key industries and centrally distributed. The net output may be decreased by directives from the central planners to "export" part of it to another region. All the supplies and demands of the plan are calculated in physical terms, and the material balances are arrived at with the assumption that the input-output relations are fixed.

Usually the demands created by the goals are too high for the available supplies. The planning commission makes recommendations to the presidium, asking it to curtail or postpone the targets and urges the economic units to upgrade their production plans. The increase in production requires a larger allocation of resources because of the input used in production. The whole procedure could be explained as "the solution of a set of simultaneous equations whose fixed coefficients are input-output relations; the known variables are the final demands, and the unknown are the gross outputs."[34] These equations are solved not only by mathematical computation but also by hard bargaining—the planning commission with the presidium and factories, the presidium with the higher authorities, and factories with the associations and ministries.

Finally, in the fall, the draft of the plan is completed and is submitted to the council for enactment. Usually it is approved without a murmur by unanimous vote, since parts of the plan are enforced from above and parts are agreed on beforehand by influential elements within the council. However, in isolated cases, the council demands a revision of the plan. After consultation by the presidium with the higher organ of government, a change may be introduced. If the revision is refused, the council usually enacts the original plan. In our research, we came across an interesting incident in which the National Council of the city of Gorzów Wielkopolski, in the province of Zielonagóra, refused to enact the Five-Year Plan because it considered the plan to be grossly deficient in the allocation of funds for necessary investment for the city. Consultation and pressure by the province did not bring any result, and finally the province council had to revise its own plan, which in the meantime had already been enacted.[35]

It is obvious from the above description that the method of planning is a highly complicated exercise which requires well-qualified personnel. For that reason and because of the limitations imposed from above, many counties accept the total framework from the provinces, and many communes either do not prepare the plan at all or just fill in the required standard form of the plan in accordance with the instructions received.[36] The province councils receive from the Council of Ministers eight directives or "annual plan indices."[37] In addition, the ministries supply the departments of the councils with "orientation indices," which are of a guiding character and are not legally binding. The annual plan indices are:

1. The gross value of output planned for the province and divided into output for industry and agriculture.
2. Production goals for the most important commodities in industry and agriculture.
3. Allocation to the province of the thirteen main groups of centrally distributed commodities (coal, steel, chemicals, etc.).
4. About 80% of the total investment in the province.
5. Total state grants to the province.
6. The plan for total employment in the province.
7. The upper limit on total wages separated into limits for the administration, the associations, and the individual enterprises.
8. Total taxes expected to be transferred to the central government.

The above indices are divided into concrete directives and expectations. Only concrete directives must be fulfilled in exact physical or monetary terms. In industrial production only the production of the most important commodities is centrally planned in physical terms. In agriculture only the plan for supply of certain basic commodities to farmers takes the form of a concrete directive; the total output of agriculture is simply a prediction. The plan of total employment is also a prediction, but the upper limit of total wages is a concrete directive. The province leadership is expected to use the predictions as exact figures in its planning, and it is expected to aim for them in its performance, but it is allowed to deflect from them in the final fulfillment of the plan. The predictions do not leave any choice in planning, but do provide room for maneuvering in the actual execution of the plans. The concrete directives have the character of the exact letter of the law and must be obeyed in planning as well as in execution. The province, in turn, determines the annual plan indices for the counties. Theoretically, the indices number about twenty, but in practice they are often much more numerous and detailed. It is clear that the independence of planning is only illusionary. Communes receive from the counties a still larger number of indices. The indices are transmitted within the province through three different channels; from the province economic planning commission to the county economic planning commission; from the province departments to the corresponding departments of the county; and, finally from the associations to their enterprises. These indices are not always identical, and it is often difficult to coordinate them at the county level.[38]

The plan of the national council determines the basic direction of the economic development of the territory under its jurisdiction. The tasks set out in the plan are compulsory for the enterprises administered by the council. The plans include the basic goals previously agreed upon for cooperatives. The calculations concerning trade and the economic activities of individuals (households, crafts, and individual agriculture) are only predictions, but they do, however, determine the direction of the council's economic policies. These policies find their formulation in the coordination of the production of local state industry, crafts, and cooperatives, and also in the allocation to individual farmers of supplies and the economic incentives which are designed to induce them to fulfill the level of production desired by the planners.

The whole planning procedure is highly complicated and disorganized, and it produces a final yearly plan which in many counties and communes is not worth the paper on which it is written.[39] It balances perfectly both vertically and horizontally, but due to its complexity and to the large number of variables which are only rough predictions (agricultural production, individual consumption, employment, etc.), it is revised, even at the province level, almost as soon as it is enacted. The changes forced by reality are made by the presidium, which informs the council at its nearest session. The plan is divided into quarterly operational plans and in practice only the quarterly plans come close to actual execution. The yearly plan is nothing more than a predetermination of the general economic policies.

The difficulties which occur in the yearly plan are, of course, greatly multiplied in the Five-Year Plan. In addition to the predictions already present in the yearly plan, the planners must estimate what the cost ratios will be in the future and must adjust their input-output ratios accordingly. For example, they have to predict the amount of plastic which should be substituted for wood in house building. Their decision on this substitution would, in turn, require the construction of a new chemical plant and, eventually, the establishment of a new pattern of raw material supply, a different housing scheme, an extension of the water, gas and electricity supply, and a new system of transportation. Because of this complexity we may expect the Five-Year Plan to be even less reliable than the one-year plans.

LOCAL BUDGET

The national councils enact local yearly budgets, starting with the commune and ending with the province councils.[40] The budgets of the provinces and counties include the budgets of all the lower councils in their territory. Finally, the local budgets are incorporated into the state budget enacted each year by parliament on the basis of the proposal of the Council of Ministers. They cover one calendar year from January 1 to December 31. They must be in agreement with the National Economic Plan and most importantly must balance expenditures with incomes. The Council of State (Presidium of the Parliament) determines directives for the composition of the budgets of the province national councils. The presidium of the province council, in turn issues the budgetary directives to the presidia of the counties and the presidia of the commune councils. The presidia of the national councils introduce changes into their budgets after their enactment by the council in order to bring them into agreement with the state budget enacted by parliament or the budgets of the higher national councils. The changes have to be submitted to the councils at their earliest session for formal approval.

The draft of the budget of a national council is prepared by its department of finance on the basis of demands for funds by other departments, and of directives issued every year by the Minister of Finance. During its work on the budget draft, the department of finance consults the planning commission and the standing committees of the national council. The final proposal of the budget is arrived at by bargaining between the department of finance, other departments, the ministry of finance, the planning commissions, the presidia of different levels and the standing committees. The principle of democratic centralism is evident in this procedure. Finally, the draft of the budget is submitted by the department of finance to the presidium. The presidium accepts the draft through its formal resolution and introduces the budget proposal at the special budgetary session of the council. The enactment of the budget by the council is usually a formality, although there have been cases in which the council has refused to accept the budget and the higher council has been forced to change its own budget.[41]

The budget of a national council is divided into parts, divisions, chapters, and paragraphs. The parts indicate which state organs are entitled to a block of funds and make them responsible for the collection of the revenues—the county national council. Divisions divide the expenditure among the main functions of government and allocate the funds for their fulfillment—education. Chapters divide the expenditure for specific tasks and provide funds for their execution—the construction of schools. Paragraphs further divide the expenditure allocated for specific tasks into funds to be spent on a particular activity—construction of a school. A transfer of funds between the parts and the divisions can be effected only by a resolution of the council. The transfer of funds from one chapter or paragraph to another may be decided upon by the presidium. National council can authorize its presidium to transfer funds between parts and divisions, and the presidium may permit the department of finance to transfer funds between paragraphs. The transfers cannot increase the total wage fund, change the total investment, or decrease the total fund designated for major renovations and repairs. The freedom of the national councils to alter their budgets is also limited by directives of the Council of Ministers and by the framework of the yearly plan.

The budgets do change in the course of the year due to modifications (discussed above) made in the original plan and to fluctuations in the revenues of the national councils. Most changes are effected by the presidium or even departments. As with the plan the approval of the council is only a formality.[42] The department of the budget composes monthly, quarterly, and yearly budgetary reports which are reviewed by the presidium. The yearly report must be approved by the national council and forwarded to the presidium of the higher national council. The yearly report of the province national council must be submitted to the Minister of Finance and to the State Control Board. All departments transmit their own budgetary reports to the corresponding ministries. Budgetary savings made by the council may be used at its own discretion.

The local budgets form an important part of the total state budget. Their share in the total outlays and revenues of the state budget amounts on an average to one-fourth. The expenditures of the central government concentrate on the development of the national economy, while the outlays of the local government are devoted to the social and economic needs of the population and to agriculture (see table 20).

Over one-third of the total expenditure of local government is concentrated at the province level (see table 21). An especially large share of the total expenditure for investment, education, culture, and social benefits is directed by the province national councils. The counties' expenditure is mostly connected with actual administration. The communes are not entrusted with large

Table 20

Percentage of Local Budgets in the Total State Outlays

	1962	1966	1970
Total percent	25	26	26
Education and culture	90	74	72
Health and social welfare	80	80	85
Agriculture	80	83	66

SOURCES: For 1962, Jan Dusza, *Budżety i Gospodarka Rad Narodowych* (Warszawa, 1962), pp. 23–24; for 1966 and 1970, calculated from: *Rocznik Statystyczny* (1968), table 3, p. 558, and *Rocznik Statystyczny* (1971), table 3, p. 600. See also: "Budgets of the People's Councils," *Polish Economic Survey*, no. 2 (January 26, 1966), p. 23.

Table 21

Expenditure of the National Councils According to Councils Level
(1960, 1965, 1970)
(%)

	1960	1965	1970
Provinces	38.6	39.8	41.1
Counties	28.3	27.3	24.3
Urban Counties	17.5	16.2	14.3
City Wards	5.1	5.0	5.2
Towns	6.1	6.6	7.2
Settlements	.5	.3	.2
Communes	3.9	4.8	7.7

SOURCE: *Rocznik Polityczny i Gospodarczy* (1971), table 15, p. 606.

funds, and they direct only a minute part of the total investment of local government, and most of their income is devoted to current expenditure, primarily for actual administration, upkeep of houses of culture, libraries, and schools, and aid for the poor and indigent. The communes spend most of the funds which are included in the budgetary division entitled National Economy for the maintenance of local roads and bridges. The expenditure for the health needs of the population is small, although the needs would warrant a much larger outlay (see chapter 2).

The expenditures envisioned in the budget of the national councils should be covered, in the first place, by their own revenues. However, they can also obtain subsidies from the central budget. These subsidies were greatly reduced between 1960 and 1965 (see table 22). At the same time direct participation in the

Table 22

Revenue Sources of the National Councils (1960, 1965, 1970)
(in Million Zlotys)

	1960	1965	1970
Payments from enterprises administered			
by the councils and from cooperatives	12,528	25,055	28,645
Taxes and fees from private economy	8,929	9,950	10,562
Other own revenues	4,958	5,314	6,301
Participation in the revenues of the			
central government	555	30,946	44,427
Subsidies from the central government	25,823	9,938	10,986
Total	54,793	81,203	100,921

SOURCE: *Rocznik Statystyczny* (1971), table 12, p. 605.
NOTE: The increase between 1960 and 1970 in the total revenues of the local government was partially due to inflation (see p. 225, table 19, note).

revenues of the central government was dramatically increased. It provided a greater financial independence to local government, commensurate with the general movement toward administrative deconcentration. The subsidies were often for the reconstruction of war-damaged buildings, and by the 1960s the need was mainly eliminated. The sources of revenue for the national councils are:

1. Payments from the enterprises administered by the councils.
2. Payments for services rendered by the organs of the councils and incomes from the council's property.
3. Revenues from local taxes and fees.
4. Participation in the revenues of the central government.

Less than half of the total revenue of the national councils is obtained from their "own" sources, the most important being the payments from the local state and cooperative enterprises (see table 22). These payments are in the form of the net profits of the state enterprises and the income tax collected from the cooperatives.[43] They are mostly collected by province, county, city, town and settlement national councils. In addition, the city, town, and settlement national councils receive large revenues as compared to their budgets, but not any net incomes from their own property, which is mainly housing.[44] The rural communes operate only a few very small local enterprises (flour mills, etc.). About thirty percent of the taxes and fees from the private economy are paid by urban crafts and small industries, and about seventy percent by private farmers.[45] The most important tax is the land tax, which accounts for more than half of all taxes paid by private agriculture.[46] The taxes and fees from private agriculture form eighty to ninety percent of the total revenue of the rural communes. Local taxes and fees collected from individuals are not an important part of the local government's total budget. They mainly enter the county treasury, as the county is the principal unit of local government in terms of actual administration.

Approximately half of the local government budget is furnished by retention of part of the revenues collected for the central government. The national councils retain part of the personal income tax and also share in the turnover tax[47] paid by industry (with the exception of sugar refineries) and in the net profits of seventeen trade and industrial associations (mostly dealing with consumer goods) which are centrally directed. The percentage of sharing is determined separately for each province by the Council of Ministers in the yearly directives on the local budget. In turn the presidium of the province national council divides the received allocation among its counties. The counties may transfer the allocation further down, and they often do so in the case of cities. Very few of the centrally distributed funds descend to the level of the communes. The provinces receive shares of the turnover tax ranging from as little as about 6–7% in the province of Katowice (heavily industrialized) to as much as 100% in the province of Koszalin (considered to be backward). All provinces, with the exception of two and of the five city provinces, received 100% of the personal income tax.[48] Direct state grants are in the form of allocations for house building and constitute only a small percentage of the total budget of local government. They did play an important part in the economies of certain cities, especially those which were heavily damaged during the war and required large capital for reconstruction, such as Warsaw, Gdańsk and Wrocław.

The degree of participation in the revenue of the central government depends on the tasks performed by the local government within the framework of the National Economic Plan and on the ability of a province to collect its own financial resources. Only the percentage of participation is fixed, and the actual revenue from the turnover tax and net profits depends on the performance of the industry located in the territory of a given province. This often makes the local budget unstable, but it forces the local officials to press the directors of the state and cooperative industries to improve their production. The national councils have a certain amount of free play with their budgets because of the fact that a large part of the local revenue depends on the performance of local or key industries, although they have to operate within the limits of the economic plan.

CONCLUSION

We can only conclude that a certain freedom in decision-making on economic matters at the level of local government is needed from the point of view of economic efficiency. The transfer of some of the responsibility for the local economy from central to local government has yet another justification, which is not of an economic, but rather of a political nature. The deconcentration of the economic decision-making leads to a situation in which the population, frustrated in its economic needs by the shortage of consumer goods and services, in its displeasure attacks the national councils, although most of the actual shortages of supplies result from the addiction of the communist leadership to the development of heavy industry and to the belief that a precisely planned economy administered by a bureaucracy is superior to the free play of economic forces.

NOTES TO CHAPTER V

[1] In this sense "capital" means stock of machinery, buildings, transportation, etc. Land includes agricultural land and all natural resources.

[2] John Montias, *Central Planning in Poland* (New Haven, 1962), p. 5; and Zygmunt Szeliga, "The Polish Economy: 1967–1968," *Contemporary Poland*, no. 2 (February 1967): 13. The V Congress of the PUWP (1968) noted the necessity of technical modernization and of increase in the productivity of labor. The technical backwardness prevented the desired development of the export of industrial products (*Uchwała V Zjazdu*, pp. 8, 9, 12, and 13).

[3] Montias, *Central Planning*, p. 6. However, the V Congress reaffirmed the dominance of centralized planning and rejected the "revisionist" arguments for introduction of market mechanism (*Uchwała V Zjazdu*, p. 16). The VI Congress continued this policy introducing at the same time deconcentration in

the actual administration of the economy (*VI Zjazd Polskiej*, pp. 187–88).

4 *Rocznik Statystyczny* (1971), table 9, p. 129; table 4, p. 375; and table 2, p. 458.

5 For example: in 1964 local production (local state and cooperative industries) accounted for 69% of the total production sold on the internal market. The increase over 1963 was 9.8%. The largest sectors in the local production were consumer goods, 31.1%; electrical machinery and metallurgical products, 19.2% and textiles and clothing, 16.2% (*Rocznik Polityczny* [1965], p. 272). The national councils directed almost all flour mills and bakeries. The share of the local state industry in the total internal market sales was: 1965, 61.9%; 1966, 60.2%; 1967, 57.9%. The decline in the share of the internal market was due to the increase in production of investments goods (from 31.0% to 34.4%) and production for export (see note 10) (*Rocznik Polityczny* [1968], p. 362). Increase in the total production of local state industry was in 1967, 7.7% over the 1968 volume, although the increase in the total industrial production was 9%. However, the increase in the total national production of consumer goods, which is most characteristic of local production, grew only by 7%. This indicated a continuous growth of the share of local production of consumers goods (*Rocznik Polityczny* [1970], p. 359 and p. 319). The expenditure of the National Councils for economic activities also grew rapidly. For example, in the Lublin Province (all councils) they increased between 1957 and 1966 by 1,280% (Zbigniew Szelog, "Wydatki Budżetowe GRN Woj. Lubelskiego W Świetle Decentralizacji Budżetowej," *Problemy Rad Narodowych*, no. 12 (Warszawa, 1968).

6 Interviews.

7 Antoni Hebda, "Wydziały a Zjednoczenia," p. 13.

8 Interviews, and also Władysław Gomułka, *VIII Plenum KC PZPR* (Warszawa, 1961), p. 61.

9 Between 1960 and 1970 their share in the GNP was relatively constant at 8–9% (*Rocznik Statystyczny* [1968], table 9, p. 79; and *Rocznik Statystyczny* [1971], table 8, p. 128).

10 For example: in 1964 the local production accounted for 3.9% of the value of the total Polish export (calculated from *Rocznik Polityczny* [1965], p. 272 and *Rocznik Statystyczny* [1965], p. 335). The share of the total production in export increased considerably over the following years and for the local state industry alone it accounted for 7.1% in 1965 and 7.7% in 1967 (*Rocznik Polityczny* [1968], p. 362). In 1969 the increase of the local state production for export was 11.5% over 1968, while at the same time the total Polish export increased by only 9% (*Rocznik Polityczny* [1970], p. 360 and *Rocznik Statystyczny* [1971], table 1, p. 410).

11 Gomułka, *VIII Plenum KC PZPR*, pp. 53–54.

12 The Enterprise Fund is used for premiums, housing, and other benefits for employees.

13 Since 1956 a larger investment has been directed to the consumer goods industries and agriculture. This has improved the standard of living considerably, but heavy industry still enjoys priority. In 1967, 31.5% of the total investment in the socialized sector of economy (state and cooperative) was devoted to heavy industry (calculated from *Rocznik Statystyczny* [1968], p. 91). In 1970 the share decreased to 26.9% (calculated from *Rocznik Statystyczny* [1971], p. 154). Heavy industry included: production of fuels, metallurgy, machine production, electrical industry, transport stock industry, and chemical indus-

try. Some of this production benefited the consumer, even if indirectly.

[14] Personal interviews.

[15] The degree of overcrowdedness is shown by the following table:

Transportation of Passengers in the Cities
(passenger-per-car/kilometer)

Year	Trams	Trolleys	Buses
1949	9.5	10.9	6.7
1955	10.5	12.8	7.1
1960	10.9	12.5	6.0
1965	11.4	12.5	6.7
1966	11.4	12.5	6.7
1967	10.3	11.1	6.0
1968	8.9	9.2	5.5
1969	9.1	8.9	5.5
1970	9.3	9.0	5.5

SOURCE: *Rocznik Statystyczny* (1971), table 28, p. 452.
NOTE: According to the Polish experts, the load should be no more than 5 to 6 passenger-per-car/kilometer (from an interview with an official of the Ministry of Communal Economy). By 1970 only buses achieved this desirable load. In fact, between 1969 and 1970 there was an increase in load for trams and trolley buses. The worst situation existed in the capital, Warsaw, where the load was 12.4 for trams, 10.5 for trolley buses and 6.3 for buses.

[16] *Mały Rocznik Statystyczny* (1939), p. 35. In 1966, only 67.5% of all urban apartments were supplied with water by pipes, only 47.8% had water closets, 40.0% bathrooms, 43.1% gas supply and 24.9% central heating (*Rocznik Statystyczny* [1968], table 5, p. 393). In 1970, in those cities which had the facilities, only 73.6% of the total population were supplied with water by pipes, 62.4% used the sewer system, and 63.4% the city gas supply (*Rocznik Statystyczny* [1971], table 17, p. 446).

[17] Calculated from, *Rocznik Statystyczny* (1968), tables 41 and 42, p. 417.

[18] *Mały Rocznik Statystyczny* (1939), p. 59. The improvement has been considerable in the countryside—from 3.1 (1931) persons per room.

[19] *Rocznik Statystyczny* (1968), table 3, p. 87; and (1971), table 3, p. 150. These figures include all investments in building construction—industrial as well as housing.

[20] This is illustrated by the following table:

Apartment Construction
(in thousands)

Year	1958	1959	1960	1961	1962	1963	1964	1965	1966	1967	1968	1969	1970
State (including the National Councils)	67.9	66.0	68.3	70.7	71.8	74.1	84.9	92.8	77.8	58.7	46.7	47.0	45.1
National Councils	33.0	33.4	33.8	38.4	42.8	46.4	51.6	55.3	42.2	27.2	18.0	14.6	14.0
Private	57.0	61.5	59.1	54.7	45.3	45.1	45.6	44.4	46.6	49.7	50.5	51.9	53.6
Cooperatives	4.1	10.1	14.7	18.8	21.6	23.2	28.1	33.3	51.6	77.3	92.1	98.1	95.5

SOURCE: *Rocznik Statystyczny* (1968), tables 11 and 12, p. 397; (1971), tables 8 and 9, p. 440; *Uchwała V Zjazdu*, p. 51.

[21] *VI Zjazd Polskiej*, pp. 121–22.

[22] The Statute of 1958, Art. 17.

[23] Decree of the Council of Ministers, February 10, 1960, *Dziennik Ustaw*, no. 18 (1960), entry 11; and for coordination of investments, Resolution of the

Council of Ministers, July 4, 1969, *Monitor Polski*, no. 39 (1969), entry 227 and *Monitor Polski*, no. 31 (1971), entry 198.

24 For example, the Minister of Forestry and Wood Industry requires the associations under his supervision to coordinate their production plans with the presidia of the province national councils (*Biuletyn Ministerstwa Leśnictwa i Przemysłu Drzewnego*, no. 8 [Warszawa 1959], entry 141).

25 Personal interviews.

26 From a speech heard by the author at a session of the Lublin Province National Council, Lublin, December 12, 1961.

27 *VIII Plenum KC PZPR*, p. 57; the Budget Act of 1960, *Dziennik Ustaw*, no. 72 (1959), entry 454; and the Budget Act of 1970, *Dziennik Ustaw*, no. 28 (1970), entry 44.

28 Speech by the chairman of the Presidium of the Lublin City National Council, Lublin, December 22, 1961. In 1968 the relationship between the Lublin City Council and the city's enterprises were basically the same. The enterprises still owed the city considerable funds.

29 Fr. Frankowiak, E. Hałas, A. Łopatka, J. Olzak, Fr. Szczerbal, "Wyniki Usamodzielnienia Rad Narodowych," *Nowe Drogi* 13, no. 10 (Oct. 1959): 125.

30 The Budget Act, July 1, 1958, *Dziennik Ustaw*, no. 45 (1958), entry 221; Bocheński and Gebert, *Zadania i Organizacja*, p. 143; and The Budget Act, November 25, 1970, *Dziennik Ustaw*, no. 28 (1970), entry 44.

31 Gebert, *Komentarz do Ustawy z Dnia*, p. 92. Jan Szreniawski, "Pozycja Prezydium Wojewódzkiej Rady Narodowej," *Annales Universitatis Mariae Curie-Skłodowska* 14, no. 11 (Lublin, 1967), p. 296.

32 See chapter 1. The quotation is from Sand and Błażejczyk, "Z Teorii i Praktyki Samorządu," p. 102.

33 Polish planners do not yet use electronic computers since the computers are scarce and have other priorities. The use of computers would make planning more detailed and hence more centralized.

34 Montias, *Central Planning*, p. 9.

35 Jerzy Szperkowicz, "Wniosek Nie Uzyskał Większości, *Świat* (Nov. 1961): 8-9.

36 Żukowski, "Biuro Gromadzkie," pp. 151–52.

37 Decree of the Council of Ministers, October 3, 1956, *Monitor Polski*, no. 91, entry 1027.

38 Hebda, *Wydziały a Zjednoczenia*, p. 16.

39 Dusza, *Budżety I Gospodarka*, p. 65. Mr. Dusza is Vice-Minister of Finance and one of the leaders of the UPP.

40 Act of Parliament on the Budget, November 25, 1970, *op. cit.*

41 Interviews, e.g., the City National Council of Toruń.

42 "Uchwała Komisji KC PZPR Do Spraw Rad Narodowych" (Resolution of the Committee for the National Councils' Affairs of the Central Committee of the PUWP), (Nov. 1966), p. 4, as quoted by Szreniawski, "Pozycja Prezydium," p. 296. On the same page Dr. Szreniawski states: "The changes in the budget are often very significant. For example, in 1966 on the basis of the 63 resolutions of the presidium of the province council (Lublin—J.P.) 1,323 changes were made."

43 The net profit transferred to the council's treasury is arrived at by subtracting from the planned profit the funds for investment, workers' housing, and other capital accumulation.

44 On balance, the administration of housing brings only losses to the na-

tional councils. This is due to the extremely low rents fixed by the central government. In 1968 the rents were increased considerably (by as much as 50%) in order to make the operation of housing economically more realistic.

[45] Dusza, *Budżety i Gospodarka*, p. 32.

[46] Ibid., p. 99.

[47] The turnover tax is the difference between the wholesale price and the factory price. The factory price is arrived at by adding the planned profit to the planned cost of production.

[48] Personal income tax is not an important item of the state revenue in the communist system of government. In Poland it provides for only about 11% of the total state expenditure.

6

COMMUNISM VIEWED FROM BELOW

Is "a view from below" the only way to analyze the functioning of the communist system? Obviously not. However, undue concentration on the "view from the top" leads to an exaggerated estimation of the control exercised by the top leaders. The view from the top, in the framework of the totalitarian model, tends to minimize the impact of human behavior. It suggests an institutionalized monolithic monster, and it prevents a meaningful arrangement of data on the behavioral patterns of the system. A traditional approach spiced with modern Western political science terminology creates a semblance of a behaviorist and scientific study, but in most cases such studies still await completion with hard data based on practical research in micropolitics.

The view from below irrevocably proves the communist political system to be far from Marx's own ideal of "populist democracy." Many of his accusations against the "formal democracy" of liberal capitalism would fit equally well present-day communism. The state has not "withered away," and the local councils have not become instruments for popular control of decision-making and of state bureaucracy. The elections, while not controlled and manipulated by the owners of private property to the detriment of propertyless, are controlled and manipulated by the party leadership, which, although not having direct legal title to the sources of production, nevertheless decides on the distribution of the fruits of the national economy. The party leaders' control of the political, social, and even moral behavior of the individual stems to a large degree from the same sources as Marx's capitalist control. In both cases, direct physical pressure in the form of political powers is less important in the normal operation of the system than the monopoly of economic incentives and disincentives.

The elections, in which the nomination of candidates is almost completely under the control of the Communist party, do not produce meaningful representation. Their existence, which is expensive and politically unproductive, is the result of the communists' devotion to their own ideology. The recall procedure, which to Marx was to be a vital weapon of popular control, serves the party as a vehicle for removal of "uncooperative" councilmen. The committees, theoretically yet another tie between the rulers and the ruled, are disregarded by the councils themselves, the leadership, and even the public. Their ineffectiveness stems from their realization of their own impotence and from the inclusion in their membership of too many state officials. The public is fully aware that the councils are not, in fact, representative. A study of public complaints clearly indicates that the individual does not demand action of his representative bodies, but begs for favors from the all-powerful bureaucrats. And yet at the same time the councils system produces a more diversified and responsive pattern of behavior than those observable in other authoritarian political structures. The unified state administration engenders a territorial fragmentation of decision-making in the process of adjusting the general policies to the local conditions and pressures. Our study indicates that while the local government bodies disregard in many instances the desires of the general public, they are highly susceptible to pressure from the local power elites and from influential individuals. This relationship is mutual, since the members of the elites, the beneficiaries of the system, exhibit the greatest propensity for support of the system.

Within the councils' structure the weight of power shifted markedly upward in comparison to Marx's original model. The principles of democratic centralism, in practical application, allocate most of the decision-making power to the provinces and, in the individual councils, to the presidia. The presidia themselves are dominated by the full-time members, the salaried state officials. The final power rests in the hands of the chairman. The system can be viewed in terms of power allocation, as a descending pyramid of chairmen, each forming his own power base in his own bailiwick and each subject to pressures from above and from below. Their political behavior is a vector of their ability and willingness to manipulate the system to their best advantage. Their motivation may be advancement of their personal careers as well as the desire to improve conditions in their localities. Their relationship to the party varies with each individual. The party's power to control the initiation of policies and even to directly interfere in administration should not be underestimated. However, most of the chairmen of the national councils are important party leaders in their own right. They are in the inner core of the leadership of the party in the province, county, or commune. Many of them have important connections at the higher levels of the party structure, with the chairmen of the provinces often having direct lines of communication to the national leaders. Theoretically, the chairmen are subordinate to the local first secretaries, but many of them have enough of an independent power base to challenge the secretaries' hegemony. The councils, after all, have their own lines of communication, which converge, at their apex, in the office of the First Secretary of the Communist party. The chairmen and the local first secretaries receive their orders from the same source, but through two different lines of communication. Because of it, each has an independent base of local authority. A struggle between the local first secretary and the chairman is not the rule of the system, but neither is it unknown.

The councils fulfill three important political functions: as implementors of national policies within the framework of the unified state administration; as an important channel of information for the national leadership; and, finally, as mobilizers of popular support. The principle of the unified state administration places the leadership of the councils in the position of manipulators of the outputs of the system. The councils, through their departments, assign the final allocation of values resulting from the national policies. The allocation may vary as to recipients, quantity, quality, and the time span in relation to the intents of the original policy pronounced at the convergence point by the First Secretary of the Communist party. The leaders of the councils, in fact, participate in the decision-making process through their ability to manipulate the rate of absorption. And since every output reverberates into inputs, the leadership of the councils plays an important role in public-policy formulation. By slowing the rate of absorption, they create the system's overload, and under these conditions further conversion cannot take place despite constant inflow of inputs. In that sense their influence on the policy formulation is of a negative rather than a positive kind.

The councils' positive effect on the inputs results from their function as one of the channels of information connecting the people with the top leadership. The leaders of the councils can adjust to their own interests the flow and the nature of information. They also participate in the policy inputs by arguing their specific interests through the official and unofficial channels of communication. They utilize for this purpose the councils' structure, as well as the party, the minor parties, the social and professional organizations, and even the media of communication. They also employ personal contacts and form individual alliances with top party and government leaders. Often they act in unison with other local office holders.

The councils' role as a channel of information is impeded by the local leadership's realization that information is one of the weapons which they can utilize for affecting the outputs in their own favor. Their freedom of action in distortion is constrained by the existence of other channels of communication which are relatively independent of the councils and of one another. This manipulation of the communication lines does not insure the complete reliability of information received by the top leadership, but it prevents gross misrepresentation since all the lines can be cross-checked against one another. In the last analysis, all the lines of communication are bureaucracies and, as such, are manipulated in the interest of specific bureaucratic groups. The system has been unable to develop sources of control and public opinion information so independent of the bureaucracies as to be effective and absolutely useful to the top leadership. The councils, although theoretically the vehicles of public control and of the impact of public opinion, are emasculated by the tight restraints on their participative faculties. Without free debate on political, social, and economic issues, the communist leadership is deprived of the channel of communication theoretically lodged in the structure of local government. The insistence on unanimity in elections and in votes on the council floor produces a seeming acceptance of official policies, but it does not inform the top leadership of the true attitudes of the population. The lack of more meaningful information prevents the central government from devising those policies most likely to achieve popular acceptance and, therefore, those which could be executed with a maximum utilization of human and economic resources. The opinions of the lower officials (commune, and perhaps also county), who are in closer contact with the population and hence better informed, filter through to the higher levels of local government, but seldom reach the central government. Under these circumstances the communist leadership, aware of its inability to ascertain truly the people's political attitudes, perhaps even misjudges the nature and strength of its opposition, and establishes social and political controls greater than are actually necessary for the system's maintenance. Our own study tempts us to assume that the party's ability to manipulate career patterns is quite sufficient for insuring the allegiance and participation of the elite. In our opinion, the loosening of direct controls over the participative functions of the councils would increase the overall efficiency of the system without endangering the system's stability. In fact, an increase in meaningful participation, even if only in local affairs, would contribute considerably to the maintenance of the nationwide political equilibrium, although in some cases it would temporarily upset the existing local political balance.

In their third role, that of mobilizers of support and acceptance and of educators of the "new socialist man," the councils fail even more than in their information-control function. The public perceives the councils as ineffectual "talking societies of mutual adoration." It considers them to be at best a bad joke or at worst a harmful collection of stupid bureaucrats. Very few individuals view the councils as viable political organizations with a life of their own. They are too closely identified with the bureaucratic structure of the state administration to be effective as independent agents of political mobilization. The public assumes the party to be in complete control of the authoritative allocation of values. Hence, it expects the party—and nobody else—to act in the role of chief mobilizer. The attitude of the individual regarding national or local policies is often determined not by the mobilization effort of his local council, but by his acceptance or rejection of the precepts of communist ideology. He is also strongly motivated by his overall integration with or alienation from the system. This is in the majority of cases predetermined by the individual's economic status and by his social and career pattern.

Some individuals recognize the future potential of the unified state administration to function as genuine and territorially deconcentrated conversion units between public demands and public policies. But first, they argue, the councils must assume an independent authority discarding the permanent appointive bureaucracy and acting without any direct interference by the party in day-to-day policy formulation and implementation.

The deconcentration of administration necessitated by the complexity of the modern industrial society allocated more authority to the local government. The growing economic responsibility and self-sufficiency of the councils was only partially the result of political pressures brought about by the 1956 limited revolution. Equally important were the administrative-economic considerations. The overcentralization, which might have had some political and economic justification in the immediate postwar period, became highly disfunctional as the communist power gained the plateau of stability and legitimacy. Also the increasing complexity of the economic structure required deconcentration of its administration, because the decision-making bottlenecks at the top would have prevented further economic progress. The decollectivization of agriculture, the definite—even if sporadic—encouragement for private crafts and some private trade, and, above all, the growing economic importance of the cooperative societies made the central planning and coordination even more haphazard than before. The central government was not able to achieve the fulfillment of its overall economic policies, when the economy was administered directly from Warsaw. The private sector, especially dominant in agriculture, had to be induced into the desired performance by persuasion and by financial and material allocation incentives. This required direct involvement and contacts at the lowest levels of the administrative structures. Finally, the increasing relative shortages of sources of production forced the planners to search for idle resources. The councils, when given certain autonomy in utilization of the local resources, contributed considerably to the tapping of economic potentialities which otherwise could not have been located by the central authorities. Politically, the deconcentration of economic administration and the allocation to the national councils of the responsibility for most of the consumer goods industry, trades, and services created a protective shield guarding the heights of the central leadership. Now the councils themselves would be the targets of popular dissatisfaction resulting from commodities shortages, antiquated services, and ineffective distribution. The central leadership could continue investment in heavy industry, abdicating at least a part of the responsibility for the general standard of living to the local government.[1]

The deconcentration and, conjointly, the growing importance of local councils were no doubt beneficial to the general public. The government was brought closer to the level of the individual citizen, and it became more responsive to, even if not more representative of, his wishes and pressures. Our study indicates, however, that the deconcentration, rather than increasing the equality of distribution and responsiveness, enhanced the political and economic power of the elite and influential. Poland and the other East-Central European communist countries are not necessarily moving toward greater democratization, if democracy means equality of opportunity and of distribution of the authoritatively allocated values. They are creating societies with a growing institutionalization of elite at local and national levels. The elite obtains special privileges in exchange for support of and cooperation with the existing system. Poland is not becoming more communistic or more democratic, but rather is moving in the direction of an elitist technocracy. The system will remain in evolutionary equilibrium as long as the top party leadership recognizes that it has increasingly to share its power with the increasingly demanding elite. It cannot afford to aggravate them to the point that members of the elite become leaders of the discontented masses, for then the top leadership would lose its control and would be replaced by a new coalition of communists and technocrats. The upheaval of December 1970 proves this point. The change of the leadership, however, occurred even before the dissatisfied elite found common cause with the striking workers. Because of this it gave more power to the new leadership, which immediately and wisely moved to pacify the masses and the elite.

In an overall evaluation, the system of local councils falls short of its theoretical-idealistic, as well as its practical, precepts. We feel that our view from below permitted discovery of the new dynamics of the communist political system. It also opened the door to an unsuspected wealth of meaningful political data which could be fitted into a more flexible theoretical framework.

NOTES TO CONCLUSION

[1] The precise mistake of Gomułka's administration, which led to its fall in December 1970, was the immediate increase in food prices. Were the prices raised gradually, province by province and by the province national councils, the workers explosion on the Baltic coast would have been isolated and directed rather toward the local government than against the center. Gomułka, by his centralized action, blew the protective cover provided by the institution of the national councils.

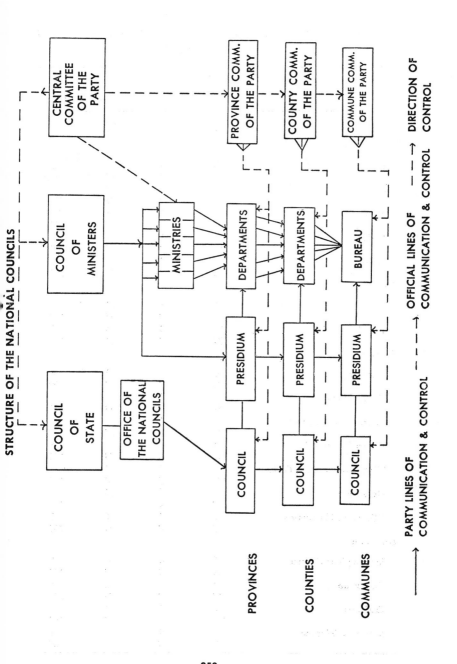

STRUCTURE OF THE NATIONAL COUNCILS

CENTRAL COMMITTEE OF THE PARTY

PROVINCE COMM. OF THE PARTY

COUNTY COMM. OF THE PARTY

COMMUNE COMM. OF THE PARTY

COUNCIL OF MINISTERS

MINISTRIES

DEPARTMENTS

DEPARTMENTS

BUREAU

COUNCIL OF STATE

OFFICE OF THE NATIONAL COUNCILS

PRESIDIUM

PRESIDIUM

PRESIDIUM

COUNCIL

COUNCIL

COUNCIL

PROVINCES

COUNTIES

COMMUNES

DIRECTION OF CONTROL

OFFICIAL LINES OF COMMUNICATION & CONTROL

PARTY LINES OF COMMUNICATION & CONTROL

"Is the National Council: state administration or self-government or both?"
(percentages in italics)

	State Adminis- tration	Self Govern- ment	Both	Total
Total Answers	46	5	24	75
	61	*7*	*32*	*100*
Age				
18–25	3	0	2	5
	60	*0*	*40*	*100*
26–35	11	2	7	20
	55	*10*	*35*	*100*
36–45	6	2	6	14
	43	*14*	*43*	*100*
46–55	10	1	4	15
	67	*7*	*26*	*100*
56+	16	0	5	21
	76	*0*	*24*	*100*
Sex				
Male	31	5	20	56
	55	*9*	*36*	*100*
Female	15	0	4	19
	79	*0*	*21*	*100*
Education				
Primary	6	0	0	6
	100	*0*	*0*	*100*
Trade School	4	0	2	6
	67	*0*	*33*	*100*
General High School	8	0	9	17
	47	*0*	*53*	*100*
Higher Technical	4	0	2	6
	67	*0*	*33*	*100*
Higher Communist Party	1	0	0	1
	100	*0*	*0*	*100*
University	22	5	10	37
	59	*14*	*27*	*100*
Other and No Answer	1	0	1	2
	50	*0*	*50*	*100*
Occupation				
Independent Farmer	5	0	0	5
	100	*0*	*0*	*100*
Housewife	4	0	2	6
	67	*0*	*33*	*100*
Craftsman	2	0	0	2
	100	*0*	*0*	*100*
Industrial Worker	1	0	0	1
	100	*0*	*0*	*100*

Appendix 2—Table 1 (continued)

	State Adminis- tration	Self Govern- ment	Both	Total
Clerk	6	0	3	9
	67	*0*	*33*	*100*
Manager	13	0	12	25
	52	*0*	*48*	*100*
Professional or Artistic	12	5	6	23
	52	*22*	*26*	*100*
Other and No Answer	3	0	1	4
	75	*0*	*25*	*100*
Social Origin				
Peasant	16	2	6	24
	67	*8*	*25*	*100*
Worker	3	0	2	5
	60	*0*	*40*	*100*
Intelligentsia	22	0	10	32
	69	*0*	*31*	*100*
No Answer	5	3	6	14
	36	*21*	*43*	*100*
Economic Status				
Very Good	10	1	4	15
	67	*7*	*26*	*100*
Good	12	1	13	26
	46	*4*	*50*	*100*
Average	18	3	6	27
	67	*11*	*22*	*100*
Bad	6	0	1	7
	86	*0*	*14*	*100*
Party Affiliation				
PUWP	11	2	10	23
	48	*9*	*43*	*100*
UPP	1	2	2	5
	20	*40*	*40*	*100*
Nonparty	33	1	8	42
	79	*2*	*19*	*100*
No Answer	1	0	4	5
	20	*0*	*80*	*100*
Location				
City	37	5	24	66
	56	*8*	*36*	*100*
Village	9	0	0	9
	100	*0*	*0*	*100*
Region				
Industrial	25	3	15	43
	58	*7*	*35*	*100*
Agricultural	21	2	9	32
	66	*6*	*28*	*100*

COMMUNIST LOCAL GOVERNMENT

NOTE: The survey as shown in this and the following tables was taken between November 1961 and April 1962. The method employed could best be called a chaotic sample. The author interviewed whomever fell into his "net"—local officials, university staff, casual aquaintances, guests at cocktail parties and dinners, auto stoppers. The questions were memorized and the same set was used in all conversations. Only on rare occasions were the answers written down immediately. In most cases the author reconstructed the responses from memory. In no way do we claim scientific purity and our findings, while interesting, cannot be treated as definite, if measured by the accepted standards of statistical sampling. Altogether about five hundred individuals were interviewed. Out of this number only eighty respondents gave a complete set of answers and were used in our tables. The meaning and purpose of most of the questions is clear from the tables and their discusstion in the text. Only a few need further elaboration. *Age:* The division into five age groups was based on the assumption that education and integration in a social and political system are variables of political attitudes. The following table illustrates the significance of the five age groups:

Age in 1961	25	35	45	55
Born	1936	1926	1916	1906
Age in 1939	3	13	23	33
Age in 1945	9	19	29	39
	Completely educated under the communist system.	University education and social integration under the communist system.	University education before the World War II. Social integration disrupted by the war and resumed after the war.	Complete education and social integration before the World War II

NOTE: By social integration we mean, an adult member of the existing social and political system with an assumed solidified career pattern.

Education: The education classification presents a problem due to changes in the system. The prewar pattern included compulsory sixth grade primary education for ages between seven and thirteen. In some cases seventh grade was provided for those children who did not enter secondary education. Alongside the general primary school there existed trade schools designed for training craftsmen. Secondary education was divided into general high school of six grades (ages thirteen to eighteen) and vocational high schools (technical), some of them extending beyond the secondary school education, but stopping short of university degrees. Normally, only the general high school diploma offered entry into universities. During the German occupation (1939–1945) the whole educational system was disrupted by the German attitude of providing only a minimum education for Poles. Universities and general high schools were abolished with only the vocational schools providing the maximum education for a few "chosen" ones. Some general high schools and some university courses were maintained in conspiracy by the Polish underground authorities. The immediate postwar period can best be described as chaotic. Although education was reestablished in general terms on the prewar pattern, students' levels of preparation varied greatly. Eventually the system evolved into compulsory education of seven grades of primary school (ages seven to fourteen), secondary schools of four grades (ages fourteen to eighteen) and four or five years at the university level. Starting with the 1961–1962 school year compulsory education was being gradually extended to eight grades (ages seven to fifteen) with the complementary reduction of high school education to three grades (ages fifteen to eighteen). In the pre- as well as the postwar period not all primary schools offered the full set of grades (six, seven or eight). The inferior schools, with three, four or five grades existed mostly in the rural areas. Their number decreased considerably in the last twenty years, but there are still primary schools in Poland which offer education short of the required compulsory eighth grade level. Some of the primary schools provide trade education (classified in our tables as trade schools) and there also exists a large number of vocational schools at the secondary level (not represented in our sample). Higher education today consists of universities, and separate higher schools of economics, higher schools of agriculture, medical academies, higher pedagogical institutes and art colleges; all classified in our sample as universities. At the same level there exist politechnical institutes, coded in the sample as higher technical education. Finally, there is the higher school of social and political studies administered by the Central Committee of the PUWP, which provides a university level of training for the leaders of the Party. The separation of individuals with the higher technical education from the rest of the university educated group was done in order to test the responses of those who are most directly identified with the process of industrialization.

Economic status: The following scale of economic standard was adopted on the advice of Polish economists with the monthly income in *zlotys* (before taxes and deductions): Very good, 3,000 and over; Good, up to 3,000; Average, up to 2,000; Bad, up to 1,000.

Region: The character of a region was classified as predominantly industrial or agricultural on the basis of its general pattern of production and employment.

Appendix 3—Table 2

"Does the activity of your national council express the will and wishes of the inhabitants of the territory under the council's authority?"
(percentage in italics)

	Yes	No	Total
Total Answers	34	38	72
	47	*53*	*100*
Age			
18–25	1	3	4
	25	*75*	*100*
26–35	13	7	20
	65	*35*	*100*
36–45	6	7	13
	46	*54*	*100*
46–55	8	6	14
	57	*43*	*100*
56 +	6	15	21
	29	*71*	*100*
Sex			
Male	29	23	52
	56	*44*	*100*
Female	5	15	20
	25	*75*	*100*
Education			
Primary	1	7	8
	13	*87*	*100*
Trade School	4	2	6
	67	*33*	*100*
General High School	8	9	17
	47	*53*	*100*
Higher Technical	2	4	6
	33	*67*	*100*
Higher Communist Party	0	1	1
	0	*100*	*100*
University	18	15	33
	55	*45*	*100*
Other and No Answer	1	0	1
	100	*0*	*100*
Occupation			
Independent Farmer	1	6	7
	14	*86*	*100*
Housewive	3	3	6
	50	*50*	*100*
Craftsman	0	2	2
	0	*100*	*100*
Industrial Worker	0	1	1
	0	*100*	*100*
Clerk	5	4	9
	56	*44*	*100*

	Yes	No	Total
Manager	16	7	23
	70	30	100
Professional or Artistic	9	11	20
	45	55	100
Other and No Answer	0	4	4
	0	100	100
Social Origin			
Peasant	12	12	24
	50	50	100
Worker	2	2	4
	50	50	100
Intelligentsia	10	22	32
	31	69	100
No Answer	10	2	12
	83	17	100
Economic Status			
Very Good	8	5	13
	62	38	100
Good	14	10	24
	58	42	100
Average	11	16	27
	41	59	100
Bad	1	6	7
	14	86	100
No Answer	0	1	1
	0	100	100
Party Affiliation			
PUWP	18	2	20
	90	10	100
UPP	3	0	3
	100	0	100
Nonparty	9	35	44
	20	80	100
No Answer	4	1	5
	80	20	100
Location			
City	32	30	62
	52	48	100
Village	2	8	10
	20	80	100
Region			
Industrial	22	19	41
	54	46	100
Agriculture	12	19	31
	39	61	100

Appendix 4—Diagram 2

INPUT—OUTPUT ANALYSIS—POLISH POLITICAL SYSTEM CAL

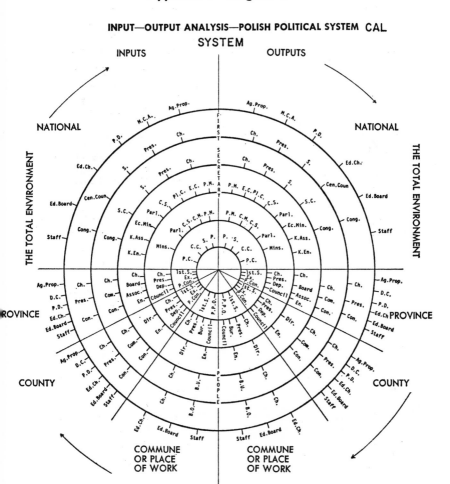

NOTE: This diagram was first published in my article: "Communist Administration in Poland Within the Frame-Work of Input-Output Analysis," *East European Quarterly* 6, no. 2 (June 1972): 230–56.

Legend to Appendix 4

(Circles Starting From the Inside)

CIRCLE 1. THE POLISH UNITED WORKERS' PARTY—THE COMMUNIST PARTY

National

P.	Politburo of the Central Committee
S.	Secretariat of the Central Committee
C.C.	Central Committee
P.C.	Party Congress

Province and County

1st. S.	1st Secretary
Ex.	Executive Committee
P. Con.	Party Conference

Commune or Place of Work

1st. S.	1st Secretary
P.P.O.	Primary Party Organization

CIRCLE 2. GENERAL ADMINISTRATION

National

P.M.	Prime Minister
C.M.	Council of Ministers
C.S.	Council of State
Parl.	Parliament *(Sejm)*
Mins.	Ministries

Province and County

Ch.	Chairman of the Presidium of the National Council
Pres.	Presidium of the National Council

Dep.	Department of the National Council
Council	National Council

Commune

Ch.	Chairman of the Presidium of the National Council
Pres.	Presidium of the National Council
Bur.	Bureau of the National Council
Council	National Council

CIRCLE 3. ECONOMIC ADMINISTRATION

National

P.M.	Prime Minister
E.C.	Economic Committee of the Council of Ministers
Pl.C.	Planning Commission
C.S.	Council of State
Parl.	Parliament *(Sejm)*
Ec. Mins.	Economic Ministries
K. Ass.	Associations of Key Industries
K. En.	Key Enterprises

Province

Ch.	Chairman of the Board
Board	Governing Board of the Association
Assoc.	Association of Local Industries
En.	Enterprise

County and Commune

Dir.	Director
En.	Enterprise

CIRCLE 4. MINOR PARTIES—THE UNITED PEASANT PARTY AND THE DEMOCRATIC PARTY

National

Ch.	Chairman of the Presidium

Province and County

Ch.	Chairman
Com.	Committee

Pres.	Presidium of the Supreme Committee	Con.	Conference
S.	Secretariat of the Supreme Committee		*Commune or Place of Work*
S.C.	Supreme Committee	Ch.	Chairman
Cong.	Congress	B.U.	The Basic Unit

CIRCLE 5. SOCIAL AND PROFESSIONAL ORGANIZATIONS

National

Ch.	Chairman
Pres.	Presidium
S.	Secretariat
Cen. Coun.	Central Council
Cong.	Congress

Province and County

Ch.	Chairman
Pres.	Presidium
Con.	Conference

Commune or Place of Work

Ch.	Chairman
B. O.	Basic Organization

CIRCLE 6. MEDIA OF COMMUNICATION

National

Ag. Prop.	Department of Agitation and Propaganda of the Secretariat of the Central Committee of the Polish United Workers' Party
M.C.A.	Ministry of Culture and Arts
P.D.	Press Department of the Minor Parties or Social or Professional Organizations, where applicable (for media owned by these organizations)
Ed. Ch.	Editor in Chief or Chairman of the Board
Ed. Board	Editorial or Managerial Board
Staff	Reporters, Correspondents, Writers, Producers, Directors, Announcers, Actors, etc.

Province or County

Ag. Prop.	Department of Agitation and Propaganda of the Executive Committee of the Polish United Workers' Party
D.C.	Department of Culture of the Presidium of the National Council
P.D.	Press Department of the Minor Parties or Social or Professional Organizations, when applicable
Ed. Ch.	Editor in Chief or Chairman of the Board
Ed. Board	Editorial or Managerial Board
Staff	Reporters, Correspondents, Writers, Producers, Directors, Announcers, Actors, etc.

Commune or Place of Work

Ed. Ch.	Editor in Chief or Director
Ed. Board	Editorial or Managerial Board
Staff	Reporters, Correspondents, Writers, Producers, Directors, Announcers, Actors, etc.

Appendix 5—Table 3

Degree of Involvement and Interest in Local Politics
(percentages in italics)

	Gladia-tor	Specta-tor 1	Specta-tor 2	Apa-thetic 1	Apa-thetic 2	Total
Total Answers	14	20	20	6	13	73
	19.1	*27.4*	*27.4*	*8.3*	*17.8*	*100*
Age						
18–25	0	0	3	1	0	4
	0	*0*	*75.0*	*25.0*	*0*	*100*
26–35	2	5	7	1	4	19
	10.5	*26.3*	*36.8*	*5.3*	*21.1*	*100*
36–45	3	5	3	0	3	14
	21.4	*35.8*	*21.4*	*0*	*21.4*	*100*
46–55	4	6	2	2	2	16
	25.0	*37.5*	*12.5*	*12.5*	*12.5*	*100*
56 +	5	4	5	2	4	20
	25.0	*20.0*	*25.0*	*10.0*	*20.0*	*100*
Sex						
Male	11	18	15	1	6	51
	21.5	*35.3*	*29.4*	*2.0*	*11.8*	*100*
Female	3	2	5	5	7	22
	13.6	*9.2*	*22.7*	*22.7*	*31.8*	*100*
Education						
Primary	0	0	0	2	5	7
	0	*0*	*0*	*28.6*	*71.4*	*100*
Trade School	1	1	2	0	0	4
	25.0	*25.0*	*50.0*	*0*	*0*	*100*
General High School	2	2	6	2	5	17
	11.8	*11.8*	*35.3*	*11.8*	*29.3*	*100*
Higher Technical	0	3	1	1	1	6
	0	*50.0*	*16.7*	*16.7*	*16.7*	*100*
Higher Communist Party	0	1	0	0	0	1
	0	*100.0*	*0*	*0*	*0*	*100*
University	10	12	11	1	2	36
	27.8	*33.3*	*30.6*	*2.8*	*5.5*	*100*
Other and No Answer	1	1	0	0	0	2
	50.0	*50.0*	*0*	*0*	*0*	*100*
Occupation						
Independent Farmer	0	0	0	2	4	6
	0	*0*	*0*	*33.3*	*66.7*	*100.0*
Housewife	0	0	2	1	3	6
	0	*0*	*3.33*	*16.7*	*50.0*	*100.0*
Craftsman	0	0	1	0	0	1
	0	*0*	*100.0*	*0*	*0*	*100.0*
Industrial Worker	0	0	0	0	1	1
	0	*0*	*0*	*0*	*100.0*	*100.0*
Clerk	0	1	5	0	1	7
	0	*14.3*	*71.4*	*0*	*14.3*	*100.0*

	Gladia-tor	Specta-tor 1	Specta-tor 2	Apa-thetic 1	Apa-thetic 2	Total
Manager	9	12	3	0	0	24
	37.5	*50.0*	*12.5*	*0*	*0*	*100.0*
Professional or						
Artistic	5	7	8	2	2	24
	20.8	*29.3*	*33.3*	*8.3*	*8.3*	*100.0*
Other and No						
Answer	0	0	1	1	2	4
	0	*0*	*25.0*	*25.0*	*50.0*	*100.0*
Social Origin						
Peasant	5	7	4	3	4	23
	21.7	*30.4*	*17.4*	*13.1*	*17.4*	*100.0*
Worker	1	1	2	0	1	5
	20.0	*20.0*	*40.0*	*0*	*20.0*	*100.0*
Intelligentsia	4	5	13	3	8	33
	12.1	*15.2*	*39.4*	*9.1*	*24.2*	*100.0*
No Answer	4	7	1	0	0	12
	33.3	*58.3*	*8.4*	*0*	*0*	*100.0*
Economic Status						
Very Good	7	4	2	2	0	15
	46.7	*26.7*	*13.3*	*13.3*	*0*	*100.0*
Good	6	8	8	0	2	24
	25.0	*33.3*	*33.3*	*0*	*8.4*	*100.0*
Average	1	8	9	3	6	27
	3.8	*29.6*	*33.3*	*11.1*	*22.2*	*100.0*
Bad	0	0	1	1	5	7
	0	*0*	*14.3*	*14.3*	*71.4*	*100.0*
Party Affiliation						
PUWP	9	9	5	0	0	23
	39.1	*39.1*	*21.8*	*0*	*0*	*100.0*
UPP	3	0	0	0	0	3
	100.0	*0*	*0*	*0*	*0*	*100.0*
Nonparty	1	8	14	6	13	42
	2.4	*19.1*	*33.3*	*14.3*	*30.9*	*100.0*
No Answer	1	3	1	0	0	5
	20.0	*60.0*	*20.0*	*0*	*0*	*100.0*
Location						
City	14	20	17	4	11	66
	21.2	*30.3*	*25.8*	*6.0*	*16.7*	*100.0*
Village	0	0	3	2	2	7
	0	*0*	*42.8*	*28.6*	*28.6*	*100.0*
Region						
Industrial	10	13	12	3	6	44
	22.7	*29.5*	*27.3*	*6.8*	*13.7*	*100.0*
Agricultural	4	7	8	3	7	22
	13.8	*24.1*	*27.7*	*10.3*	*24.1*	*100.0*

NOTE: *Gladiator* is, was, or would like to be a councilman; *Spectator 1* takes part in meeting with his councilman and/or attends sessions; *Spectator 2* reads literature or listens to mass communication concerning the council; *Apathetic 1* shows no interest; *Apathetic 2* has a negative attitude toward his council.

Appendix 6—Diagram 3

PARTICIPATION OF THE FOUR AGE GROUPS
(GLADIATORS & SPECTATORS 1 & 2)

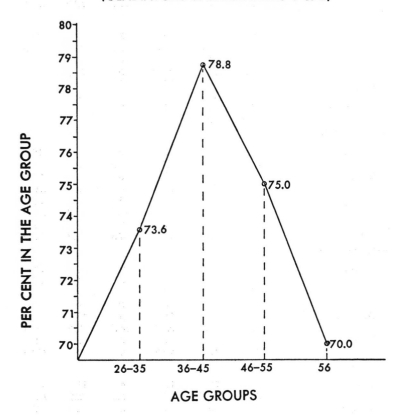

Appendix 7—Table 4

"How do you evaluate the work of your council?"
(percentages in italics)

	Positively	Negatively	Total
Total Answers	39	36	75
	52.0	*48.0*	*100.0*
Age			
18–25	2	3	5
	40.0	*60.0*	*100.0*
26–35	14	6	20
	70.0	*30.0*	*100.0*
36–45	9	5	14
	64.3	*35.7*	*100.0*
46–55	6	9	15
	40.0	*60.0*	*100.0*
56+	8	13	21
	38.1	*61.9*	*100.0*
Sex			
Male	34	21	55
	61.8	*38.2*	*100.0*
Female	5	15	20
	25.0	*75.0*	*100.0*
Education			
Primary	2	6	8
	25.0	*75.0*	*100.0*
Trade School	5	1	6
	83.3	*16.7*	*100.0*
General High School	9	8	17
	52.9	*47.1*	*100.0*
Higher Technical	2	4	6
	33.3	*66.7*	*100.0*
Higher Communist Party	0	1	1
	0	*100.0*	*100.0*
University	21	15	36
	58.3	*41.7*	*100.0*
Other and No Answer	0	1	1
	0	*100.0*	*100.0*
Occupation			
Independent Farmer	2	5	7
	28.6	*71.4*	*100.0*
Housewife	2	4	6
	40.0	*60.0*	*100.0*
Craftsman	0	2	2
	0	*100.0*	*100.0*
Industrial Worker	0	1	1
	0	*100.0*	*100.0*
Clerk	6	2	8
	75.0	*25.0*	*100.0*

Appendix 7—Table 4 (continued)

	Positively	Negatively	Total
Manager	15	8	23
	65.2	34.8	100.0
Professional or Artistic	14	10	24
	58.3	41.7	100.0
Other and No Answer	0	4	4
	0	100.0	100.0
Social Origin			
Peasant	16	9	25
	64.0	36.0	100.0
Worker	2	3	5
	40.0	60.0	100.0
Intelligentsia	11	23	34
	32.4	67.6	100.0
No Answer	10	1	11
	90.9	9.1	100.0
Economic Status			
Very Good	9	5	14
	64.3	35.7	100.0
Good	15	11	26
	57.7	42.3	100.0
Average	14	14	28
	50.0	50.0	100.0
Bad	1	5	6
	16.7	83.3	100.0
No Answer	0	1	1
	0	100.0	100.0
Party Affiliation			
PUWP	19	3	22
	86.4	13.6	100.0
UPP	2	1	3
	66.7	33.3	100.0
Nonparty	14	31	45
	31.1	68.9	100.0
No Answer	4	1	5
	80.0	20.0	100.0
Location			
City	35	31	66
	53.0	47.0	100.0
Village	4	5	9
	44.4	55.6	100.0
Region			
Industrial	24	22	46
	52.2	47.8	100.0
Agricultural	15	14	29
	51.7	48.3	100.0

BIBLIOGRAPHY

GENERAL WORKS ON POLAND

1. Barnett, Clifford R., et al. *Poland: Its People, Its Society, Its Culture*, New Haven: HRAF, 1958.
2. Benes, Vaclav L. and Norman F. G. Pounds. *Poland*, London: E. Benn, 1970.
3. Bethell, Nicholas. *Gomulka: His Poland, His Communism*, New York: Holt, Rinehart and Winston, 1969.
4. Bromke, Adam. *Poland's Politics: Idealism vs. Realism*, Cambridge, Mass.: Harvard University Press, 1967.
5. Dziewanowski, M. K. *The Communist Party of Poland: An Outline of History*, Cambridge, Mass.: Harvard University Press, 1959.
6. Galbraith, John K. *Journey to Poland and Yugoslavia: 1958*, Cambridge, Mass.: Harvard University Press, 1958.
7. Gibney, Frank. *The Frozen Revolution, Poland: A Study in Communist Decay*, New York: Farrar, Straus and Cudahy, 1959.
8. Halecki, Oscar, ed., *Poland*, New York: Praeger, 1957.
9. Hiscocks, Richard. *Poland, Bridge for the Abyss?*, London: Oxford University Press, 1963.
10. Karol, K. S. *Visa for Poland*, (tr. by Mervyn Savill) London: MacGibon & Kee, 1959.
11. Korbonski, Stefan. *Warsaw in Chains*, New York: Macmillan, 1959.
12. Kruszewski, Anthony Z. *The Order-Neise Boundary and Poland's Modernization*, New York: Praeger, 1972.
13. Kuncewicz, Maria, ed. *The Modern Polish Mind*, London: Secker & Warburg, 1963.
14. Lane, Arthur, Bliss. *I Saw Poland Betrayed*, Indianapolis: Bobbs-Merrill, 1948.
15. Lednicki, Waclaw. *Russia, Poland, and the West*, London: Hutchison, 1954.
16. Lewis, Flora. *Case History of Hope: The Story of Poland's Peaceful Revolution*, New York: Doubleday, 1958.
17. Morrison, James F. *The Polish People's Republic*, Baltimore: Johns Hopkins University Press, 1968.
18. Pirages, Clark. *Modernization and Political Tension Management: Case Study of Poland*, New York: Praeger, 1972.
19. Pounds, Norman J. G. *Poland Between East and West*, Princeton, N.J.: Van Nostrand, 1964.
20. Rozek, Edward J. *Allied Wartime Diplomacy: A Pattern in Poland*, New York: Wiley, 1958.

21. Sharp, Samuel. *Poland, White Eagle on a Red Field*, Cambridge, Mass.: Harvard University Press, 1953.
22. Shneiderman, S. L. *The Warsaw Heresy*, New York: Horizon, 1959.
23. Staar, Richard F. *Poland, 1944–1962: The Sovietization of a Captive People*, Baton Rouge: Louisiana State University Press, 1962.
24. Stehle, Hansjakob. *The Independent Satellite, Society and Politics in Poland since 1945*, New York: Praeger, 1965.
25. Syrop, Konrad. *Spring in October—The Polish Revolution of 1956*, New York: Praeger, 1957.
    Syrop, Konrad. *Poland*, London: Hale, 1968.
26. Zawodny, J. K. *Death In The Forest*, Notre Dame, Ind.: University of Notre Dame Press, 1962.
27. Woods, William. *Poland: Eagle in The East*, New York: Hill and Wang, 1968.

BIBLIOGRAPHY

WORKS QUOTED

Almond, Gabriel and Verba, Sidney. *The Civic Culture.* Princeton: Princeton University Press, 1963.

B., Cz. "Jak Przekształca Się Nasz System Planowania i Zarządzania." *Nowe Drogi* 12 (April 1958).

Babiuch, Edward. "Szczera Rozmowa na Wsi." *Nowi Drogi* 15 (June 1961).

Bigo, Tadeusz; Jendrośka, Jan; Wołoch, Józef. *Pozycja Ustrojowa Komisji Rady Narodowej.* Wrocław, Warszawa, Kraków: Ossolineum, 1966.

Biskupski, Kazimierz. *Władza i Lud.* Warszawa: Książka i Wiedza, 1956.

Bocheński, Tadeusz and Gebert, Stanisław. *Zadania i Organizacja Pracy Rad Narodowych.* Warszawa: Wydawnictwo Związkowe CRZZ, 1966.

Bocheński, T.; Gebert, S.; Starościak, J. *Rady Narodowe, Ustrój i Działalność.* Warszawa: Wydawnictwo Prawnicze, 1971.

Borkowski, Janusz. "Formy Działania Prezydiów Rad Narodowych," *Problemy Rad Narodowych, Studia i Materiały,* no. 9. Wrocław, Warszawa, Kraków: Ossolineum, 1967.

Burda, Andrzej. *Rozwój Ustroju Politycznego Polski Ludowej.* Warszawa: Państwowe Wydawnictwo Naukowe, 1967.

Chwistek, Józef. "Wpływ Instytucji Wiążących Zaleceń I Opinii Na Prawne I Faktyczne Pozycje Komisji Rad Narodowych." *Problemy Rad Narodowych, Studia i Materiały,* no. 12. Wrocław, Warszawa, Kraków: Ossolineum, 1968.

Czyżewski, Wacław. *Więc Zarepetuj Broń.* Warszawa: Wydawnictwo Ministerstwa Obrony Narodowej, 1964.

Djilas, Milovan. *The New Class.* New York: Praeger, 1960.

Dusza, Jan. *Budżety i Gospodarka Rad Narodowych.* Warszawa: Zjednoczone Stronnictwo Ludowe, 1962.

Dziennik Urzędowy (The Official Gazette of the Council of Ministers).

Dziennik Urzędowy Ministerstwa Finansów (The Official Gazette of the Ministry of Finance).

Dziennik Ustaw Polskiej Rzeczypospolitej Ludowej (The Official Gazette of the Polish People's Republic). Warszawa. (Before 1951 called *Dziennik Ustaw Rzeczypospolitej Polskiej*).

Ehrlich, Stanisław; Maneli, Mieczysław; Wesołowski, Włodzmierz; and Zawadski, Sylwester. *Spór o Istotę Państwa.* Warszawa: Książka i Wiedza, 1961.

Engels, Frederick. *The Origin of the Family, Private Property and the State,* Chicago: C. H. Kerr & Co., 1902.

——. *Herr Eugen Dühring Revolution in Science (Anti-Dühring),* New York: International Publishers, 1935.

Frankowiak, Fr.; Hałas, E.; Łopatka, A.; Olzak, J.; and Szczerbal, Fr. "Wyniki Usamodzielnienia Rad Narodowych." *Nowe Drogi* 13 (Oct. 1959).

Gebert, Stanisław. *Komentarz do Ustawy z Dnia 25 Stycznia 1958 o Radach Narodowych*. Warszawa: Wydawnictwo Prawnicze, 1961.

――――. *Komentarz do Ustawy o Radach Narodowych*.Warszawa: Wydawnictwo Prawnicze, 1964.

Gomułka, Władysław. *Przemówienia, 1959*. Warszawa: Książka i Wiedza, 1960.

――――. *Przemówienia, 1960*. Warszawa: Książa i Wiedza, 1961.

――――. "Referat 1-go Sekretarza K.C., Sprawozdanie Komitetu Centralnego I Wytyczne Rozwoju PRL w Latach 1966–70." *Nowe Drogi* 18 (July 1964).

――――. "Referat Wprowadzający 1-go Sekretarza KC PZPR Tow. Władysława Gomułki." *III Plenum KC PZPR—Wybory do Sejmu i Rad Narodowych*. Warszawa: Książka i Wiedza, 1965.

――――. "Przemówienie do IX-go Plenum Komitetu Centralnego PZPR." *Nowe Drogi* 13 (June 1959).

――――. *Stanowisko Partii Zgodne Z Wolą Narodu*. Przemówienie Wygłoszone Na Spotkaniu Z Warszawskim Aktywem Partyjnym 19 Marca 1968 r. Warszawa: Książka i Wiedza, 1968.

Groszyk, Henryk. "Geneza i Istota Centralizmu Demokratycznego." *Annales Universitatis Mariae Curie-Skłodowska*. Sectio D, vol. 4, no. 5 (1957).

Gwiżdż, Andrzej and Zakrzewska, Janina, eds. *Konstytucja i Podstawowe Akty Ustawodawcze Polskiej Rzeczypospolitej Ludowej*. Warszawa: Wydawnictwo Prawnicze, 1958.

Hazard, John N., *The Soviet System of Government*. Chicago: The University of Chicago Press: 1960.

Hebda, Antoni, "Wydziały a Zjednoczenia w Świetle Przepisów, Praktyki i Propozycji." *Gospodarka i Administracja Terenowa* 2 (December 1961).

Instytut Nauk Prawnych Polskiej Adademii Nauk. *Problemy Rad Narodowych —Studia i Materiały*, no. 1. Warszawa: Państwowe Wydawnictwo Naukowe, 1964.

――――. *Problemy Rad Narodowych—Studia i Materiały*, nos. 3, 9, 10, 12, 14. Warszawa: Ossolineum, 1965, 1967, 1968, 1969.

Iserzon, Emanuel. "Kierunki Reformy Orzecznictwa Karno—Administracyjnego." *Państwo i Prawo* 11 (November 1961).

――――. "Kontrola 'Związanej' i 'Swobodnej' Działalności Administracji." *Kontrola Państwowa* 7 (March 1962).

Iwaszkiewicz, Jarosław. "Przemiany Polaków." *Polityka* 12 (November 1968).

Izdebski, Z. "Zespoły Obywatelskie w Administracji Jako Wyraz Realizacji Konstytucyjnej Zasady Udziału Mas w Rządzeniu Państwem." In *Problemy Rad Narodowych, Studia i Materiały*, no. 1. Warsawa: Państwowe Wydawnictwo Naukowe, 1964.

Janikowski, Mieczysław. *Próba Tamtych Dni*. Warszawa: Wydawnictwo Ministerstwa Obrony Narodowej, 1964.

Januszko, Zbigniew. "Rola Rad Narodowych w Zarządzaniu Gospodarką." *Nowe Drogi* 15 (March 1961).

BIBLIOGRAPHY

Jarosz, Zdzisław. *System Wyborczy PRL*. Warszawa: Państwowe Wydawnictwo Naukowe, 1969.

Jaroszyński, Maurycy. *Zagadnienia Rad Narodowych*. Warszawa: Państwowe Wydawnictwo Naukowe, 1961.

Kasperski, Witold. "Spółdzielczość Mieszkaniowa Wobec Nowych Zadań." *Gospodarka i Administracja Terenowa* 2 (December 1961).

Kolaja, Jiri. *A Polish Factory*. Lexington: University of Kentucky Press, 1960.

Kołodziejczyk, Tadeusz. "Nowy Garnitur." *Polityka* 10 (April 2, 1966).

————. "Wysoka Rada Podlegać Raczy," *Polityka* 10 (April 16, 1966).

Korbonski, Andrzej. *Politics of Socialist Agriculture in Poland, 1945–1960*. New York and London: Columbia University Press, 1965.

Lenin, V. I. *The State and Revolution*. In *Collected Works*, vol. 25. Moscow: Progress Publishers, 1964.

————. "All Power to the Soviets." *Pravda*, no. 99 (July 18, 1917). In *Collected Works*, vol. 25. Moscow: Progress Publishers, 1964.

Leoński, Zbigniew. *Rady Narodowe—Zasady Organizacji i Funkcjonowania*. Warszawa, Poznań: Państwowe Wydawnictwo Naukowe, 1965.

Machnienko, Aleksander and Skrzydło, Wiesław. "Komissii Viekhovo Organa Gosudarstvennoi Vlasti Socialisticheskovo Gosudarstva." *Annales Universitatis Mariae Curie-Skłodowska*, sectio G, vol. 8, no. 6 (1961).

Mały Rocznik Statystyczny (Little Statistical Yearbook). Warszawa: Główny Urząd Statystyczny, 1939.

Maneli, Mieczysław. *O Funkcjach Państwa*. Warszawa: Państwowe Wydawnictwo Naukowe, 1963.

Marx, Karl. *The Civil War in France*. London: Martin Lawrence, Ltd., 1933.

Marx, Karl and Engels, Friedrich. *The Communist Manifesto*. New York: Appleton-Century-Crofts, Inc., 1955.

"Między Zjazdami-Rolnictwo." *Trybuna Ludu* (November 9, 1968).

Mikołajczyk, Jadwiga. "Radny—Anonim?" *Trybuna Ludu* (April 13, 1964).

Mikołajczyk, Stanisław. *The Rape of Poland: Pattern of Soviet Aggression*. New York: Whittlesey House, 1948.

Milbrath, Lester W., *Political Participation*. Chicago: Rand McNally & Co., 1965.

Milosz, Czeslaw. *The Captive Mind*. New York: Alfred A. Knopf, 1953.

Miśkiewicz, Marian. "Z Krytyki Wyciągamy Wnioski." *Nowe Drogi* 15 (June 1961).

Monitor Polski (The Official Gazette of the Government of the Polish People's Republic). Warszawa.

Montias, John. *Central Planning in Poland*. New Haven: Yale University Press, 1962.

Norojek, Winicjusz. *System Władzy w Mieście*. Wrocław, Warszawa, Kraków: Ossolineum, 1967.

COMMUNIST LOCAL GOVERNMENT

Nowak, Stefan. "Social Attitudes of Warsaw Students." *The Polish Sociological Bulletin*, nos. 1–2 (January–June 1962).

Ostapczuk, Bronisław. "Nowe Aspekty Sytuacji Prawnej Prezydiów Rad Narodowych." *Państwo i Prawo* 18 (October 1963).

Ostrowski, Krzysztof and Przeworski, Adam. "Local Leadership in Poland." *The Polish Sociological Bulletin*, no. 2 (1967).

Petranko F. "People's Power." *Izvestia* (December 5, 1964), in *The Current Digest of the Soviet Press*, 16, no. 49 (December 30, 1964) p. 15.

Piekalkiewicz, Jaroslaw. *Public Opinion Polling in Czechoslovakia, 1968–69. An Analysis of Surveys Conducted During the Dubcek Era.* New York: Praeger, 1972.

————. "Communist Administration in Poland Within the Framework of Input-Output Analysis." *East European Quarterly* 6 (June 1972), pp. 230–258.

III Plenum KC PZPR—Wybory do Sejmu i Rad Narodowych. Warszawa: Ksiązka i Wiedza, 1965.

Prezydium Miejskiej Rady Narodowej w Grudziądzu. *Materiały Informacyjne dla Radnych Miejskiej Rady Narodowej i Wydziałów Prezydium MRN*, no. 1/62. Mimeographed. Grudziądz, Feb. 1962.

Prezydium Wojewódzkiej Rady Narodowej w Opolu. *Materiały z Sesji Sprawozdawczej Wojewódzkiej Rady Narodowej w Opolu.* Opole: Opolskie Zakłady Graficzne, 1961.

Radni Rad Narodowych. Seria "Statystyka Polski-Materiały Statystyczne," no. 59. Warszawa: Główny Urząd Statstyczny, 1970.

Riggs, Fred W. "Agraria and Industria." In *Toward the Comparative Study of Public Administration*, edited by William J Siffin. Bloomington, Indiana: Indiana University Press, 1959.

Rocznik Polityczny i Gospodarczy (Political and Economic Yearbook) Warszawa: Państwowe Wydawnictwo Ekonomiczne.

Rocznik Statystyczny. (Statistical Yearbook). Warszawa: Główny Urząd Statystyczny.

Rot, Henryk. *Akty Normatywne Rad Narodowych i Ich Prezydiów.* Warszawa: Wydawnictwo Prawnicze, 1962.

Rozmaryn, Stefan. *Konstytucja Jako Ustawa Zasadnicza PRL.* Warszawa: Państwowe Wydawnictwo Naukowe, 1961.

Różański, Henryk. *Problemy XXII Zjazdu KPZR—Budowa Kommunizmu w ZSRR a Rozwój Współpracy Krajów Socjalistycznych.* Warszawa: Ksiązka i Wiedza, 1962.

Rybicki, Zygmunt. Działalność i Organizacja *Rad Narodowych w PRL.* Warszawa: Ksiązka i Wiedza, 1965.

————. *System Rad Narodowych w PRL.* Warszawa: Państwowe Wydawnictwo Naukowe, 1971.

Rylke, Maksymilian. "Kompetencje Rad Narodowych Stopnia Powiatowego w

BIBLIOGRAPHY

Sprawowaniu Funkcji Koordynacji Terenowej." *Państwo i Prawo* 19 (October 1964).

Sand, Kazimierz and Błażejczyk, Martin. "Z Teorii i Praktyki Samorządu Robotniczego w Polskiej Rzeczypospolitej Ludowej." *Annales Universitatis Mariae Curie-Skłodowska*, sectio G, vol. 7, no. 3 (1960).

Shulman, Marshall D., "Changing Appreciation of the Soviet Problems." *World Politics* 10 (July 1958).

Siffin, William J., ed. *Toward the Comparative Study of Public Administration*. Bloomington, Indiana: Indiana University Press, 1959.

Skrzydło, Wiesław. "Zasady Ustawodawstwa o Radach Narodowych w Praktyce." In *Z Problematyki Rad Narodowych*. Lublin: Wydawnictwo Lubelskie, 1961.

————. "System Partyjny PRL i Jego Wyraz w Ustroju Politycznym Państwa." *Państwo i Prawo* 14 (July 1959).

————. "Partie Polityczne w Systemie Przedstawicielskim PRL." *Ruch Prawniczy i Ekonomiczny* 21 (April 1959).

Skrzydło, Wiesław and Sand, Kazimierz. *Wybory do Sejmu i do Rad Narodowych*. Rzeszów: Prezydium W.R.N., 1961.

Smoktunowicz, Eugeniusz. "Funkcje Kierowniczo-Koordynacyjne Prezydium W Stosunku Do Wydziałów I Innych Jednostek Organizacyjnych Podporządkowanych Radzie Narodowej." *Problemy Rad Narodowych, Studia i Materiały*, no. 9. Wrocław, Warszawa, Kraków: Ossolineum, 1967.

Sobiesiak, Józef. *Brygada Grunwald*. Warszawa: Wydawnictwo Ministerstwa Obrony Narodowej, 1964.

Sokolewicz, Wojciech. *Przedstawicielstwo i Administracja w Systemie Rad Narodowych PRL*. Wrocław, Warszawa, Kraków: Ossolineum, 1968.

Sokolewicz, Wojciech and Zawadzki, Sylwester. "Wyniki Badania Uchwał Rad Narodowych i Ich Prezydiów." In *Problemy Rad Narodowych*, no. 3 Warszawa: Ossolineum, 1965.

Sorgenicht, Klaus et al., eds. *Verfassung Der Duetschen Demokratischen Republik. Dokumente, Komentar*. 2 vols. Berlin: Staatsverlag Der D.D.R., 1969.

Starościak, Jerzy. *Decentralizacja Administracji*. Warszawa: Państwowe Wydawnictwo Naukowe, 1960.

————. *Wprowadzenie Do Prawa Administracyjnego Europejskich Państw Socjalistycznych*. Warszawa: Państwowe Wydawnictwo Naukowe, 1968.

Surmaczyński, Marian. "Aktywność Radnych i Ich Satysfakcja Z Pracy Społecznej (Na podstawie badań empirycznych w województwie wrocławskim). *Problemy Rad Narodowych, Studia i Materiały*, no. 14. Wrocław, Warszawa, Kraków: Ossolineum, 1969.

Swearer, Howard R. "Popular Participation: Myth and Realities." *Problems of Communism* 9 (Sept.–Oct. 1960).

Świerkowski, Ryszard. "Rada Odwołała Przewodniczącego." *Perspektywy* 4 (January 7, 1972).

Szczerbal, Franciszek. "Usprawniać Pracę Rad." *Nowe Drogi* 15 (February 1961).

COMMUNIST LOCAL GOVERNMENT

Szcypiarski, Andrzej. "Polska 1918." *Polityka* 12 (November 9, 1968).

Szeliga, Zygmunt. "The Polish Economy, 1967–1968." *Contemporary Poland* 1 (February 1967).

Szelog, Zbigniew. "Wydatki Budżetowe GRN Woj. Lubelskiego W świetle Decentralizacji Budżetowej." *Problemy Rad Narodowych, Studia i Materiały*, no. 12. Wrocław, Warszawa, Kraków: Ossolineum: 1968.

Szperkowicz, Jerzy. "Wniosek Nie Uzyska Większości," *Świat*, (November, 1961).

Szreniawski, Jan. "Komisje Rad Narodowych w Systemie Terenowych Organów Władzy PRL." *Annales Universtatis Mariae Curie-Skłodowska*, sectio G., vol. 6, no. 4 (1960).

————. "Prezydium Rady Narodowej—Model i Dewiacje." *Annales Universitatis Mariae Curie-Skłodowska*, sectio G, vol. 14, no. 6. Lublin: 1967

————. "Pozycja Prezydium Wojewódzkiej Rady Narodowej." *Annales Universitatis Mariae Curie-Skłodowska*, sectio G, vol. 14, no. 11. Lublin: 1967.

Szymczak, Tadeusz. "System Powoływania I Skład Prezydium Rady Narodowej." *Problemy Rad Narodowych, Studia i Materiały*, no. 9. Wrocław, Warszawa, Kraków: Ossolineum, 1967.

Talmon, J. L. *The Origin of Totalitarian Democracy*. New York: Praeger, 1961.

Thomas, S. B. *Government and Administration in Communist China*. New York: International Secretariat, Institute of Pacific Relations, 1955.

Trotskii, Lev. *My Life; An Attempt at Autobiography*. New York: C. Scribner's Sons, 1931.

Turski, Ryszard. *Dynamika Przemian Społecznych w Polsce*. Warszawa: Wiedza Powszechna, 1961.

Typiak, Piotr. *Praca w Gromadzie*. Warszawa: Ludowa Spółdzielnia Wydawnicza, 1960.

Uchwala V Zjazdu Polskiej Zjednoczonej Partii Robotniczej. Warszawa: Ksiażka i Wiedza, 1968.

Wachowicz, Franciszek. "Rady Oglądane Z Bliska." *Trybuna Ludu*, (May 28, 1965).

Wagner, W. W. *Polish Law Throughout the Ages*. Stanford, California: Hoover Institution, 1970.

Weber, A. *Podziemne Rady Narodowe w Walce o Polskę Ludową*. Warszawa: Ksiażka i Wiedza, 1954.

Wendel, Adam and Zell, Zygmunt. Warszawa: Ksiażka i Wiedza, 1968.

Wentlandt, Mieczysław. "Struktura Osobowa Prezydiów Rad Narodowych W Latach 1944–1965." *Problemy Rad Narodowych, Studia i Materiały*, no. 10. Wrocław, Warszawa, Kraków: Ossolineum, 1967.

Wesołowski, Włodzimierz. "Stara i Nowa Klasa." *Kultura* 6 (November 1968).

Wiatr, Jerzy J. "Elections and Voting Behavior in Poland." Ann Arbor, Michigan: International Political Science Conference, 1960. Unpublished paper.

BIBLIOGRAPHY

————. "Economic and Social Factors of Electoral Behavior." *The Polish Sociological Bulletin*, no. 1–2 (January–June 1962).

————. *Społeczeństwo, Wstęp Do Socjologii Systematycznej.* Warszawa: Państwowe Wydawnictwo Naukowe, 1968.

Wróblewski, Jan. "Formy Pracy Rady Narodowej m. Łodzi." *Zeszyty Naukowe Uniwersytetu Łódzkiego, Prawo*, no. 17 (1960).

Wycech, Czesław. "Owocnych Obrad—Dla Dobra Robotników, Chłopów i Całego Narodu-Przemówienie Powitalne Prezesa NK ZSL Czesława Wycecha NA IV Zjeździe PZPR," *Trybuna Ludu* (June 16, 1964).

Zakrzewski, Witold. "Z Zagadnień Działalności Uchwałodawczej Rad Narodowych i Ich Prezydiów w. Woj. Krakowskim w Latach 1955 i 1962." In *Problemy Rad Narodowych—Studia i Materiały*, no. 3. Warszawa: Ossolineum, 1965.

Załuski, Zbigniew. *Czterdziesty Czwarty.* Warszawa: Czytelnik, 1968.

Zawadzka, Barbara and Zawadzki, Sylwester. "Ewolucja Składu Rad Narodowych." *Problemy Rad Narodowych, Studia i Materiały*, no. 10. Wrocław, Warszawa, Kraków: Ossolineum, 1967.

Zawadzki, Sylwester. *Rozwój Więzi Rad Narodowych z Masami Pracującemi w Polsce Ludowej.* Warszawa: Państowe Wydawnictwo Naukowe, 1955.

————. "Spór o Istotę Dyktatury Proletariatu." *Państwo i Prawo* 18 (October 1963).

————. "Kierunek Pogłebienia Democratyzmu Systemu Rad Narodowych." *Nowe Drogi* 15 (August 1961).

Zawodowe Studium Administracyjne przy UMCS w Lublinie. *Z Prolematyki Rad Narodowych.* Lublin: Wydawnictwo Lubelskie, 1961.

Zell, Zygmunt. "Funkcje Kontroli Społecznej Komisji Rad Narodowych." *Państwo i Prawo* 15 (June 1960).

————. "Analiza Tematów Sesji Ubiegłej Kadencji." *Gospodarka i Administracja Terenowa*, no. 9 (September, 1969).

XXII Zjazd Kommunistycznej Partii Związku Radzieckiego. Warszawa: Książka i Wiedza, 1961.

"V Zjazd PZPR." *Nowe Drogi*, no. 12 (December 1968).

VI Zjazd Polskiej Zjednoczonej Partii Robotniczej (VI Congress of the Polish United Workers' Party). *Uchwała O Dalszy Socjalistyczny Rozwój Polskiej Rzeczypospolitej Ludowej.* Warszawa: Trybuna Ludu, 1971.

VI Zjazd Polskiej Zjednoczonej Partii Robotniczej. Podstawowe Materiały i Dokumenty. Warszawa: Książka i Wiedza, 1972.

Żukowski, Zygmunt. "Biuro Gromadzkie W świetle Przepisów i Praktyki." *Problemy Rad Narodowych, Studia i Materiały*, no. 14. Wrocław, Warszawa, Kraków: Ossolineum, 1969.

INDEX